They Came From a Land Down Under

Duncan Mackay

First published in the United Kingdom in 2024 by
The Choir Press

ISBN 978-1-78963-480-8

Contents

To my late father, David Mackay. I finally wrote the book I promised you that I would! I hope that I have done you and Jimmy proud.

Preface

I was eight years old when the 1974 FIFA World Cup finals were staged in West Germany. It was an event I had been excited about since finding out it was happening after arriving in the country in the summer of 1972, along with my father, David, a member of the Royal Corps of Signals in the British Army, and mother, Joan. It was the latest posting of a nomadic childhood that had already included spells in Malta, Cyprus, Hong Kong and Singapore.

My earliest sporting memory is of the 1972 Olympic Games in Munich, which were held shortly after we landed in West Germany. I remember my mother and father getting extremely excited about an athlete from Northern Ireland called Mary Peters winning the gold medal in the pentathlon. I also recall them sitting transfixed in front of the small black-and-white television as members of the Palestinian Black September terrorist organisation broke into the Olympic Village and took 11 Israeli athletes, coaches and officials hostage in their apartments.

I was too young to understand what the death of the 11 Israelis in a botched rescue plan meant, and just continued to look forward to the World Cup. I only knew two things about the World Cup: one, that England had won it in 1966 and, secondly, that when anyone talked about it they always spoke of a Brazilian player called Pele. I was determined to learn more about it before it started.

I was vaguely aware that I had an uncle called Jimmy, whom I had once met and who was a professional footballer in Australia after emigrating there from Scotland. But they never mentioned him on the British Forces Broadcasting Service, whose radio station was the main conduit for my parents to stay connected with home and who did regular Saturday reports on English and Scottish football. Therefore, I never gave him much thought.

When I began saving everything I could find associated with the World Cup, my father must have told me that Jimmy was playing for Australia and they were trying to qualify for West Germany 1974. But I did not listen. The World Cup was for players like Bobby Moore, Johan Cruyff and Franz Beckenbauer; players I was quickly learning about, not my dad's brother.

By then, my father had lived more of his life outside Scotland than he had spent there. Like most Scots, though, he remained fiercely proud of his roots. He had been born and raised in Craigmillar, an area about three miles south-east of Scotland's capital, Edinburgh. The town is best known for Craigmillar

Castle, a settlement dating back to the 14th century which has a historic link to Mary, Queen of Scots. She went there to rest after the birth of her son, the future James VI, the first monarch to rule both Scotland and England.

Craigmillar Castle provides a splendid background to a town which has always suffered social deprivation

It remains one of the best-preserved medieval castles in Scotland, but then, as now, its striking splendour was in stark contrast to the rest of Craigmillar. Industrialisation in the area started in the late 19th and early 20th centuries, with it becoming a hub for the Scottish brewing industry. A group of seven breweries sprung up during this period, thanks to them identifying the good railway link and also taking advantage of the local aquifers providing excellent water for brewing.

To help house the workers needed to service the breweries, an estate was constructed immediately under Craigmillar Castle. It consisted mainly of tenements; a type of building shared by multiple dwellings. Typically, they were flats or apartments on each floor with a shared entrance stairway access, and were popular in Scotland. They were built mainly in Edinburgh and Glasgow to provide high-density housing for the substantial number of people moving to the city as a result of the Industrial Revolution. They were usually overcrowded, and disease quickly spread in areas where sanitary facilities were often inadequate.

As a child, my father, born in April 1930, remembered Craigmillar as a place of strong women and old men as most of the young men had volunteered or been called up to fight in the Second World War. The White House (or 'The Whitehoose', as everyone there called it), an Art Deco-listed building, was a popular place for the old men to stand around and reminisce about their experiences in the previous Great War – the 'war to end war'.

They had served in places like Passchendaele, a village that gave its name to a battle that served as a vivid symbol of the mud, madness and senseless slaughter of the Western Front, and many had been injured. They were the lucky ones. Up to half a million British and German troops had been killed there during one of history's deadliest battles. My grandfather had been gassed there when he was a young man, and suffered as a result for the rest of his life.

Art Deco-listed building The White House was a pub central to Craigmillar life when David and Jimmy Mackay were growing up there

Social deprivation was a major problem, and it was the kind of place that most youngsters wanted to get out of as soon as possible. That is why, when the British Army offered my father an escape, he grasped it with both hands in the hope of making a better life for himself.

His younger brother, Jimmy, had seen a similar opportunity as a 21-year-old in 1965, when he signed up for a two-year working holiday in Australia. He was just one of dozens of young men from all over Europe attracted by the chance to play soccer – as it was known there to differentiate it from rugby, which most Australians considered football – in an exciting new country where it was assumed it was always sunny and warm.

I first became aware of how good a footballer my Uncle Jimmy was sometime in the middle of 1973. My father showed me a cutting from a Sydney newspaper, which included a photograph of Jimmy, about how Australia had beaten Iran 3–0 and were now favourites to qualify for the World Cup. The very same World Cup that I had been obsessing about for so long!

Included inside the envelope sent by Jimmy's wife, Marilyn, was a small tin badge depicting a kangaroo wearing football boots and kicking a ball. Around the edge were the words 'Australia – Socceroo'. From then on, I was telling everyone at school that my uncle was going to play in the World Cup. The idea sounded so ridiculous that my teacher called my mother in for a meeting to warn her about my 'fantasies'. Imagine her shock when my mum told her that it was the truth.

The same scenario happened a few months later, when a new teacher at the school did not believe that I was going to be away for a few days because I was going to Hamburg to watch my uncle play for Australia in the World Cup against East and West Germany. Before the match against West Germany, we visited the Socceroos training camp, where I enjoyed a kickabout with the players, and the coach, Rale Rasic, praised my heading ability.

Just to add to the unlikeliness of the story, I ended up going back to school a day later than arranged. Our family had missed the last train home after the match against West Germany and were getting ready to spend a night on a bench at the station, until a nun took pity on us and arranged accommodation at the local convent.

The Socceroos were a team of part-time players mostly born outside the country who pulled off one of the most remarkable feats in Australian sport history

The story of the 1974 Socceroos has been captured excellently by many writers and journalists down the years, but I have always thought that the entire journey deserved to be told in one book. Plus, I promised my dad, who died in 1994 shortly after getting back to England from a trip to Australia to visit Jimmy, that one day I would write it. On the following pages, I hope that I have captured the spirit of the team and accurately recorded the challenges they faced and how they overcame them.

At the time, I was too young to appreciate the magnitude of what this group of special players – mostly immigrants, all part-timers subject to racial abuse, and dismissed as second-rate no-hopers – achieved.

They qualified for the World Cup finals at a time when only 16 countries competed in the tournament, rather than the 48 who will take part in the 2026 tournament. What accentuated the achievement of that performance in 1974 was the fact that England, the old country where the modern game had originated and who only eight years earlier had lifted the World Cup trophy, did not qualify.

There was incredulity, even some anger, at the fact that Australia were taking part and England were not. But no team had ever had a longer campaign or travelled further to reach the finals than the 1974 Socceroos, playing 11 matches in five countries, in temperatures ranging from 100 degrees Fahrenheit to below freezing.

During the 1960s and 1970s, soccer was denigrated as 'wogball', but the Socceroos' qualification for that World Cup went a long way towards shaking off that image. The Socceroos are now *expected* to qualify for the World Cup finals (and have appeared in every one since 2006).

Australian footballers are multi-millionaires who represent some of Europe's biggest clubs, and are household names. Australia has a national league that will soon celebrate its 50th anniversary. There is a devoted army of supporters happy to analyse the team's tactics, performances and players in minute detail on social media. Satellite television now shows wall-to-wall live football from all over the world.

It is unlikely any of this would have happened if it had not been for the 1974 team. This was a group of players who achieved history, but who mostly went back to their old lives after returning home from West Germany. Certainly, none of them grew rich on the back of being the first footballers from Australia to play in the World Cup finals. But they blazed a trail for the likes of Tim Cahill, Harry Kewell and Mark Viduka to become international stars and extraordinarily rich.

In many ways, the Socceroos' story is the story of Australia. Of a country where migration has always been important. Just as immigrants helped build football in Australia and transformed it into the most popular participation sport in the country, the new Aussies powered the economy and turned it from a predominantly British nation into one of the most multicultural societies in the world.

The national soccer team has always reflected the realities of the ethnic make-up of Australia better than competing sporting codes, politics, business and the media. From the early days when the Scots were the predominant force to the Greeks and Italians, to the present-day African Australians that are starting to break through at Socceroos level, the team has reflected the changing face of the country for 100 years.

In my professional career as a journalist, I ended up making the Olympic Games my speciality. It has taken me all over the world, including many times to Australia. On every occasion I have visited, the subject of my Uncle Jimmy and his role in Australian soccer has come up at some stage. Every time, my heart swells with pride knowing the special place he and those 1974 Socceroos have in Australian sporting history.

This is their story.

Author's Note

I would like to make a couple points of clarification. To make the book as authentic as possible, I have mostly used the term soccer throughout the book as that is what the sport has been called in Australia for most of its history as a way to differentiate it from rugby football and Australian rules. Secondly, the term Socceroos as a nickname did not come into usage until 1972, thus it has not been used to describe the national team before then.

Prologue

The name's Mackay, Jimmy Mackay

13th November 1973, Bielefeld, West Germany

My father, David Mackay, had been sitting cross-legged in front of the eight-inch black-and-white television in the corner of the front room of our second-floor apartment in Bielefeld in West Germany for hours since he got home from work. At least, that is how it seemed. He was flicking incessantly between the two channels the TV could receive, hoping he could somehow conjure it up to tell him what had happened more than 5,600 miles away.

The news he was desperate to find out about was whether his younger brother, Jimmy Mackay, and the Australian soccer team he represented, had won their play-off match against South Korea in Hong Kong, which was seven hours ahead of where we were. The winner would qualify for the following year's FIFA World Cup, set to take place here in West Germany.

My father had had a long and distinguished career in the Royal Corps of Signals, and he was nearing the end of his final overseas posting. He had been called up to do his National Service when he was 19 years old and decided he liked it so much he would enlist as a regular and stay.

At the time of being conscripted, he had been training as a cabinet maker at a coffin maker's workshop in Edinburgh. He was working alongside another Scottish teenager who had recently been invalided out of the Royal Navy and was polishing the caskets as he pursued his dream of becoming an actor while playing non-league football for Bonnyrigg Rose.

It was an idea my dad tried to dissuade the fellow youngster from seriously following. He told him one day after work down the pub that people would always need coffins and that it was a much safer career path to follow.

The two lost touch when my father left to join the army. The next time he heard of his former colleague was in 1962, when Sean Connery appeared in a new British film *Dr. No*, playing the lead role of a character called James Bond. It was a story my father loved telling and laughing at himself about.

My father was the second oldest of four brothers and a sister. The youngest, James, or Jimmy as everyone called him, was born in December 1943 as the Second World War reached its final stages.

David started his National Service while his younger brother was still at primary school, where his talent for sport, particularly football and table tennis, was already standing out.

As my father's career progressed, he increasingly began spending longer periods away from Scotland, including being part of the United Nations Peacekeeping forces sent to Korea and Cyprus. On visits home, he caught up with Jimmy's successes.

Former James Bond actor Sean Connery ignored advice to give up dreams of becoming an actor

As a young footballer, Jimmy was recruited by Connery's old club, Bonnyrigg Rose. From there he was spotted and joined Airdrieonians. They were a Scottish professional team from the town of Airdrie, in the Monklands area of Lanarkshire. Airdrie were playing their tenth consecutive season in the First Division, the top flight of Scottish football, in 1964–1965. They had been promoted as champions in 1954–1955, which coincided with a change of the league structure.

My father was a passionate Heart of Midlothian supporter, so he must have had mixed feelings when Jimmy made his debut for Airdrie against this team at Tynecastle Park in the opening Scottish First Division match of the season. Airdrie were totally outclassed as Hearts ran out 8–1 winners.

It set the tone for that season, one of the most remarkable in the history of Scottish football. Hearts faced Kilmarnock at Tynecastle Park on the last day of the season with a two-point lead, knowing all they needed to do was to avoid a defeat by two goals. But Kilmarnock won 2–0 to clinch the title on goal average.

The Glasgow giants, Rangers and Celtic, languished back in fifth and eighth place, respectively. It was the only time that both of the Old Firm clubs had failed to finish in the top three of the top tier of Scottish football in the same season.

My father was on leave at the time and attended that final match against Kilmarnock, where he fully expected to see Hearts crowned Scottish champions for the first time in five years. He never quite got over it, I fear. Hearts have not won the Scottish championship since.

It was sad news for Airdrie and Jimmy as well. They were relegated after finishing 17th out of the 18 teams. He had played five league matches and scored one goal, along with three matches in the Scottish League Cup. At 21,

Jimmy's career was at a crossroads. But with National Service having ended in 1963, he was at least free to go where he wanted.

My father tried to encourage Jimmy to contact some clubs in England and arrange trials. But just as Connery had done several years earlier, Jimmy ignored the career advice. He decided instead, in the summer of 1965, to travel to Australia for a two-year 'working holiday' with a group of friends. Before he left, he wrote to a number of football clubs in Australia, advising them that he was coming and wondering if there would be any opportunities for him to play.

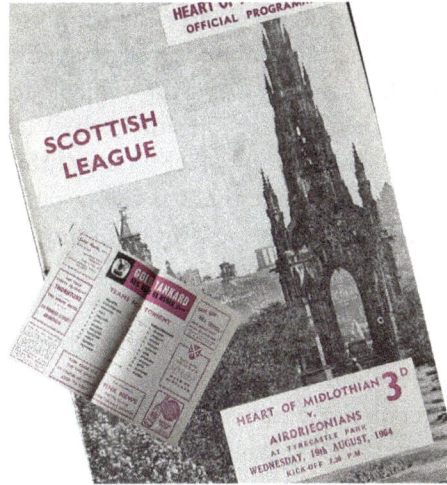

Jimmy Mackay made his debut for Airdrieonians in August 1964 against Heart of Midlothian at Tynecastle Park in a match his side lost 8-1

South Melbourne Hellas, a club with its roots in the city's Greek community, got in touch to offer him a contract. It was then, in the close-knit Australian football community, that word got out that a talented young Scottish footballer was on his way. Among those alerted to the fact was Duncan MacKay, who was no relation to our family.

Duncan MacKay's 10-year career in Scottish football had included captaining Celtic, playing 236 matches for the club and appearing 14 times for his country. After losing his place at Celtic, MacKay had joined Third Lanark in November 1964. Founder members of both the Scottish Football Association and Scottish Football League, Third Lanark were already beginning to implode. At the end of the 1964–1965 season, they were the only team to finish below Jimmy's Airdrie.

It was former Celtic captain Duncan MacKay who persuaded a young Jimmy Mackay to play for Melbourne Croatia after arriving in Australia

Like Jimmy, Duncan MacKay decided to seek a new challenge, although at 28 years of age, he was older and far more experienced. He had accepted an offer to play and coach Melbourne Croatia, which, as the name suggests, drew its support from the Croatian community. At the time, Australia's clubs were largely drawn along ethnic lines. Duncan MacKay was the star name at a time when Melbourne Croatia were spending big in a bid to become the top side in the Victoria League.

When Duncan MacKay heard that Jimmy was on his way, he made it his mission to ensure that the youngster signed for Melbourne Croatia. He would undoubtedly have known of Jimmy as he had scored his only goal for Airdrie in their 2–1 victory against Third Lanark a few days before Duncan MacKay joined them.

To help make sure he signed Jimmy, Duncan MacKay was at the airport to greet him and his friends when they landed. Of course, Jimmy was overwhelmed at being met upon arrival by such a well-known name from his homeland. He willingly allowed himself to be hustled away to sign for one of South Melbourne Hellas' fiercest rivals.

Jimmy Mackay, fifth from right in back row, was part of the Melbourne Croatia side crowned Victoria State League champions in 1968

Fortunately, the furore that the incident caused died down after a few weeks. Jimmy did eventually move to South Melbourne Hellas many years later, after helping Melbourne Croatia win the Victoria League in 1968. In 1970, by now having turned his working holiday visa into something more permanent and having started the process of becoming an Australian citizen, he was called up to represent his new country.

In 1970, I have a vague recollection, as a five-year-old, of Uncle Jimmy visiting my father, my mother Joan and me in Singapore, where my dad had been posted, and staying overnight. It would have been the first time my dad had seen him since he emigrated to Australia and I had been born.

Two years later, when I was seven, we moved to West Germany, where my father was part of British Forces Germany in Herford. The British Army of the Rhine had been established after the end of World War Two, with the mission of defending West Germany. It remained there for the rest of the Cold War.

For me, an early passion for football was beginning to develop, especially with West Germany set to host the 1974 FIFA World Cup. Unlike today, only 16 countries qualified for the finals, and there had already been celebrations in our household when Scotland qualified for the first time since Sweden 1958, and England, the 1966 champions, were knocked out. But having your uncle play in the World Cup was something else.

My father had been trying to follow Jimmy's Australia since they had begun their World Cup qualifying campaign with a 1–1 draw against New Zealand in Auckland in March 1973. In those pre-internet days, this was not an easy task, but my dad managed to track Jimmy, usually via results in the small print of two-day-old editions of the *Daily Mirror* from London and the occasional telephone call, as they got past New Zealand, Iraq, Indonesia and Iran.

It left them facing a two-legged final qualifying round against South Korea. The first game, on 28th October in Sydney, finished goalless, and then the second leg, on

Jimmy Mackay decided to stay in Australia, assumed citizenship and ended up a national hero

11th November in Seoul, ended 2–2 with Australia coming from two goals down. Away goals did not count double in those days, so a replay was arranged in the neutral venue of Hong Kong just two days later. Jimmy had called on the way to update my father. The tension in our apartment that day was high. Even at such an early age, I could tell how much this meant to my father.

There was no news until, finally, an item came on at the end of a news bulletin which had been headlined by German Chancellor Willy Brandt addressing the fledgling European Parliament and the continuing saga of the OPEC oil embargo which was crippling the continent.

The presenter said: '*Australien hat Südkorea geschlagen und sich für die FIFA-Weltmeisterschaft 1974 in Westdeutschland qualifiziert.*'

('Australia has beaten South Korea to qualify for the 1974 FIFA World Cup in West Germany.')

It was accompanied by grainy footage of a stunning right-footed volley curving and arching over the South Korean goalkeeper and into the top left-hand corner of the net.

Once the pandemonium, which must have shaken the whole apartment block, had died down, my dad turned to my mother and said: 'I'm sure that was our Jimmy that scored that goal.'

At which point, the telephone rang. It was Jimmy, still up celebrating and preparing for the journey home. A team of predominantly part-time players from diverse backgrounds, all drawn to Australia for the promise of a better life, had left the country a few days earlier largely as unknowns and were now returning as heroes.

Jimmy *had* scored that goal.

CHAPTER ONE

Wogball

When the First Fleet, a flotilla of 11 British ships, sailed into Botany Bay in 1788, it brought with it 1,040 people, nearly half of them convicts. Along with the members of society Britain did not want, they travelled with a broad range of provisions and equipment. These included two bulls, seven cows, one stallion, three mares, 44 sheep, 32 pigs, four goats and poultry.

The First Fleet also introduced something to Australia that would last for much longer and help define the nation – sport.

Many of the sailors, officers and convicts were steeped in the emerging British sporting traditions, particularly horse racing, cricket, boxing, other blood sports like cockfighting, and even pedestrianism, the now-antiquated term for foot racing.

Before the First Fleet had left Portsmouth, Britain had already begun to codify sport. In Scotland, the Honourable Company of Edinburgh Golfers was founded in 1744, a decade before the Society of St Andrews Golfers, which would later become the Royal & Ancient Golf Club, still one of the game's main governing bodies. Three major horse races – the St Leger, the Oaks and the Derby – were all created between 1776 and 1780. The Marylebone Cricket Club, the organisation which still plays a leading role in setting the laws of the sport, was founded in 1787.

The early settlers in Australia naturally had more pressing concerns at first, but sports, above all, cricket and horse racing, soon left their mark. In many towns, a cemetery and horse racetrack were among the first things built, then a church and then a cricket pitch.

From 1788 to 1868, Britain transported more than 160,000 convicts to Australia. In addition, nearly 200,000 free settlers and assisted immigrants chose to migrate from Britain to Australia to start a fresh life. Many of the later settlers brought with them a new sport that was sweeping Britain – football. The first modern set of laws were drawn up in 1863, the same year the Football Association in England was founded.

For a long time, it was widely assumed the first game of football in Australia was played in 1880 between the Wanderers and the King's School on Parramatta Common in Sydney and organised by John Walter Fletcher.

Subsequent research, however, by Victoria University historian Ian Syson, discovered that an earlier game had taken place on Saturday, 7th August 1875, in Woogaroo, just outside of Brisbane. The *Queenslander* reported that Brisbane Football Club met the inmates and warders of the Woogaroo Lunatic Asylum on the football field in the grounds of the Asylum.

'... play commenced at half-past two, after arranging the rules and appointing umpires; Mr. Sheehan acting as such for Brisbane, and Mr. Jack for Woogaroo,' the newspaper reported. 'One rule provided that the ball should not be handled nor carried.'

Another publication, *The Footballer*, also noted in its section on 'Football in Queensland' that the 'match was played without handling the ball under any circumstances whatever (Association rules).'

Fletcher may not have organised the first football game in Australia, but he was undoubtedly a key figure in the development of the sport there. He had graduated from the University of Oxford and emigrated to Australia in 1875 where he began working as a teacher. After settling in Sydney suburb Woollahra, Fletcher started to work towards the establishment of association football in the region. He called a meeting at the Aarons Hotel in Sydney, and the first club, Wanderers, was formed on 3rd August 1880, with Fletcher as its secretary.

The Wanderers' first game was that one against King's School, a rugby-playing educational establishment. The Wanderers, wearing a white jersey, cap, knickerbockers and blue stockings, with a badge over the left breast representing the Southern Cross, the radiant star group that helped early sailors find their way to Australia, won 5–0 in front of a crowd reported to be 1,000.

In 1882, Fletcher formed the New South Wales English Football Association, Australia's first soccer association and one of the first to be established outside the United Kingdom. The word 'English' was necessary to distinguish the association from organisations related to rugby football, which had already been established as the most popular code of football in the Sydney area.

In Victoria, more than 20 years before Fletcher had formed his soccer association, an Australian called Thomas Wentworth Wills had helped found Australian rules football. In May 1859, in Melbourne, he was one of seven men who helped formulate the rules for a game viewed today as uniquely Australian. It was, in fact, a compromise of the various brands of football played at English public schools. Aged 14, Wills had been sent to England to attend Rugby School, where he had played an early version of rugby football.

Australian rules captured the imagination of Victoria but failed to catch on in New South Wales, where rugby was the passion. But soccer clubs were formed in Victoria and inter-state matches between them and New South Wales began as early as 1883. Shortly after the turn of the 20th century, as well as Victoria and New South Wales, there were football associations operating in Queensland, Western Australia, Tasmania and South Australia.

It might have been isolated from the rest of the world by distance, but Australian soccer made a significant early contribution to the future of sport. In 1911, Australian teams Sydney Leichhardt and HMS Powerful were the first to use squad numbers on their backs. A year later, numbering in football would be ruled as mandatory in New South Wales. Countries around the world, including England in 1928, gradually began to adopt the concept, which made it easier to identify players. FIFA copied the idea for the first time at the 1950 World Cup finals in Brazil.

Fledgling plans to form a national governing body for soccer began in 1911, when the Commonwealth Football Association was formed. At its second conference, held in April 1914 at the Grosvenor Hotel in Brisbane under the chairmanship of Mr R J Holiday from South Australia, a potentially major step forward was agreed. The meeting decided 'to forward fraternal greetings to the Australian Olympic Committee, and to assure it of the hearty co-operation of the Commonwealth Football Association', also stating that the Association desired that the necessary steps should be taken for the representation of soccer football at Berlin.

Within four months of that conference, Australia was engaged in World War One and sport took a back seat, including the cancellation of those 1916 Olympics in Germany's capital. More than 416,000 Australians enlisted during the War, with over 330,000 serving overseas.

A total of 50,000 Australians fought in the Allied campaign in Gallipoli in 1915. The whole Gallipoli operation cost 26,111 Australian casualties, including 8,141 deaths. Despite the heavy losses, Australian – and New Zealand – soldiers were seen to have displayed great courage, endurance, initiative and discipline.

In Australia, the battle played an important part in fostering a sense of national identity, and those at home were proud of how their men had fought so valiantly, despite the horrendous conditions. It has been estimated that 4,000 soccer players from Australia participated in World War One, with 500 of them killed.

When the soldiers returned home to Australia after the end of the War in 1918, sport gradually resumed. In 1921, the Australian Soccer Football Association was formed with its headquarters in Sydney. The following year, a national team was established and toured New Zealand. Both Australia and New Zealand's first official internationals were played against each other during this tour.

They played three matches at Carisbrook in Dunedin, Athletic Park in Wellington, and Auckland Domain. The results were two 3–1 wins to New Zealand and a 1–1 draw in Wellington. New Zealand would go on to win four of the first six matches between the two countries, with Australia picking up

Australia played its first international match during a tour to New Zealand in 1922

one victory in the first game between the teams in Australia in Brisbane in 1923.

From 1923 to 1954, the sides played for the 'Soccer Ashes' trophy, a razor case carried by Queensland Football Association secretary Private William Fisher at the landing of Gallipoli. It contained the ashes of cigars smoked by the teams' captains, Australia's Alex Gibb and New Zealand's George Campbell, after the sides' first international match in Australia and was inspired by the Ashes urn awarded to the winner of the series between Australia and England in cricket.

Gibb is recognised as Australia's first international captain and was awarded cap number one retrospectively, in 2000, by Football Federation Australia for the match against New Zealand in 1922. Like so many of those who were to follow him, Gibb was of Scottish heritage. He was born in Leinster in Ireland but was raised to Scottish parents in Musselburgh. Gibb played at local clubs Musselburgh Union, Newton Grange and Musselburgh Athletic before moving to Queensland when he was about 22.

The 'Soccer Ashes' trophy disappeared for 70 years before the grandchildren of former Australian Soccer Football Federation chairman Sydney Storey, who died in 1966, discovered the prized possession in pristine condition. It had been diligently stored alongside a collection of century-old footballing artefacts in the garage of their family home. Upon recovery of the trophy, the first edition of the match since 1954 was scheduled for October 2023, at the home of

Premier League club Brentford, in London, with Australia winning 2–0.

The arrival of more British settlers after World War One helped ensure the popularity of football continued to grow. In the 1920s, the term 'British Association Football' was replaced by 'soccer' in order to signify its difference from Australian rules football, often referred to as 'footy' and considered by many Australians as 'our game'. Even as interest in the sport grew, soccer still lagged behind Aussie rules, rugby and cricket.

In 1923, China's national team visited Australia for a three-month tour which aroused much interest. They played 24 games, including five 'Test matches' against Australia. Australia won the first three games, China the fourth, and the fifth ended in a draw.

The founding fathers of Australian soccer fulfilled a major ambition in 1925, when the Football Association in England sent a team to tour the country. Billed in the local press, of course, as 'England', the tourists enjoyed a 100 per cent success record and averaged 5.5 goals per game. There were four 'Test matches' against Australia, although these were not recognised as full internationals.

The English manager, John Lewis, later criticised the Australians for bringing on substitutes and breaching the rules of amateurism by paying players £1 per day, a £5 bonus and compensation for time lost at work. In the light of how Australia's players were to be treated in the future, this was somewhat ironic.

The onset of World War Two led to another period when sport was no longer that important. Almost a million Australians, both men and women, served in the War. They fought in campaigns against Germany and Italy in Europe, the Mediterranean and North Africa, as well as against Japan in Southeast Asia and other parts of the Pacific. The

A team from the Football Association in England toured Australia in 1925, with the visitors winning all their matches

Australian mainland came under direct attack for the first time as Japanese aircraft bombed towns in North West Australia and Japanese midget submarines attacked Sydney Harbour.

Total battle casualties among Australian troops were 72,814, with 34,000 killed. Over 31,000 Australians became prisoners of war. Of these, more than 22,000 were captured by the Japanese, a third of whom subsequently died.

After the War, sport gradually returned to normal as the troops returned home to Australia. In 1949, Leichhardt-Annandale defender Joe Marston received a letter from a scout at English Second Division club Preston North End inviting him for a trial. Marston broke into Preston's first team the following year and helped the club earn promotion to the First Division, where in 1952–1953 they were beaten to the English League title by Arsenal only on goal average.

In 1954, Marston became the first Australian to play in the FA Cup final at Wembley Stadium as Preston were beaten 3–2 by West Bromwich Albion. Marston played in the same Preston side as Tom Finney and Tommy Docherty. He appeared in 197 consecutive league and cup matches for the club and in 1955 was appointed team captain.

Marston returned home to Australia in 1956 due to homesickness, despite pleas from Preston for him to stay. On his final home appearance, Finney had led the crowd in giving him a standing ovation and the local band played *Waltzing Matilda* and *For He's a Jolly Good Fellow*. Marston blazed a trail that in years to come would be followed by many others.

In 1958, Marston was player-coach and captain as Australia played five matches at home against English Division One side Blackpool, who included Stanley Matthews, watched by a combined audience of 94,110. Australia lost all five matches, including 5–2 and 8–2 in the two matches at Sydney Sports Ground, 4–2 at the Brisbane Cricket Ground and 8–0 at the Olympic Park in Melbourne. Australia's best performance was in the fourth match of the series at the Adelaide Oval, when they lost only 1–0. Marston's performances were still good enough for Matthews to try to persuade him, unsuccessfully, to return to England.

For all of Marston's great success in England, it was clear that Australia's national team still had a long way to go to become competitive on the international stage.

Shortly after Marston had left the country to pursue his career in England, a team representing the English Football Association toured the country again in 1951. The FA XI started their tour with a 4–1 win over Australia at the Sydney Cricket Ground in front of a crowd of 46,014. They then won by a series of huge scores, including 13–1 in Adelaide and 17–0 in a second match in Sydney.

'Australia could not handle the mud, whereas England revelled in it and ran rings around the Australians,' the *Sydney Morning Herald* wrote of the second game. 'It became almost farcical. Our players spent more time on their backs in the mud than on their feet. One spectator commented, "The only time they were on their feet was when the band played *God Save the King.*"

The FA won all seven matches against Australia, scoring 55 goals and conceding just four. Sheffield Wednesday striker Jackie Sewell scored 14 goals, including six in the 17–0 victory. Overall, the FA played a total of 21 games in Australia, scored 157 goals and Sewell finished with a final total of 35. In a match against Victoria before a record crowd for soccer of 29,652 at the Melbourne Cricket Ground, the FA won 7–0 and Sewell scored all of the goals.

Relations between the FA touring party and the Australian Soccer Football Association were strained throughout the tour, with the English unhappy at their treatment. The FA tour leader, David Wiseman, had accused their hosts of 'niggardly economy, adopting a bargain-price attitude and treating the players like a fourth-rate side'.

At one point, Wiseman claimed he had drafted a letter to Football Association secretary Sir Stanley Rous asking for him to recall the team. 'Our players have complained that they are drawing 5,000 pounds sterling gates and then being asked to accept third-rate meals and living conditions,' he told the *Daily Express* in London.

The matches against the Football Association in 1951 were billed as 'Australia versus England', although they were very one-sided, with the visitors winning 13-1 in Adelaide

The Australians hit back by revealing that they had invested £40,000 in the tour but, as it was watched by a total of 190,020 spectators, they probably recouped their money. In the end, Wiseman announced he had decided to drop his protests 'to carry on for the sake of the many pleasant people we have met out here'.

The same year as Marston left England, Melbourne hosted the 1956 Olympic Games and Australia qualified for the football tournament as hosts. They defeated Japan 2–0 in the first round, with goals from Graham McMillan and Belfast-born Frank Loughran, before losing 4–2 to India in the quarter-final. The gold medal was won by a Soviet Union team that included legendary goalkeeper Lev Yashin.

The 1950s saw a further large influx of British and Southern European migrants to Australia that led to an explosion in the popularity of soccer. According to data from 1945 to 1985, more than four million European settlers landed in Australia. The majority of them were from the United Kingdom and Ireland, but many also came from Southern Europe.

The European immigrants, especially those from Italy, Croatia and Greece, became the impetus for soccer development in Australia. They brought with them a huge passion for the sport that they were keen to continue in their adopted country. Some of the new migrants did not speak English, and soccer provided an important gateway into communities, breaking down cultural and language barriers.

The English Football Association scored 55 goals in seven matches, including beating Australia 17-0 in one match

The most prominent soccer clubs in Australian cities during the 1950s and 1960s were based around migrant-ethnic groups. Ethnic soccer clubs in Australia were founded in the 1950s and 1960s. Names like Sydney Croatia, Pan-Hellenic, Eastern Suburbs Hakoah, Preston Makedonia, Melbourne Croatia, Marconi Stallions, South Melbourne Hellas or St. George Budapest left no one in any doubt as to which communities those teams had their roots in.

But some Australians began to resent the amount of immigrants from non-English-speaking countries, and many viewed soccer as a game 'for foreigners' in contrast to the rugby codes and Australian rules. Many started to refer to the sport as 'wogball', a term designed to be a racial slur to describe Southern European immigrants from Croatia, Greece, Italy, Macedonia, Malta, Serbia, Spain and Turkey.

Many of the blazers who ran the Australian Soccer Football Association were horrified at how these new immigrants were taking over the sport. The established order wanted no part of the 'wogs' and 'wog clubs'. Immigrants who hoped to play soccer were regularly faced with closed doors when they tried to join established local clubs. They were not welcome, no matter how good they were. It was part of the reason so many migrant communities established their own clubs.

The activities of these new clubs were widely covered by *Soccer World*, a weekly national newspaper published in Sydney. Established by Hungarian immigrants in 1958, *Soccer World* – also known as 'the green paper' as it was printed in the colour of the most famous Hungarian club, Ferencvaros, but also because that was the colour of the daily newspaper in Hungary in the pre-communist era – promised to 'act as a link between Australians and New Australians in bringing them together on the field of sport'.

The driving force behind the new publication was Marcell Nagy, a former president of the Hungarian Football Association before fleeing Budapest in 1957 shortly after the Soviet Union crushed the revolution in the country. Nagy was at one time a member of the FIFA Executive Committee who had played a major part in the development of European soccer between the two World Wars. He was instrumental in the formation of the Mitropa Cup, forerunner of the European Cup.

In 1962, Andrew Dettre, another Hungarian, began writing for *Soccer World*. His regular job was working for the *Daily Telegraph* in Sydney and he was supposed to not write for any other publications, so invented the pen name 'Paul Dean'. Dean was a combination of 'DE' for Dettre and 'AN' for Andrew. Dettre took over as editor-in-chief in 1963 and would become one of the most influential, if not the most influential, voices in Australian soccer for many years.

Soccer World, a newspaper set up by Hungarian immigrants, was edited for many years by Andrew Dettre and chronicled the growth of the sport in Australia

Dettre's sidekick was Lou Gautier, the second son of a roving business executive who was born in 1936 in Wuhan in China. He was educated at boarding school in France, where he grew to love football. The family later emigrated to Australia when Gautier was in his teens. Gautier tried a number of jobs, including one as a wool quality estimator, before joining *Soccer World* where he became an important chronicler of Australian soccer's early failures and later successes.

Unfortunately, the formation of clubs along ethnic lines also sometimes led to tensions from overseas being continued in the new country. 'We should not allow the sporting clashes of these teams to deteriorate into nationalistic warfare,' *Soccer World* warned on the eve of the 1961 season. 'Not one Sydney team can claim to be fully Austrian, Hungarian, Italian or even Australian. All are mixtures and that's how it should be.

'If all of them, Australians and Poles, Italians and Greeks, Hungarians and Jews, realise that the success or failure of the team they follow in no way reflects upon their national character, we will have a splendid season.'

Crowd violence at big matches was not unusual. One of the worst incidents came in April 1965, on the same day as the annual Anzac Day remembrance events to commemorate the role of Australian and New Zealand troops in war. A Federation Cup match at Wentworth Park, in Sydney, between South Coast United and Pan-Hellenic, a club founded by Greek immigrants, was abandoned.

South Coast's Jim Kelly, a defender who had captained English First Division club Blackpool before emigrating to Australia, was attacked by a Pan-Hellenic supporter. While Kelly's teammates took their own retribution on the 27-year-old fan, Jim Condos, kicking and punching him, other fans used corner flags as weapons as they fought players and each other. The match referee was also attacked, suffering broken ribs and a bump on his head, and having his teeth kicked in.

The Australian press condemned what had happened. The *Sydney Morning Herald* wrote that it 'was the worst exhibition this State has seen of the mass hysteria and rioting which soccer provokes overseas.' The incident was called 'The Battle of Wentworth Park' and 'The Anzac Day riot'. The *Sydney Morning Herald* concluded that 'Australians would not attend a sport that allowed hooligans to assault players and referees.'

The violence meant that hostility towards soccer among Australians continued to grow. In one incident, vandals attacked a ground in Melbourne, attempted to burn it down and left graffiti saying 'Down with soccer' and 'Go Home Wogs'.

In the absence of a national competition, the most important league in Australia was the New South Wales First Division. It was filled with suburban clubs like Canterbury, Auburn, Granville, Corrimal and Gladesville. In 1955, the league was expanded to 12 teams, with two ethnic community clubs, Sydney Prague, formed by immigrants from Czechoslovakia, and Sydney Austral, a club founded by the Dutch community, joining.

The New South Wales Second Division contained the majority of the new ethnic clubs, and they attracted big crowds and were financially well resourced, which was in contrast to the top tier of the competition. In 1956, Sydney Hakoah, a Jewish club that played in distinctive blue and white striped shirts featuring the Magen David badge, won the Second Division but were denied promotion.

Walter Sternberg, the president of Hakoah and prominent Sydney businessman, convened a meeting of disgruntled clubs in his Bellevue Hill home. Among them were Canterbury and Auburn, who saw the commercial opportunities being wasted by not embracing the migrant soccer movement.

At the meeting, a breakaway governing body, the New South Wales Federation of Soccer Clubs, was formed. A new First Division was launched that year in 1957. The rebel group quickly gathered momentum. Soon, all other states in Australia followed suit.

The Australian Soccer Football Association had become a FIFA member only a year earlier and, even then, only because it was affiliated with the world body through its membership of the English Football Association. The old guard claimed 'the wogs had hijacked the game', but no one was listening. Any influence or control they had over the sport had disappeared almost overnight.

There was a new pioneering spirit in Australian soccer. There were startling innovations, such as games on Sundays and matches at night under floodlights, neither of which was heard of in any sport in Australia before soccer's new era came along.

Clubs also began importing quality, high-profile players from Europe, many of them attracted by the lifestyle that Australia offered and the significant amount of money the clubs could pay them. The problem was that the Australians were not paying the European clubs any transfer fees for these prized assets.

Among the first to make the move to Australia was Leo Baumgartner, a striker for Vienna side FK Austria Wien. He had toured Australia with his club in 1956 and enjoyed the experience so much that he contacted Sydney Prague. The following year, along with another player, Karol Jaros, Baumgartner arrived to play in the newly launched New South Wales League. He made a massive impact and was nicknamed 'The Little Professor of Soccer'. Half of the FK Austria Wien side who had toured Australia followed him and moved to clubs there.

Sydney Hakoah and Sydney Austral, plus two Melbourne sides, Wilhelmina and Hakoah, soon began importing players from clubs in Austria, the Netherlands and, later, Israel. All the clubs claimed the players had come as migrants, not footballers, and therefore they did not need to pay transfer fees.

Adolf Blutsch, one of the Austrians who returned to Australia after touring with FK Austria Wien, explained the attraction of playing there to Vienna newspaper *Welt Am Montag*. 'Earnings of players in Australia cannot be compared with those in Austria,' said the midfielder, who spent two seasons with Sydney Hakoah before going home. 'When I went out there, straight after my arrival, they placed a house at my disposal; with bonuses and other extras, one could even put some neat sums aside.'

The European clubs were understandably angry at losing some of their best players for no compensation and complained to FIFA. To rub salt into the wounds, many of the European players who moved to start new lives were then transferred between clubs in Australia for fees.

FIFA sided with the European clubs and in April 1960 announced the

Austrian club FK Austria Wien toured Australia in 1958, and half the team returned to play there

suspension of Australia's membership. FIFA general secretary, Helmut Kaser, left the Australians in no doubt he believed they were guilty of duplicity. 'It would be an error on your side to believe that only Australia has immigrants,' he said. 'The Austrian and Dutch players – to mention only those – did not immigrate to Australia and incidentally become members of a football club. On the contrary, you wanted to recruit good footballers in Europe and made them look like immigrants.'

A similar situation had occurred in Colombia in 1949, when their national league had broken away from FIFA and began signing some of the world's top players without paying transfer fees. Colombia was banned from international competition for five years until, in 1954, an agreement was reached which saw the foreign players return to their home countries.

Australia's suspension led to the bizarre situation in 1961 when a squad representing the English Football Association, including Finney and future England World Cup-winning captain Bobby Moore, landed in Australia during a tour of Asia, Oceania and North America but were not allowed to play any matches against local opposition.

In September 1961, the chairman and treasurer of the New South Wales Federation of Soccer Clubs, Henry Seamonds, led a delegation that visited Melbourne to discuss plans with the state's top clubs for a national knockout cup to be played in Sydney. The scheme was ambitious, with clubs to be flown in for matches which were to be played over a five-week period.

Seamonds, an English-born, Sydney-raised gynaecologist, also announced that they planned to go ahead with the formation of a new Australian Soccer Federation based on the top clubs in each state. Victoria was, at first, reluctant to commit itself to this new project. Seamonds issued an ultimatum to Victoria: 'Join us, or we will go ahead without you, and you will lose your top players to our organisation. If you do not come in now, we will not admit you in future.'

The Victorian State League clubs sent a group, led by Theo Marmaras of South Melbourne Hellas, on a fact-finding mission to the other states to gauge opinion about whether they thought the new national governing body was a good idea. The consensus was overwhelmingly positive, and it led to Victoria agreeing to back the new Australian Soccer Federation.

Soccer in Victoria was fighting its own civil war at the time, and Marmaras was also involved in the campaign that, in 1962, saw the Victorian Amateur Soccer Football Association disbanded and replaced by the Victorian Soccer Federation.

Marmaras had been born on the Greek island of Lemnos and followed his brother to Australia in 1923, when he was 13, with no English and no money. Spotting an opportunity, Marmaras had opened the Melbourne Oyster Bar, importing rock oysters from Sydney and distributing them all over the country by air, a venture that made him rich. He was charismatic, popular and nicknamed the 'Oyster King'.

When the Australian Soccer Federation was officially formed in November 1961, Marmaras was elected as president of the new body after Victoria and Tasmania had joined forces. New South Wales were furious as they had expected Seamonds, the architect of the proposal, to be given the post. After only a few minutes, Marmaras deferred to Seamonds and took the position of vice-president. It was an early warning of how inter-state alliances could affect major decisions that would impact on the future of the sport in Australia.

Ever since FIFA had suspended Australia, its president, Sir Stanley Rous, the former secretary of the Football Association in England, had been travelling regularly to the country to try to broker a compromise. But he had made it clear that they needed to be able to negotiate with one body that had the support of everyone in the sport. The formation of the Australian Soccer Federation finally appeared to offer that opportunity.

There seemed to be a setback in February 1963 when Seamonds suffered a heart attack and died during a lunch break of a meeting of the Australian Soccer Federation in St Kilda. It followed a particularly heated debate on the issue of the readmission of Australia to FIFA. Marmaras was appointed chairman, while New Zealand-born William Walkley, the founder and managing director of the petrol company Ampol, took over as president.

Walkley promised, when he was elected, that he was determined to be more than just a figurehead. One of the first things he did was to arrange for the new organisation to take control of the assets of the Australian Soccer Football Association, thus ending a legal battle between the two rival bodies.

Walkley had first become interested in soccer when he realised that so many people from overseas were making their homes in Australia. He claimed it was 'the sport that could do most to bring old and new Australians together and aid the newcomers' assimilation'.

Walkley and Ampol were great benefactors of Australian sport, including soccer. From 1958, Ampol donated the winner's cup and prize money for the pre-season competition in New South Wales and arranged for pre-season inter-state champions to meet in a national knockout competition.

Walkley turned to Michael Weinstein to help solve the crisis with FIFA. Weinstein had been born in Poland but, as a teenager, fled to Russia after Adolf Hitler's forces invaded Poland in September 1939 to start World War Two. Weinstein completed his schooling in Russia before starting a law degree.

Sir William Walkley, main picture; Michael Weinstein, top right, and Theo Marmaras, bottom right, all contributed to getting FIFA to lift its international ban

When the Germans launched Operation Barbarossa, a massive three-pronged invasion of the Soviet Union in June 1941, Weinstein was accepted into the Soviet Army's officer school and became a tank commander. He fought almost all the way to Berlin and was with the forces that 'liberated' the land of his birth.

Weinstein was wounded several times, including somehow surviving his tank being blown up in one battle, and awarded a number of medals for bravery and leadership. He lost a finger and carried shrapnel in his body as reminders of World War Two for the rest of his life.

At the end of the War, Weinstein was put in charge of the prosecutor's office in the Polish city of Lodz where, by chance, he met a cousin who informed him that his mother, Eva, and his only sister, Madzia, had somehow survived the death camp at Auschwitz. Following periods in Austria and Italy, in 1949, Weinstein and his wife followed his mother and sister to Melbourne. He arrived fluent in Polish, Russian, German and Italian – but no English. Weinstein enrolled on an English course and started a successful construction business.

It was football that provided Weinstein with the opportunity to really make his mark in Australia. He played with Melbourne Hakoah reserves but was not really up to the standard required. Weinstein quickly became team manager at the club and, within a year, was its president. He was the ideal man to cut through all the bureaucracy that was hampering Australia being readmitted to FIFA.

FIFA refused to readmit Australia until fines of £48,000 were paid – the country used the Australian pound until 1966, when it switched to the Australian dollar. Gradually, relations with FIFA improved and they dropped their demand to £30,000. A figure of £18,500 was eventually agreed and, in July 1963, members of the Australian Soccer Federation unanimously voted to meet FIFA's demands. Walkley sent Weinstein to FIFA headquarters in Zurich with a cheque that it was assumed he underwrote.

FIFA finally lifted Australia's ban from international football, which meant they could enter the 1966 World Cup, to be held in England.

CHAPTER TWO

Trailblazers

Australia were among 21 countries that entered the 1966 FIFA World Cup qualification rounds for the African, Asian, and Oceanian zone. The entries of the Philippines, beaten 15–1 by Malaysia at the 1962 Asian Games in Jakarta, and Gabon were rejected on the grounds that they had not paid the requisite entry fee and that they were not members of FIFA, respectively. It left 16 countries from Africa, two from Asia and one from Oceania.

Most countries in Asia had turned down the chance to take part in the qualifying rounds, citing lack of organisation, financial resources and the fear they would be embarrassed. But North and South Korea had both entered. South Africa were among the African countries who put in their entry forms, despite having been expelled from the Confederation of African Football in 1958 due to its government's Apartheid policy.

FIFA had followed suit by formally suspending South Africa at its Congress in 1961 in London. A few days later, Football Association secretary, Sir Stanley Rous, was elected as the world governing body's president to succeed another Englishman, Arthur Drewry, who had died in March of that year.

Sir Stanley was adamant that sport, and FIFA in particular, should not embroil itself in political matters. Against fierce opposition, he resisted attempts to expel South Africa from FIFA. The suspension was lifted in January 1963 after a visit to South Africa by Sir Stanley in order to investigate the state of the sport in the country. The decision caused outrage, particularly in Africa.

The lifting of their suspension meant South Africa were eligible to enter the World Cup, but it would have been impossible for them to have participated in the African zone as no one would have played them. So, they were moved to the Asia/Oceania zone with Australia and North and South Korea.

At FIFA's Congress in October 1964, which took place during the Olympic Games in Tokyo, there was a larger contingent of representatives from African and Asian associations, and they forced through the suspension of South Africa's membership. South Africa, however, was not formally expelled from FIFA until 1976, after Sir Stanley had lost his position as president. They were only re-admitted in 1991 following the release from prison of Nelson Mandela and the dismantling of the Apartheid system.

The issue of South Africa was not the only topic that the African countries were angry about. In January 1964, FIFA had announced that the line-up for the 16-team finals would include 10 countries from Europe, including hosts England, four from Latin America and one from the Central American and Caribbean region. That left just one place to be fought for by Africa, Asia and Oceania, an area representing 70 per cent of the world's population.

With many African countries finally beginning to gain independence from the European countries who had ruled them for decades, they considered it an insult that FIFA did not think they were worthy of their own place at the World Cup finals. Since the World Cup had first taken place at Uruguay in 1930, Egypt, at Italy 1934, had been the only African country to take part in the finals.

Besides claiming Africa deserved a place on playing merits alone, they also complained that the costs of arranging a play-off between Africa's top teams and their counterparts from Asia and Oceania was 'onerously' expensive and linking the continents was 'completely unjustified'.

Ghana, the 1963 African champions, coordinated the protests. Ohene Djan, a member of FIFA's Executive Committee and Ghana's director of sport, sent a telegram to Zurich making Africa's dissatisfaction clear. 'Registering strong objection to unfair World Cup arrangement for Afro-Asian countries STOP,' he wrote to FIFA's headquarters. 'Afro-Asian countries struggling through painful expensive qualifying series for ultimate one finalist representation is pathetic and unsound STOP At the worst, Africa should have one finalist STOP Urgent – reconsider.'

In July 1964, the African countries agreed they would boycott the World Cup if FIFA did not change their mind and allocate them a direct place at England 1966. Tessema Yidnekatchew, a former Ethiopian international and deputy president of the Confederation of African Football, helped Djan with the campaign. He called FIFA's decision 'a mockery of economics, politics and geography'.

FIFA were not for turning. 'As the decisions of the Organising Committee are final, I do not think that for the prestige of FIFA it would be a good solution to alter the decisions even if some of Tessema's arguments appear reasonable', FIFA secretary general Helmut Kaser wrote to Sir Stanley.

So, in October 1964, on the same weekend that the Confederation of Africa had successfully lobbied for South Africa to be suspended, the continent's leading football teams carried out their threat. Following a unanimous vote, all 15 of Africa's remaining countries announced they were withdrawing from the 1966 World Cup.

Sir Stanley claimed he was 'shocked to hear that the African countries had decided to withdraw from the World Cup'. The FIFA Executive Committee tried to fine each of the African countries 5,000 Swiss francs, but this was later dropped.

A path to England 1966 was beginning to open up unexpectedly for Australia, with only three countries now left in the African, Asian, and Oceanian zone. In the chaos, Sir Stanley admitted that he feared North Korea would also decide to withdraw to avoid having to play neighbours South Korea. The two were technically still at war after only an armistice was signed at the end of their conflict in 1953. Australia had participated in the Korean War on the side of the South, sending 17,000 troops from the army, navy and air force. A total of 340 Australians had been killed, including 43 reported missing.

When the draw had originally taken place, Australia, North Korea, South Korea and South Africa had been due to take part in a four-team qualifying tournament in Japan. The winners were then scheduled to meet three African countries who had emerged as the winners from that zone on a home- and-away basis.

Sir Stanley was right to fear that the situation in Korea would cause further disruption. Except it was the South, not the North, who proved to be the problem. South Korea claimed it was them that had inherited FIFA membership in 1947, when the United Nations recognised Korea's independence, and that North Korea was an affiliate member of their association. They also objected to North Korean symbols, including the flag, being displayed on the international stage.

The search to find a host to stage the truncated qualifying group dragged on through the first half of 1965. North Korea lacked a FIFA-standard stadium to stage an international match. They did not have diplomatic relations with most countries outside China and the Soviet Union. At one point, Australia was mentioned as a possible venue, even though the government in Canberra would almost certainly have refused visas to the North Korean party. Malaysia also ruled out staging the tournament on the grounds they would not admit North Korea. They were followed by Hong Kong.

Sir Stanley even discussed hosting a play-off in England between Australia and South Korea just two weeks before the World Cup kicked off, with no mention of North Korea.

In the end, an unlikely solution emerged. Norodom Sihanouk had been crowned king of Cambodia in 1941 and the country had secured independence from France in 1953. He had abdicated in 1955 in favour of his father, Suramarit, so he could get directly involved in politics. Sihanouk's political party, Sangkum, won the general elections that year, and he became prime minister. He governed the country under one-party rule and suppressed political dissent. After his father died in 1960, Sihanouk assumed a new position as chief of state of Cambodia.

At a meeting of what would later become the Non-Aligned Movement, Sihanouk met Kim Il-Sung, North Korea's Supreme Leader. The two became close friends, with Sihanouk later claiming Kim was the closest he had to family after the death of his mother. It was therefore an extension of the country's friendship with North Korea when Sihanouk offered Cambodia's capital Phnom Penh as a neutral venue for the World Cup qualifying tournament.

Cambodia had built several new facilities, including a 60,000-capacity Olympic Stadium, to host the 1963 Southeast Asian Peninsular Games. But Cambodia had to withdraw due to the political situation at the time, which would descend into the genocidal rule of the Khmer Rouge in 1975.

Cambodia had diplomatic relations with North and South Korea, as well as Australia, so in July 1965, FIFA accepted their offer. South Korea was not so keen, though, and withdrew for 'logistical reasons', although it was widely believed it was an excuse to avoid having to play their neighbours from the north. Australia also voiced objections before, in October, finally agreeing to take part in a two-legged play-off for the last place at England 1966.

Australia had not played an international match since 1958, when they had drawn 2–2 with New Zealand at Carlaw Park in Auckland. Before that, their previous game had been in 1956, against India in a friendly after they had knocked Australia out of the Olympics in Melbourne. The Indians proved that was no fluke with a thumping 7–1 victory at the Sydney Sports Ground.

After FIFA had finally lifted their ban on Australia in 1963, English Division One club Everton had toured the country the following year. Australia were coached by Jim Kelly, a former teammate of the great Sir Stanley Matthews at English Division One club Blackpool. He had emigrated to Australia in 1961, playing for South Coast United and making such an impact that, by the end of his first year, three Sydney newspapers had voted him Player of the Year. After taking over as player-coach, Kelly led South Coast to the New South Wales championship in 1963.

Kelly picked the best players he had available, including Leo Baumgartner and Karl Jaros, two of the Austrians whose decision to play in Australia had led to the FIFA ban, and former Real Madrid goalkeeper Adauto Iglesias. Even Kelly, however, could not bridge the gap that had grown between Australia and the rest of the world during the country's isolation. Everton won 8–2 at the Olympic Park in Melbourne and 5–1 at the Royal Agricultural Showground in Sydney, in front of big crowds of 32,453 and 39,794, respectively.

Everton had been followed in 1965 by Torpedo Moscow from the Soviet Union and another English Division One side, Chelsea. Torpedo won their match 2–0, but Australia showed signs of improvement against a Chelsea team managed by Tommy Docherty, drawing 2–2 at the Royal Agricultural Showground in Sydney and 1–1 at Olympic Park in Melbourne. The London club's squad included the 22-year-old Terry Venables, a future Australian coach.

For the matches against Chelsea, Australia had been coached by Tiko Jelisavcic, a Yugoslavian who had played for Partizan Belgrade and BSK Belgrade. The striker had moved to Australia in 1962 to join Yugal, a club in Sydney founded six years earlier by Yugoslav immigrants.

Jelisavcic was an inside forward who was flown in just in time to help Yugal win the New South Wales League Second Division by scoring the only goal in a match against rivals Balgownie. He then scored four goals in the final of the Australian Cup at Wentworth Park in Sydney as Yugal beat St George Budapest 8–1 in front of a crowd of 11,014.

English First Division club Everton became the first international side to visit Australia after FIFA lifted its ban in a tour sponsored by British tobacco manufacturer W.D. & H.O. Wills

By 1965, Jelisavcic was the player-coach at Hakoah in Sydney, who were enjoying a successful season, so was probably the obvious choice to lead Australia into their first World Cup adventure. The Australian Soccer Federation sent telegrams to 20 players informing them that they had been selected. The squad was made up of seven Scots, five Englishmen and five Australians, plus an Irishman, a German and a Hungarian.

Geoff Sleight, an English winger who had played for Bolton Wanderers and Wigan Athletic, had been chosen for the squad, despite having only arrived the year before to play for Sydney Prague. 'In those days if you were a Pom, you could get it [naturalised] after a year and become Australians,' he said. Other nationalities newly arrived in Australia often had to wait for five years until they were given citizenship.

Other Englishmen in the squad included 23-year-old left-back Stan Ackerley, a former Manchester United youth team player before having a brief spell with Oldham Athletic and then drifting into non-league football with Kidderminster Harriers and Altrincham. He had immigrated in 1963 to

Australia, where he joined Slavia in the Victorian State League. He quickly made an impression and the following year New South Wales State League club APIA Leichhardt paid £4,500 for him.

Among the five Australians chosen was 22-year-old St George Budapest striker Johnny Warren. Warren had two soccer-playing older brothers who had introduced him to the game. A few doors up the road in Botany, which sits on the northern shore of Botany Bay, where the First Fleet had landed in 1788, lived Johnny Watkiss.

Watkiss had been born in Willenhall in England, but his parents had immigrated to Australia when he was young. The youngsters fuelled each other's passion for soccer, and they had both played together for Canterbury-Marrickville.

There, they had come under the influence of Joe Vlasits, known to everyone as 'Uncle Joe'. He was a Hungarian who, in 1947, had migrated to Australia, where he had quickly become involved with local Sydney clubs. Vlasits had helped mould a group of promising young players, including Warren and Watkiss, into what became known as the 'Canterbury Babes' that went on to win the New South Wales League twice.

Watkiss was slightly older than Warren, at 24, and had already been called up by Jelisavcic for the matches against Chelsea. He justified his selection by scoring goals in both matches. Warren admitted in his autobiography, *Sheilas, Wogs and Poofters*, that after the telegram notifying him of his call-up for the World Cup matches, he went 'into the bathroom to cry my eyes out'.

Jelisavcic appointed the 27-year-old Les Scheinflug as captain. He had been born in German town Buckeburg and had arrived in Australia in 1955, as a 17-year-old, with his parents. He joined Sydney Prague, where he played alongside Baumgartner, 'The Little Professor', and Herbert Ninaus, another of the Austrians who had moved to Australia after the FK Austria Wien tour in 1957. Cambodia was to be the start of a long association between Scheinflug, Australia and the World Cup.

Jelisavcic decided that the ideal preparation for the squad would be a month-long training camp in Cairns, on the tropical north-east coast of Queensland, where the hot and humid conditions would help them get ready for what they were set to face in Phnom Penh. Apart from the 20 players, Jelisavcic did not have an assistant but there were two team managers in charge of planning.

They were Jim Bayutti, an Italian immigrant who in 1954 had helped found APIA Leichhardt. He owned a construction company that employed hundreds of Italians who flocked to start a new life in Australia.

The other manager was Ian Brusasco, born in Australia to Italian parents who had fled that country in 1923 because of his father's opposition to Benito

Mussolini. Felice Brusasco was president of Azzurri Football Club in Brisbane and asked his son to take over as the secretary to help out.

Brusasco accepted, despite never having seen a game of football after being brought up on rugby union at school. He promised his father he would help him for 12 months but ended up playing a leading role in the revolution that shaped the formation of the Australian Soccer Federation, becoming a dominant figure in setting up the Queensland Soccer Federation.

Australia's first World Cup squad in 1965. Back row: Jim Bayutti (manager), Ian Brusasco (official), Nigel Shepherd, Billy Rice, John Roberts, Billy Rorke, John Watkiss, Les Scheinflug, Billy Cook, Lou Lazzari (masseur), Tiko Jelisavcic (coach). Middle row: Pat Hughes, Ian Johnson, Archie Blue, Roy Blitz, David Todd, Johnny Warren. Front row: Geoff Sleight, Ron Giles, Hammy McMeechan, John Anderson, Jim Pearson, Steve Herczeg, Stan Ackerley.

Australia's team for its first World Cup qualifying match against North Korea in Phnom Penh was coached by Yugoslavian Tiko Jelisavcic and included seven Scots and five English players

The only other assistance Australia's fledgling World Cup team received was from Lou Lazzari, a masseur.

Jelisavcic was a strict, authoritarian coach brought up in Eastern European culture. When the squad gathered at the YMCA in Cairns, he informed them that there was to be no drinking and no sex. He immediately caused resentment among his squad by ignoring one of his own key rules and allowing his wife, Seka, to join the camp.

Jelisavcic worked his players hard by making them train twice a day in the oppressive heat, telling them that it would help prepare them for what they were about to face in Cambodia. The players received £5 a day as compensation for the time they were missing by being away from their day jobs.

Most of the players found Jelisavcic's approach to training unstructured and boring. 'We did some running for fitness, but apart from that, it was very poor or virtually non-existent,' said Sleight. 'There was also no organisation on set plays, such as corners and free kicks, for or against. In fact, there was not even an acknowledgement of the need for set plays to be practiced. There was no consideration given to technique or the shape of the team;

the players involved simply brought their own technique and skills if they had them.'

Even though the squad spent a month together, they did not really bond. 'There was little camaraderie, togetherness or team spirit,' said Sleight. 'There were cliques within the group, including a split between "probables" and "possibles", and players who came from the same club side tended to stick together.'

The Australians played only two matches during the training camp, both against local sides. They beat a Far North Queensland XI 17–0 with Steve Herczeg, a Hungarian refugee whose family had settled in South Australia, scoring six goals. A week later, they beat local Ingham side Herbert River-Roma 12–0, with Herczeg scoring another four, and Scottish-born Hammy McMeechan also hitting four.

It was hardly the sort of preparation to get ready for the most important matches in Australian soccer history. 'We were in camp for four weeks in north Queensland, but we never played any serious preparation matches,' said Scheinflug. 'All we did was run in the morning and in the afternoon because we knew Phnom Penh would be hot. We never saw the ball.'

In the second warm-up match, Scheinflug suffered an injured ankle which he was still struggling to shake off when the team arrived in Cambodia.

The players were overwhelmingly confident, however, that they were going to beat North Korea. 'For the whole four weeks in the training camp, and even during the trip over to Cambodia, I can remember all the boys talking about what they were going to do after the World Cup in England,' Warren wrote in his autobiography. 'Everyone seemed to think it was a mere formality to go and beat the North Koreans, even though we knew nothing about how they played.'

Some players even speculated that the North Koreans may not bother turning up.

Australia had little idea what was happening in soccer outside their own country, apart from in England, highlights of which were shown weekly on television. They had even less idea about football in North Korea, a country more of a mystery back then than it is now. To be fair, at that point, few people in the world had any idea about how good North Korea was at football.

The World Cup was important to Kim Il-Sung, who saw football as an opportunity to display his ideology of '*Juche*' – 'self-reliance' – to the world by fielding a winning national team. North Korea had been officially formed in 1948. It came after Korea had been divided into two zones along the 38th parallel at the end of the Second World War, with the north occupied by the Soviet Union and the south by the United States.

The Korean War had started in 1950, when troops from the north had invaded the south. More than 2.5 million Korean civilians were killed during the War, and North Korea's capital, Pyongyang, was largely destroyed during bombing by the United States and its allies. The country began a period of self-isolation which continues until this day.

The Chollima Movement, named after a Chinese mythological flying horse, was launched by Kim and was intended to promote rapid economic development. The Chollima was supposed to be able to accomplish the most difficult tasks and lead heroes to victory, showing absolute effort and sacrifice – physical and mental – for the sake of the homeland. As the 'economic miracle' promised by Kim failed to materialise, North Korea's footballers came to be the showcase for the Chollima philosophy.

The North Koreans had already been in a training camp for several months by the time they arrived in Phnom Penh, working on their fitness and tactics and being brainwashed with how their mission was to sacrifice themselves for their 'eternal leader'. The players trained with elastic bands on their legs to strengthen their muscles. The goalkeeper, Lee Chang-Myung, only five foot five inches tall, was made to leap hundreds of times per day towards the crossbar until he was able to touch it slightly above his elbow.

The team had played five official friendly matches before departing for Cambodia, winning all of them without conceding a goal. This included a 4–0 victory against Khmer, 3–0 wins against Indonesia, Guinea and China, and a 1–0 win over North Vietnam. Altogether, in the preceding two years, the North Koreans had played 34 matches, winning 30 of them and losing only two.

Les Channing, a journalist who closely followed what was happening in football in Asia, was among the few to have seen North Korea in action and warned the Australians not to underestimate their opponents.

'Frankly speaking, something more than mere speed and stamina will be required to defeat the North Koreans,' he wrote in *Soccer World*. 'The North Koreans have a good knowledge of modern football techniques. Their play is a combination of speed, stamina, strength, superb ball control on the ground and in the air. Tigerish first-time tackling, crisp shooting and excellent teamwork.'

The Australians travelled to Phnom Penh via Bangkok, where relations with Jelisavcic were strained even further when he was caught cheating at cards. Team managers Bayutti and Brusasco called a team meeting, where they were made aware of how angry the players were and that any confidence they had in Jelisavcic had now been totally eroded. There was little choice, however, but for the party to continue towards Cambodia with Jelisavcic at the helm.

Security was tight when the Australians touched down in Cambodia for what would be the national team's first match recognised by FIFA. Sihanouk had skilfully managed to avoid Cambodia getting dragged into the war in neighbouring Vietnam. But in May 1965, he had broken diplomatic relations with the United States, ended the flow of American aid, and turned to China and the Soviet Union for economic and military assistance. Sihanouk had blamed America for recent cross-border air attacks by South Vietnam that had killed Cambodian citizens.

Herczeg remembered, after arriving, hearing the 'sound of gunfire all around' – a forerunner of what the Australian soccer team were to face regularly on trips in the future.

The Australians were surprised to discover, after landing seven days before the first match, that not only had the North Koreans turned up but they had been there for two weeks already, getting acclimatised.

The event was a major public relations opportunity for Sihanouk, and he was determined not to waste it. After arriving, the Australians were escorted to the Hotel Le Royale, a stunning French colonial building, which was luxury after a month in a YMCA.

Jelisavcic remained the strict disciplinarian. He allowed the players to relax by the hotel swimming pool after training sessions conducted in 90-degree heat but banned them from entering the water. Jelisavcic believed that swimming would lead to stiff muscles.

Before the opening match, both the Australian and North Korean teams were paraded through Phnom Penh in open-top buses on a 'royal progress' tour. Thousands of Cambodians lined the streets to catch a glimpse of the foreign footballers. A lavish welcome reception and dinner was arranged and attended by Sihanouk, and a special performance of Cambodia's royal ballet entertained the guests. The Australians were 'treated like kings', it was reported.

For all of Jelisavcic's rules, little attention was paid by the Australians to what they were eating and drinking. Everyone ate the local food and drank the water. At one official dinner, the Australian party were fed snake, at which most of them drew the line.

It was not long before the squad began going down with stomach problems. The goalkeeper, John Roberts, estimated that he lost a stone and a half while he was in Cambodia and reported that he engaged in a constant battle with roommate Watkiss as to who would get to use the toilet. The illness that swept through the squad meant that winger Roy Blitz, an Englishman who had played for Fulham's youth team, missed the first leg of the tie.

Still, none of this did anything to shatter the confidence of the Australian management that they would beat North Korea. A few days before the first leg on 21st November, Jelisavcic and Bayutti went to watch the North Koreans train at the Olympic Stadium. They had hoped to remain anonymous but were recognised by local football officials, who guided them to the VIP section next to the North Korean delegation.

Jelisavcic claimed he was not overly impressed by what he had seen. 'We shall beat them,' he told Australian Associated Press reporter Jim Shrimpton.

Australia's players did not quite share their coach's confidence, with doubts beginning to creep in after watching North Korea train. 'They immediately appeared very fast and very skilful,' Warren admitted in his autobiography. 'Most of the Korean players had up to 60 or 70 international caps under their belts, and all of them were full-time soccer players and army personnel.

'We, on the other hand, were very much part-time players. I knew quite well that our team was largely inexperienced at international level, and it was now becoming clear that the opposition was not the pushover we were expecting.'

Two days before the first match, the North Korean squad had played a gentle nine-a-side warm-up match, and then stayed behind to watch the Australians take part in a full-scale practice match between the 11 'probables' against the nine 'possibles', who were supplemented by Jelisavcic and a local Cambodian player. 'It sounds crazy, but that's what happened,' Sleight, playing for the main team, said.

Yet, even after everything they had seen and found out about the North Koreans, the Australians remained sufficiently confident of winning for the squad to organise a sweepstake as to what the final score would be.

Sihanouk had ordered officials in Cambodia to ensure that the Olympic Stadium was full for the first leg. Before the match kicked off in front of a crowd of 60,000, he presented both teams with a specially minted medal. The Australians gave each of their North Korean opponents an Aboriginal boomerang as a mark of respect.

From the start, in a match played in temperatures approaching 100 degrees, it was clear that the North Koreans were going to live up to the billing given by Channing of having 'speed, stamina, strength, superb ball control on the ground and in the air'. The Cambodian crowd were fully behind their friends from North Korea and cheered them on enthusiastically.

Australia, playing in an attacking 4-2-4 formation and wearing green shirts with white shorts, were totally overwhelmed from the first whistle. They did well to keep the score down to just one at half-time after Pak Doo-ik had put the red-shirted North Koreans ahead in the 15th minute. In the second half, the North Koreans' intense preparations really began to show as they scored three goals during an 11-minute period. Pak Seung-zin scored in the 54th minute, then Im Shung-hwi in the 58th and then Han Bong-zin in the 65th.

Scheinflug, who had needed an injection on the ankle he had injured before they left Cairns just to be able to play, managed to pull one back for Australia in the 70th minute with a penalty. More than half of Australia's team were suffering from stomach problems as a result of eating the local food and drinking the water. In those days, substitutes were not allowed, so they all had to battle on. 'In the second half, those sick boys couldn't run,' remembered Sleight.

'We were buggered,' was how Scheinflug described it, so it was no surprise North Korea took advantage by adding more goals from Pak Seung-zin and Han Bong-zin in the 80th and 88th minutes, respectively, to give them a 6–1 victory. The final goal summed up the skill the North Koreans possessed as they sliced through Australia's defence with a series of quick-passing.

'We were completely out of our depth,' Warren, who watched from the bench, admitted. 'We hadn't known our opponent, and we weren't properly match fit.'

How Jelisavcic thought his team of part-timers could beat a well-drilled team like North Korea is a mystery. Afterwards, he admitted sheepishly that 'the Koreans are world-class.'

Scheinflug was in no doubt that they were let down badly by their coach. 'We could have done much better with a coach who could give us more information about the opposition and a doctor who could advise us what not to eat and drink in Cambodia,' he said.

There was silence on Australia's team bus heading back to the hotel until Sleight broke the ice. 'I said that things could have been worse; that if we hadn't scored, we could have lost 6–0,' he recalled. 'I also had a 6–1 scoreline in the sweep! My bet had actually been on a 6–1 win for us, but the others had felt that was such an outrageous suggestion that they had let me have it on both teams. I won the sweep – every cloud has a silver lining.'

Bayutti was on the bus and furious with Sleight's frivolous attitude. He was dropped for the next match and, apart from a brief few minutes as a substitute in a friendly, never played for Australia again.

Sleight returned home to England the following year at the end of his three-year contract with Sydney Prague. He played non-league football for several clubs, including Macclesfield Town, Mossley and Frickley Athletic, and later became chief scout at then Premier League club Leeds United. Sleight earned enough from playing soccer in Australia that when he returned to the United Kingdom, he had saved more than £1,000 to put down as a deposit on a new house.

North Korea's performance in that first match had set alarm bells ringing even louder thousands of miles away in London. The British government were growing increasingly fearful of a country with whom they had no diplomatic relations qualifying for England 1966.

Moving the tournament from England altogether was even considered by Prime Minister Harold Wilson, though that was quickly dismissed due to the 'undesirable political repercussions' it might provoke. Between them, the Football Association and the Foreign Office hoped that somehow Australia could pull off a sporting miracle to avoid them having to figure out how a team representing a *de facto* enemy of the British state would be allowed to play in England.

The Australians, of course, had no idea of how much was riding on their performance in the second leg three days later on 24th November. The margin of the defeat in the first leg did not mean that Australia's World Cup hopes were over. In those days, aggregate did not count. If Australia won, there would be a replay.

For the second leg, Roberts was replaced by 20-year-old Bill Rorke after criticism of the goalkeeper's display in the first game. Roberts never played for his country again, but the performance did not appear to harm his career as he became one of the first Australian-born players to establish himself in English football with Blackburn Rovers, Chesterfield, Bradford City, Southend United and Northampton Town.

Rorke's selection was one of five changes and marked a change of tactics by Jelisavcic, who told his players to mark their rivals individually but still attack whenever the opportunity presented itself.

It looked like a remarkable comeback could be on the cards when, in the 15th minute, Scheinflug, still playing in pain due to his ankle injury, put Australia in front against the run of play in front of 55,000 fans. John Anderson, a Scots-born winger who played for South Melbourne Hellas, immediately missed an opportunity to double Australia's lead. It proved a costly miss as, in the 18th minute, Kim Seung-il equalised for North Korea.

The Australians gave a far better account of themselves in the second leg but were ultimately no match for their full-time opponents as Pak Seung-zin scored his third goal of the tie in the 53rd minute before Kim Seung-il his second of the game a quarter of an hour from the end. English journalist Eric Batty, a writer for *World Soccer*, claimed that 'Australian sport has never been so embarrassed'.

Lou Gautier, though, believed that Australia had been beaten by a team that was set to shock the world at England 1966. 'This North Korea will be a tough customer and it will be anything but outplayed,' he predicted in *Soccer World*. 'The Australian team provided their own assessment, and they were unanimous that North Korea was a far superior team to those they had recently played against like Everton, Chelsea and Torpedo Moscow.'

Any remaining respect that the players had for Jelisavcic disappeared in the final few minutes of the second match. Billy Rice, the Belfast-born centre-back, had given everything in the two matches in the heat and humidity, despite being one of the players to suffer from diarrhoea. He was terribly ill at half-time but still went out for the second half. Towards the end of the match, Rice collapsed and was carried off by his teammates. Jelisavcic demanded, 'Let the bastard walk!' The players were not slow in letting Jelisavcic know what they thought about him.

Following the humbling experience against North Korea, the Australian Soccer Federation commissioned a special report from key officials involved in the planning and preparation. Among the reasons Jelisavcic blamed was 'insufficient adjustment to the extremely heavy tropical climatic conditions', the 'first international match played outside of Australia' and 'a huge number of spectators'. He also claimed that the players had suffered 'stage fright' because of the 'importance of the match'.

Co-managers Bayutti and Brusasco also provided suggestions to help improve the team for future World Cup campaigns, including closer links with Asia. Apart from an oblique reference by Brusasco to a 'slight disharmony', there was no mention of Jelisavcic being a cheat at cards and of the players' general lack of respect for him.

The Australian team did not return home immediately as the Australian Soccer Federation had organised a five-game tour of Asia, partially to help offset the cost of the trip to Cambodia.

It was not the only piece of bizarre scheduling by the Federation as they had arranged for the final of the Australian Cup, between APIA Leichhardt and Sydney Hakoah, to take place at Wentworth Park in Sydney on the same day as the first leg of the World Cup qualifying game.

The match ended 1–1 after extra time and a penalty shootout, one of the first played anywhere in the world, was ordered. This was abandoned with the score at 13–13 due to the fading light. The two teams met again in a replay on 24th November – the same day as the World Cup second leg in Phnom Penh – with Sydney winning 2–1, despite missing their player-coach Jelisavcic. APIA, meanwhile, were forced to play the final without several key players, including Roberts, Pat Hughes, Ackerley and Watkiss.

The first match of the post-World Cup tour came in Phnom Penh only two days after their humbling at the hands of North Korea. Still tired, they played a 0–0 draw against Cambodia's national team in a match that was significant because it was the first time Warren appeared in an Australian shirt.

From there, the party travelled to Hong Kong to take part in a mini tournament called the Scandinavian Airlines System Cup, featuring the host country and Swedish club side AIK Stockholm. The Australians were knocked out as they lost 1–0 to Hong Kong.

After that, Australia played a game against a Hong Kong FA XI, which featured nine players from Taiwan. It was a hard, bruising game before a hostile crowd of 13,800, with the Australians giving as good as they got. The *China Mail* described it as a 'degrading, disgusting, despicable so-called soccer spectacle'. Australia won 3–1 thanks to a hat-trick from Archie Blue. Blue was a Glasgow-born striker who had played in the English Football League for Exeter City and Carlisle United, before moving to Australia in 1963 to join Footscray JUST.

Towards the end of the game, as tempers boiled over, Australia had Scottish-born defender Billy Cook sent off. It is claimed that when dismissing him, the English referee, Fred Parlett, told the former Kilmarnock player, 'Son, I'm going to send you off for your own good.'

After the final whistle, the local fans threw stones at the Australian players as they left the field, and then tried to storm their dressing room. The team had to stay there for two hours until officials managed to control the situation enough to smuggle them out in a police van. Shrimpton, the Australian Associated Press reporter covering the tour, recalled having to file his match report from underneath a table to avoid the rocks being flung through the windows.

Gautier claimed that the reason the home fans were so upset was nothing to do with the Australians' physical approach, but the fact that they had backed their team heavily at the bookmakers to beat their opponents. 'At the final whistle, the crowd's hostility was directed as much to its own players, and the Chinese team, too, had to be escorted home in a police Black Maria,' he wrote in *Soccer World*. It was not the last time that an Australian soccer side touring Asia would find itself needing police protection from angry supporters.

Several months later, the Hong Kong Football Association published the results of an inquiry into the crowd disturbances. The Association's secretary, Joseph Wong, admitted the Australians were nothing to do with the trouble and 'they had played hard, but clean and fair football'. The Hong Kong FA 'put the blame for the riot on some of their own players for inciting the crowd with unsportsmanlike conduct and antics'.

It was a relieved Australian squad that left Hong Kong for the finale of their tour in Malaysia. The team played Malaysia's national team on consecutive days at the Perak Stadium, on a site in Ipoh once used to detain communist supporters during the Malayan Emergency between 1948 and 1960. Australia won the first match 1–0 with a goal from Jim Pearson, a Scot who had played for Greenock Morton and Aberdeen before emigrating to Australia in 1962.

By now, Australia were really on top form and concluded the tour with a 3–0 victory against Malaysia in front of less than 300 spectators, thanks to goals from English-born Dave Todd, Ian Johnstone and Scheinflug.

Australia's first trip to Asia came at a huge personal cost for Scheinflug. 'The ankle injury I suffered in that trial in Ingham affected my career,' he said. 'It was never handled properly, and I was given injections to be able to play against Korea. When I came back from Cambodia it got worse and I did not play for nearly a year. I was given more injections, but it never healed properly.'

All the players involved in Australia's matches in Cambodia are convinced that they would have performed more credibly if they had played these friendlies before the games against North Korea and not after. 'Had we gone to Asia for our preparation and played tough opponents, instead of staying in

Cairns and thrashing local sides, we would have had a better chance,' Ackerley said. 'The Federation probably could not afford to send us away for a whole month.'

The North Korean team had received 'The People's Hero Award' upon their return to Pyongyang from Cambodia but, three days after the second match against Australia, had gone back into a training camp at a military barracks in preparation for the World Cup.

Australia's results against North Korea did not look quite so bad after their opponent's performance at England 1966. Before the tournament started, the North Korean team had been talked up by the Communist Party of Great Britain, who gave the team plenty of coverage in their daily newspaper the *Morning Star*.

In the lead-up to the tournament, the North Koreans were described in the pages of the paper as the 'dark horses of the battles' for the trophy and the 'mystery team' of the tournament, who had 'sensationally defeated Australia' but were still regarded as '100-1 outsiders for the World Cup'.

A column in the *Morning Star*, before North Korea's first game of the tournament, added: 'All we know of North Korea is that the team has trained together for the last two years – plus their devastating performances against Australia … but even this is not as informative as it might seem. Australia are no great shakes in the world of soccer, ranking, possibly, at Third Division level.'

North Korea's qualification continued to cause all sorts of diplomatic problems behind the scenes. South Korea lobbied hard for the North Korean flag to be banned from the World Cup. This was turned down, but the Foreign Office in London did order that a set of commemorative stamps showing the flags of all 16 competing countries at the tournament be withdrawn by the Post Office.

The presence of North Korea also precipitated a major change in World Cup protocol, when the original plan to have both nations' anthems played before each match was altered. Instead, the anthems were played only before the opening game of each country and before the final in a bid to minimise the amount of times the North Korean national anthem *Aegukka* was played.

North Korea lost their opening match 3–0 against the Soviet Union at Ayresome Park in Middlesbrough before drawing 1–1 with Chile, Pak Seung-zin equalising two minutes from the end. In the final group match, North Korea caused one of the biggest shocks in history when they beat the two-time World Cup winners Italy 1–0 with a 42nd-minute goal from Pak Doo-ik, another of the players who had scored against Australia.

The crowd of 17,829 that day included 18-year-old Peter Wilson, a local footballer destined later to become a major figure in the history of Australian soccer.

The victory meant the North Koreans qualified for the quarter-finals, where they met Portugal at Goodison Park in Liverpool. Backed by 3,000 fans from Middlesbrough, who had taken the team to their hearts, North Korea raced into a 3–0 lead inside 25 minutes – Pak Seung-zin scoring again. Inspired by Eusebio, Portugal pulled the match back to win 5–3, but it demonstrated just how good a team North Korea were.

At least one group of English football fans – beside those of the *Morning Star* – would not have been surprised by North Korea's performance. 'When I was in England on holiday, I was asked by the *Daily Express* to write three columns about North Korea, who were 500-1 to even score a goal,' Ackerley revealed.

'Nobody knew anything about them. I wrote amongst other things that I would not be surprised if they made the semi-finals. Well, they were three-up in the quarter-final against Portugal, so I was not far off the mark. The newspaper articles were a consolation of sorts because I got paid much more than I would have been had we qualified.'

The performance of North Korea at that World Cup is still celebrated. In 2002, many of the surviving members of the team were granted permission by the government in Pyongyang to return to England to take part in a documentary film *The Game of Their Lives*.

When the team travelled back to Goodison Park, there to meet them were Todd and Sleight, two of the Englishmen who had been part of Australia's squad in Phnom Penh. 'It was amazing,' Todd said.

Englishman Dave Todd, Australian international number 173, still treasures the cap he was rewarded for playing against North Korea

'And we met them all. There were only seven of their players left, but Everton issued them with Everton shirts with their names on the back.'

In 2015, Todd and Sleight travelled back to Sydney for Australia's own special 50th anniversary reunion of the Cambodia squad. Warren, who had died in 2004, was among those missing, along with Jelisavcic.

Jelisavcic's period in charge of Australia was not a success, and he had left with little respect from the players he had led in their historic campaign. What no one was aware of at the time was the legacy he was to bestow on Australian soccer, thanks to a meeting he had had two years earlier with another Yugoslavian footballer in Belgrade. His name was Zvonimir Rasic.

Football Federation Australia held a 50th-year anniversary reunion for Australia's 1965 World Cup qualifying squad

After leaving Australia, Jelisavcic later re-emerged as the coach of Nigeria's team, where he was more successful. He led them to third-place finishes in the Africa Cup of Nations tournaments in 1976 and 1978, before moving to coach in Mexico, where he was killed in a car crash in 1986 at the age of 57.

During the reunion, the team of 1965 spent some time with the Socceroos of 2005, who had ended Australia's 32-year absence from the World Cup finals when they qualified for Germany 2006.

'These pioneers laid the foundations of the future World Cup qualifying campaigns and broke new ground under trying conditions, and with extremely limited resources, as they travelled to play in a place totally foreign to them,' David Gallop, the chief executive of the Football Federation of Australia, said in a speech. 'Considering the challenges they faced, and the magnitude of what they were up against, these trailblazers epitomise what it means to represent your country. They have, and will continue to leave, a lasting legacy for Australian football.'

CHAPTER THREE

Fergie time

Australia's return to international football had not gone to plan, and the way they had been outplayed in Phnom Penh by North Korea had opened many people's eyes to how far they still had to go to compete with the best sides in Asia, let alone the rest of the world.

Australia's application to join the Asian Football Confederation in 1964, after FIFA had lifted their ban, was rejected. Jim Bayutti, the co-manager during Australia's matches in Cambodia, had then launched plans to establish the Oceania Football Confederation, together with Sid Guppy, chairman of the New Zealand Football Association, and FIFA president Sir Stanley Rous.

Other key officials within FIFA were not so keen on the establishment of a separate confederation representing Oceania. FIFA general secretary, Helmut Kaser, was a leading opponent and claimed, 'It was felt this name had no real meaning.' The Australian Soccer Federation were reduced to sending FIFA a summary from the *Encyclopaedia Britannica* to prove that Oceania really did exist.

The Oceania Football Confederation was officially given recognition by FIFA at its Congress in London on the eve of the 1966 World Cup, with Australia, Fiji, New Zealand and Papua New Guinea as the founding members, and French-controlled New Caledonia given associate membership.

In 1968, the first Oceania Football Confederation Congress was held at the Metropolitan Motel in Brisbane, and Sir Willam Walkley and Ian McAndrew, the president and secretary of the Australian Soccer Federation, respectively, were elected to the same positions for the new organisation.

Bayutti remained a passionate believer that Australia needed to establish closer links with Asia if the sport in the country was to progress. He lobbied for Australia to take part in the Merkeda Tournament, an annual event in Kuala Lumpur which attracted some of the continent's top teams. Australia accepted an invitation to compete in 1966 but then withdrew because they could not afford to fund the trip.

In the end, Australia played only one match in 1966, when a team containing mainly Sydney-based players met Roma during the Italian club's tour. The team was coached by Joe Marston, who since returning from English First Division club Preston North End in 1956, due to homesickness, had played for and then managed APIA Leichhardt.

This was actually Marston's second spell coaching Australia as he had also led them when English side Blackpool, including Sir Stanley Matthews, had toured the country in 1958 and again the following year when Scottish club Heart of Midlothian visited.

Only four of the players involved in Australia's matches against North Korea – Bill Rorke, Pat Hughes, Billy Rice and Johnny Watkiss – played against Roma at the Royal Agricultural Showground in Sydney on 13th June before a disappointing crowd of 5,469. The Australians were captained by Trevor Edwards, who had been part of Wales' squad at the 1958 World Cup in Sweden, before moving to Australia six years later to play for Sydney Hakoah. Also included was Bruce Morrow, who had played for Australia at the 1956 Olympic Games in Melbourne when he had scored both goals in their 4–2 defeat against India in the quarter-finals.

It was Morrow who put Australia ahead against Roma in the 66th minute before the guests equalised in the last minute with a freak goal. The ball got stuck in the mud, deceiving Rorke and Edwards, and allowed Giuseppe Tamborini to make it 1–1. 'Were the Romans happy?' wrote Andrew Dettre in *Soccer World*. 'They embraced and kissed as if they had just won the European Cup instead of merely drawing with a scratch Australian XI that had never trained together before the match.'

When Bayutti returned from the 1966 World Cup, where he saw England lift the trophy with a 4–2 victory over West Germany at Wembley Stadium, he was put in charge of Australia's preparations for Mexico 1970. He promised matches in 1967 against Scotland and Manchester United, regular training camps and an overseas tour lasting up to two months, including games in Hong Kong, Singapore, Malaysia, India and Iran. 'We haven't got a moment to waste,' he said.

But plans to enter a team for the qualifying competition for the 1968 Olympic Games in Mexico City were shot down by the Australian Olympic Federation. They claimed they did not want to 'look ridiculous' on the international stage.

During the 1966 World Cup, Bayutti and McAndrew had invited several countries to take on Australia's fledgling international team. In the end, the only one that honoured the commitment they had made was Scotland, who were planning a major worldwide tour in 1967 to help their own preparations for qualifying for the next World Cup. The news that they would play a three-match series was greeted with much excitement among the thousands of Scottish ex-pats in Australia.

The status of the matches caused controversy from the start in a row that rumbled on for more than half a century. When the announcement was made, Bayutti claimed the matches would also have added significance because they

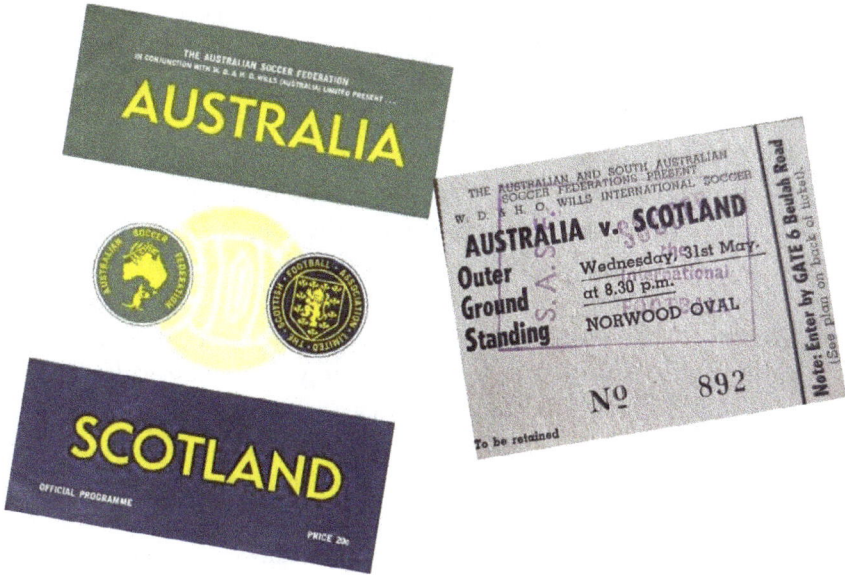

The Australian Soccer Federation insisted the matches against Scotland were full internationals

would be the first international matches recognised by FIFA to be played in Australia. FIFA confirmed this when they included the upcoming games in their monthly bulletin as full internationals.

This was contradicted by Scottish Football Association secretary Willie Allan, who warned that the squad sent on the world tour would be a mixture of established international and up-and-coming youngsters. 'Under no circumstances should they be labelled a Scottish international team,' he told the *Glasgow Herald* newspaper. 'Our newly-won prestige, both at international and club level, is too precious for that.'

Scotland announced its preliminary squad in the middle of March 1967 for the month-long tour that would start in Israel and then travel to Hong Kong before arriving in Australia. After a week there, they would go on to New Zealand and Canada before heading home.

The squad included several well-known names such as Celtic's Tommy Gemmell and Willie Wallace, Rangers' John Greig and Ronnie McKinnon, Leeds United's Billy Bremner and Peter Lorimer, and Sheffield Wednesday's Jim McCalliog. It also included several names not that widely known outside the United Kingdom, including 19-year-old Leeds winger Eddie Gray and a striker called Alex Ferguson.

The 25-year-old Ferguson had been rewarded for a remarkable couple of seasons at Dunfermline, during which he had scored 66 goals in 89 appearances.

It was made clear that the final strength of the Scottish squad would depend on players' commitments to their clubs.

In April, a Scottish side captained by Greig, and including Gemmell, McKinnon, Wallace, Bremner and McCalliog, beat neighbours England 3–2 at Wembley Stadium. It was England's first defeat since lifting the World Cup the previous year, making Scotland 'world champions' in the words of many of their supporters. It ensured legendary status for Scotland's new manager, Bobby Brown, a former Rangers player who had been appointed to the national role having impressed at St Johnstone.

That victory at Wembley was one of the major highlights of 1967 and part of 'Scottish football's finest year'. Scotland's top club sides made a massive impact in European football. Celtic, making their debut in the tournament, became the first British side to win the European Cup by beating Inter Milan 2–1 in Lisbon. A week later, Glasgow rivals Rangers narrowly failed to make it a double when they lost 1–0 to Bayern Munich in the final of the European Cup Winners' Cup in Nuremberg. Kilmarnock, meanwhile, reached the semi-final of the Inter-Cities Fairs Cup before losing to Leeds United.

The success in Europe of the clubs, along with Leeds United, had a huge impact on the squad chosen by Scotland for their tour. Out of the original party of 17, 11 had to drop out. On 29th April, the day of the Scottish Cup final between Celtic and Aberdeen, the Scottish Football Association held an emergency meeting to decide whether they should cancel the tour or go ahead with a much-weakened squad.

In the end, they decided to continue with their plans, and among the replacements drafted in was Arsenal's Frank McLintock, Burnley's Willie Morgan, Huddersfield Town's Joe Harper and Chelsea's Eddie McCreadie, a member of the team that had beaten England at Wembley. But McCreadie was then withdrawn by his club, Chelsea, after they reached the FA Cup final, and Arsenal prevented McLintock from joining the tour. Brown continued to defend the venture. 'This is no holiday,' he said. 'This is a strictly business assignment.'

Soccer World led the protests about the number of reserves in the party. Under a front-page headline, 'THIS DILUTED SCOTCH ISN'T WHAT WE WANT!', they claimed the Australian Soccer Federation should have 'called the tour off'. The newspaper asked, 'Why should it be the Australian fans who get the second (if not third) best of everything?'

Scotland's governing body came in for especially harsh words from *Soccer World*. 'This whole sorry business proves once again what many of us have known already: the Scottish FA is one of the most unfortunate football organisations in the world,' they wrote. 'It has no control over the Anglo-Scots (players who are with English clubs) and, in the off-season, not even with the Scots.

'Time and again, Scotland has failed to achieve any success at all at full international level – not because their players were untalented, but their organisation was weak.'

The only positive aspect, according to *Soccer World*, was that 'their team will be much weaker than expected and thus the three matches will be much closer.'

Australia's mainstream press were also extremely critical of the composition of Scotland's travelling party. 'The original team has been so whittled down that it even includes players who have never even represented their English clubs in the first-team,' the *Daily Mirror* in Sydney wrote. 'And they have the arrogant unmitigated nerve to announce this is only a flag-waving tour, a goodwill tour to show how Scottish football is played. We should by rights meet them with a team of Aboriginals, who have never seen a Scottish team before. We are footing the bill and we have every right to expect the chance of seeing the best.'

The *Daily Mirror* claimed the Australian Soccer Federation were as responsible as the Scottish Football Association. 'It was obvious we were being taken for a ride months ago,' the newspaper wrote. 'Why on earth could they not have been tough and told the Scots to get back to haggis bashing? We should have the Scots we expect – the best or nothing.'

The editorial concluded with the hope that their early tour opponents did not 'beat these cocky Scots en route before we have the chance to get at them.'

Mind you, Australia's preparations were not much more organised. At the beginning of April, they announced a preliminary squad of 46 players, including 27 from New South Wales, for the series against Scotland. Members were nominated by the Australian Coaching Federation in each of the states in conjunction with the Australian Soccer Federation's National Team Sub-Committee. At this stage, a coach to replace Tiko Jelisavcic had not been appointed.

It was more than three weeks after this preliminary squad was made public before it was revealed that Jozef Venglos was the surprise choice of Bayutti to coach Australia against Scotland. The 31-year-old had only arrived in the country from Czechoslovakia less than a year earlier. Venglos had played as a midfielder for Slovan Bratislava for 12 years until 1966, the year he had toured Australia with them, and also represented Czechoslovakia at B level before his career was ended by hepatitis.

Venglos had been appointed by Sydney Prague in August 1966 to replace Stefan Cambal, a member of the Czechoslovakia side who had reached the 1934 World Cup final, where they were beaten by hosts Italy. Venglos, a qualified physical education teacher, had only been in the country a few weeks when *Soccer World* reported that 'his coaching methods are so novel and interesting that his coaching classes are extremely well attended.'

Venglos may have impressed the soccer community in Australia, but his teaching qualifications were not recognised in the country, so at first no school was able to employ him. To complement his modest salary as Sydney Prague coach after his arrival, Venglos worked as a factory hand, where his roles included keeping machinery clean and helping out wherever he was needed. It is unlikely anyone there realised they were sharing the factory floor with a man destined to become one of Europe's top soccer coaches. In the end, Venglos managed to get a job as a PE teacher in a Sydney high school.

At the same time Venglos was beginning to carve out his coaching career in Australia, the six-year spell in the country of his predecessor, Jelisavcic, was ending. He was soon to pay the price for a series of poor results at Sydney Hakoah and, at the end of 1967, left Australia for good.

When the preliminary squad for the matches against Scotland was cut to 18, it contained seven survivors from Australia's 1965 tour of Asia. They included goalkeeper Rorke, defenders Nigel Shepherd, Rice, Billy Cook and Watkiss, midfielder Pat Hughes and striker Johnny Warren. The selection of Hughes and Cook must have been particularly special as both had been born and started their careers in Scotland.

Hughes had played in the Scottish junior leagues in West Dunbartonshire with Duntocher Hibernian before immigrating to Australia in 1960 to join APIA Leichhardt. He had captained Australia on the Asian tour in the matches against Cambodia, Hong Kong and the first game in Malaysia.

Cook had seemed destined for a fine career in Scotland after captaining the country's under-15 schoolboys' team. English Division One club Everton had been interested in signing him, but his father thought he was too young to move to Liverpool. So, on leaving school, he began his electrician apprenticeship, while impressing on the football field with hometown side Galston Amateurs. From there, he had moved to junior side Ardrossan Winton Rovers, before quickly joining Kilmarnock.

Under the former Rangers winger Willie Waddell, Kilmarnock were enjoying the best period in their history, which would peak in 1964–1965 with them winning the Scottish League. It was difficult for Cook to break into the side, so, in 1963, after just 15 appearances, he accepted an offer to join Victoria State League club Slavia Melbourne.

Luckily, Cook's sending-off for his 'own good' in the 1965 match against the Hong Kong XI, which had ended in a riot, did not seem to have been held against him by the Australian selectors. Hughes and Cook were two of seven Scottish-born players included in the squad.

A couple of new names set to make a big impact in the future were also picked. They were 20-year-old strikers Ray Baartz, who had recently joined Sydney Hakoah for an Australian record transfer fee of £5,600 from Adamstown Rosebud in Newcastle, and Melbourne Hungaria's Atti Abonyi.

It is doubtful that Venglos had much say in the squad's selection as the final choice was made by Bayutti after consultation with several officials from the other states in Australia. Selection by committee at that time was not unusual in several countries. Even in Scotland, a group of officials had chosen the team until the appointment of Brown, who had demanded the authority to be allowed to pick who he wanted.

The discrimination that 'wogball' still faced establishing itself as a mainstream sport was demonstrated when the Australian Soccer Federation tried to book the Sydney Cricket Ground to host the first full international to be played in the country and a match which was gaining unprecedented attention. The trust that ran the ground, however, turned them down because the game was due to take place on a Sunday. Most people, though, assumed it was more to do with the fact they did not want to be associated with soccer.

'Let us not fool ourselves any longer,' *Soccer World* wrote in an editorial. 'Soccer, in the eyes of some higher ups in this country, is still a dirty word. To them, it's not the world's greatest and most popular sport – which in fact it is – but is synonymous with foreigners, over-publicised riots and, alas, a clear threat to rugby. This being so, they do everything in their power – or beyond – to stifle the natural growth of soccer.'

Scotland's party arrived in Sydney on 27th May, the day before the opening match against Australia, having beaten Israel 2–1 in Tel Aviv and Hong Kong 4–1, where their visit coincided with the start of large-scale anti-government riots.

Brown was met at the airport by a hostile Australian media, who claimed the Scottish party contained 'third-rate' players and made much of the fact it was an 'insult to Australia'. He continued to defend the strength. 'The team has a great deal of quality,' he told the reporters. 'Every player has considerable first-team experience.'

The status of Scotland's touring party remained a matter of dispute. The Scottish Football Association were still insisting that no full caps would be awarded to players who appeared in any of the matches on the tour. Allan, the Scottish FA secretary, angrily refuted claims that Australia had been deceived. 'Australia knew what the situation was from the start,' he said. 'There was no suggestion of deception.'

The Australian Soccer Federation continued to claim the matches would be full internationals, despite the furore and Scotland's admission that this was not their best team. 'In welcoming Scotland to Australia, I also want to thank our visitors for enabling us to stage our very first full home internationals,' Bayutti wrote in the match programme. 'We know we have a great deal to learn from

Scotland, but we are willing to learn. There is no reason why Australia, which has produced so many champions in other sports, cannot one day compete with the best on equal terms in soccer.'

Scotland's visit down under was partly funded by a sponsorship deal between the Australian Soccer Federation and W.D. & H.O. Wills, 'the makers of Craven Filter cigarettes'. The British tobacco manufacturing company had sponsored several tours to Australia by visiting European club sides since FIFA had lifted its ban. Its advert in the programme for the Scotland matches claimed they were honoured to help bring them over 'to play Australia in a series of "Full International" matches, the first ever played here'.

With the Sydney Cricket Ground refusing to back down on their refusal to stage the opening match in the series, the game instead took place at the Royal Agricultural Showground at Moore Park. The Showground was best known for hosting the annual Sydney Royal Easter Show since 1882. But it also had a rich sporting heritage, having been the venue in 1907 for the first game of rugby league in Australia when New South Wales played against a group from New Zealand.

The Showground contained an egg-shaped speedway track measuring 509 metres, which also doubled as a venue for harness racing. Promoters claimed the speedway track was the fastest in the world – it was certainly one of the most dangerous. By 1967, it had claimed the lives of 25 riders. There was also a hint of danger when one spectator decided to run around the track waving a Scottish flag at half-time. He was lucky to get away with being jeered and slow handclapped by angry Australian fans.

A crowd of 34,792 had gathered to watch a match that *Soccer World* described as 'modern, defensive football at its worst … Both teams used packed retreating defences and used those well – but had little or no idea of attacking. As a result, the match was a rather dull, sometimes boring struggle, a series of hard clashes, crunching tackles – and little else.'

Venglos employed a 4-3-3 formation that he stuck to throughout the series which saw Australia mark the occasion by wearing gold shirts and green shorts with white socks for the first time. It was reported that the young coach was 'going to take no chances that Australia's full first international ended in humiliating defeat … the occasion was far too important for the Australians to play the game by instinct. Acutely aware that the hard facts of international football soccer these days justify the end rather than the means, Australia was going to take no chances.'

This pragmatic approach would be a feature of Australia's approach to international football for several years and was often criticised by supporters who did not understand.

Soccer World had been portraying McCalliog, the Sheffield Wednesday striker who had scored Scotland's third goal in their 3–2 win against England at Wembley Stadium the previous month, as the star of the team. They were less impressed after seeing him in action in the blue of Scotland. 'It's staggering to think that McCalliog could be worth $300,000 on the British market – they are either woefully short of talent or sickeningly full of cash over there,' they wrote.

Nevertheless, McCalliog played a major role in the only goal of the match. His shot in the 31st minute was turned onto the post by Australian goalkeeper Peter Fuzes, a Hungarian who had fled to the country in 1957 as a 10-year-old. There to push the ball into an empty net on the rebound was the Dunfermline striker Ferguson. The front page of the following week's *Soccer World* showed Ferguson, wearing the number 10 shirt, running away to celebrate his goal as Fuzes and Scottish-born defender Alan Marnoch looked on despairingly.

Ferguson, a former apprentice toolmaker from Govan in Glasgow, certainly justified his pen-portrait in the match programme, which described him as having a 'reputation for taking half-chances. Is probably the best "snapper-up" of goals in Scotland today.'

What the programme did not mention was that Ferguson also had a reputation in Scotland of being a dirty player, using his elbows to maximum effect. In the first match of the tour, against Israel, he had broken the nose of their star player, Mordechai Spiegler.

During the match in Sydney, Ferguson clashed several times with Alan Westwater, yet another of the Scots facing their country of birth. Westwater had been born in the Bridge of Allan, and his father, Willie, had played professional football for Morton before transferring to Bankstown in Sydney in 1957. Alan had returned to Scotland in 1963, for a period, to play for Stirling Albion but had returned three years later and joined Pan-Hellenic in Sydney.

Westwater was praised by *Soccer World* for fighting 'like a demon' and not allowing himself to be 'overawed by the Scots' reputation', which seemed to upset his opponents. 'Ferguson almost managed to turn the match into a brawl with his roughness and antics and he alone will really be "remembered" by the Sydney fans,' the newspaper reported.

'Ferguson angered the crowd with his hard, at times deliberately rough, play. Although he scored the winning goal, he seemed more interested in settling scores of private feuds throughout the match.'

Among those praised for giving Scotland such a hard game was Baartz, making his international debut and described as 'Australia's most dangerous forward', and defender Watkiss, hailed as the 'best man on the field' and 'better than any Scot on view'.

Brown, the Scotland manager, came out to defend his players, particularly Ferguson, against accusations of rough play and the level of their performance.

Jim McCalliog, foot raised, and Alex Ferguson, right, were part of Scotland's team that won the opening match of their 1967 tour in Australia 1–0, thanks to a goal from the future Manchester United manager

He instead claimed it was the Australians' fault. 'I can't recall any match of this standard where the tackling was so brutal,' he said. 'It was downright dangerous to be caught in possession.

'I think the critics have been unfair to the Scottish players. We are being treated as a full international team, which we are not. Due to circumstances well known, including the success of teams like Celtic, Rangers, Kilmarnock and Leeds United in cup competitions, I brought a young and inexperienced squad of players to Australia.

'These players met something they had never experienced before when they played at the Showground on Sunday. The big crowd, the international atmosphere and the way the Australian team fought. All this was new to some members of the Scottish team. I am sure we shall put on a better exhibition in the remaining two matches in Adelaide and Melbourne, and I look to Australia to play better too.'

The next match, three days later on 31st May, at the Norwood Oval in Adelaide saw Baartz score his first international goal. Heart of Midlothian's Jim Townsend had put Scotland ahead in the 25th minute with a fabulous 30-yard shot before Baartz equalised nine minutes later, much to the joy of the 10,315 crowd. Scotland scored the winner in the 68th minute through Morgan, who, according to *Soccer World*, gave a 'scintillating display'.

Venglos was delighted with his team's performance. 'It would have been something of an upset had we beaten the tough, skilful Scottish side,' he said.

Australia's performance from its 'gallant part-timers' showed real progress, claimed *Soccer World*. 'Any Australian team up to only three years ago would have collapsed in face of the pressure Scotland exerted in the dying stages and would have conceded another three or four goals,' they wrote.

The final game in the series, at Olympic Park in Melbourne on 3rd June, once again showed why Ferguson was the 'best snapper-up of goals in Scotland'. He scored both of Scotland's goals, in the 61st and 82nd minutes, as his side won 2-0 before a crowd of 22,138. *Soccer World* were far more complimentary on this occasion about Ferguson's performance, calling him 'classy' and claiming he should 'rate special mention … though it is unlikely that Australians will remember [him] a year from now.'

Overall, *Soccer World* were quite positive about the visit of Scotland, despite having originally wanted their tour cancelled after the withdrawal of so many top players. 'Sydney fans would not have recognised the Scots the way they played in Adelaide and Melbourne,' wrote Lou Gautier in his summary of the two matches. 'They performed as true British professionals and turned on some polished soccer in the tradition of some of the best teams which toured Australia in the past.

'Yet, despite the Scots' brilliance, they could only beat Australia narrowly. The Australian team gained accrued prestige from their clashes against Scotland. They, too, lifted their game to heights no other Australian team had reached.'

Gautier was also impressed with the debut of Abonyi, who he predicted had done enough to have 'secured a permanent berth in the Australian squad for the next few years'. It epitomised the progress the national team had made since the rude awakening they had received against North Korea in Cambodia less than two years earlier.

'When one considers that the team has only been together for a fortnight and that the players were part-timers opposed to well-heeled professionals, we must take our hats off to this gallant band who did Australia soccer proud in six historical days which may mark a new era in the history of our national team,' Gautier wrote.

There were no Scottish journalists on the tour, but Brown spoke to the *Sunday Mail* after the Australian leg of the tour was completed. 'We are delighted that we have won all three matches,' he said. 'Believe me, they really took these matches seriously and we did well to win them all. I also think that despite the early criticism we won over the fans and our visit here has been very worthwhile.'

One consequence of the Australian party being together for two weeks was that Warren lost his job as a result of being away for so long. In the end, it worked out better for him as his club, St George Budapest, appointed him as their full-time promotions officer, a role for which he was ideally suited.

After leaving Australia, Scotland travelled to play matches in New Zealand and Canada. Games included a 7–2 victory over Canada, with Harper scoring five goals. Ferguson finished the top scorer on the tour with a total of nine goals in seven matches, including the three against Australia. All the players who travelled received a payment of £200 for taking part in the trip.

When he got home to Scotland, Ferguson left Dunfermline and joined Rangers for £65,000, a record fee for a transfer between two Scottish clubs. He scored 35 goals in 66 appearances for the Glasgow club before moving on to Falkirk and Ayr United, where he ended his playing career in 1974. After the world tour, Ferguson was never selected for Scotland again.

Once he had finished playing, Ferguson embarked on a coaching career which saw him achieve unprecedented success. First, at Aberdeen, he won three Scottish League championships, four Scottish Cups and both the UEFA Cup Winners' Cup and the UEFA Super Cup. Then, in 1986, he moved to England to take over Manchester United, where he established himself as one of the greatest coaches in history. Ferguson won a record 38 trophies, including 13 Premier League titles and five FA Cups. He also lifted the UEFA Champions League twice.

A year before joining Manchester United, Ferguson had also taken over as Scotland's manager, following the death of Jock Stein, and was in charge for a two-legged World Cup qualifying play-off against Australia. Scotland won the first leg at Hampden Park in Glasgow 2–0 before drawing the return 0–0 in Melbourne at Olympic Park, where 18 years earlier he had scored those two goals.

West Bromwich Albion full-back Dougie Fraser, who played in all three of Scotland's matches against Australia in 1967, claimed that it was during that tour he first identified Ferguson as a future manger. 'He had that sort of aura ... I just couldn't put my finger on it, but there was something there,' Fraser said. 'He knew what he was talking about and, without over-emphasising, you could see he was destined for something. He looked like he had some sort of leadership qualities.'

Ferguson was knighted in the 1999 Queen's Birthday Honours list for his services to the game. But he still regularly reflected on his disappointment at the absence of any form of official recognition to mark the international matches he had played for Scotland during that epic 1967 tour.

Then, in 2005, a book was published, *My Father and Other Working-Class Football Heroes*, by British broadcaster Gary Imlach, about his father, Stewart.

Stewart Imlach had made four appearances for Scotland in 1958 – against Hungary, Poland, Yugoslavia and France. The latter two games took place at that year's World Cup finals in Sweden. However, prior to the 1970s, caps were only issued to those who appeared in matches against the other home countries, so Imlach never received a memento to mark his appearances. Following concerted public pressure, the Scottish Football Association bowed to the popular will in 2006 and officially capped all players affected by the previous rule.

That led to a new campaign for the Scotland tour of 1967 to be re-assessed. In 2021, shortly before Sir Alex's 80th birthday, it was announced that the matches against Australia, Canada and Israel on that trip had been elevated to full internationals. Sir Alex joined several other players, including Townsend, who had scored for Scotland in the second match against Australia in Adelaide, in being awarded a special cap.

They were all presented with the honour during Scotland's match against Israel at Hampden Park in October 2021. 'Sir Alex has never been fully recognised for his achievements on the pitch as an international player, but we are able to correct that tonight,' Scottish Football Association president Rod Petrie said when awarding Sir Alex his cap.

The row over the status of Scotland's tour to Australia was resolved in 2021 when the matches were upgraded to full internationals and caps awarded to the players involved, including Sir Alex Ferguson

It was also finally recognition, 54 years after the matches had taken place, that Bayutti and sponsor, tobacco manufacturer W.D. & H.O. Willis, had been right all the time. Australia's matches against Scotland had been their first full internationals to be played at home.

When Australia travelled to Glasgow in 2000 to play Scotland in a friendly at Hampden Park, Ferguson was asked for his memories, for the match programme, of those matches against Australia 33 years previously. He did not recall the negative attention his performances had attracted and instead focused on the tough approach adopted by Scotland's rivals.

'In Australia, the games were very physical. There was an Italian, Giacometti, who I think had a kick at everybody,' Ferguson said. 'At the time, the Australian team was a collection of players who had recently emigrated from Italy, Greece and England. I think there was even a Scot playing for them.'

John Giacometti was a striker who played for APIA Leichhardt, having joined them from Italian Serie C club Lecco in 1962. 'He gave the fans drama and comedy,' it was claimed. Giacometti scored a remarkable 103 goals in 104 matches for APIA between 1963 and 1968. But his only appearances for Australia were in the three matches against Scotland.

It is a historical curiosity that shortly after Ferguson and Scotland had landed in Australia, they were joined by Manchester United. Matt Busby's side arrived having recently been crowned as English League champions – the last time they would lift the title until they triumphed again in 1993 under Ferguson.

Manchester United had left England on a major tour just four days after being crowned champions, and had already played a series of matches in the United States and New Zealand before arriving in Australia.

The schedule was gruelling. The squad of 18 players and eight officials left Manchester on board BOAC flight BA537 at 3.30pm on 15th May to Los Angeles via New York City. They did not land back home until 30th June after a 30-hour flight from Perth.

The team played a total of 12 matches, including eight in six Australian cities in 28 days. During their time down under, Manchester United stayed in eight different hotels and took 12 flights, including the one back to Manchester.

In the official tour itinerary issued to each player, they were instructed that 'each member of the party must take charge of their own luggage. The maximum weight allowance is 44 lbs per person and there is a very heavy charge for all excess weight. In order to include the skips in the over-all allowance, members are asked to ensure that their luggage does not weigh more than 40 lbs, including hand luggage, and to leave a margin on the return journey for articles of presents accumulated.'

The party were also told, 'you are allowed to take up to a maximum of £15 in sterling notes, which you may spend or exchange abroad if you wish.' But they were warned not to make a 'false declaration or conceal excess notes; these are serious offences and may lead to heavy penalties.'

The arrival of Busby's team caused a lot of excitement, so much so that instead of its usual green masthead, *Soccer World* switched to a red one for the duration of their stay. Negotiations for the tour had started early in 1966, and the Australian Soccer Federation had made it a condition that Manchester United send their strongest side, including Bobby Charlton, George Best and Denis Law, which is why he was not part of the Scotland squad. United took their commitments seriously, and the club trainer, Jack Crompton, insisted the squad train every day.

Manchester United's eight matches in Australia did not include one against the national side, instead meeting a series of state representative teams. They won seven of the eight matches, scoring 33 goals and conceding only three.

The only game they failed to win was the third match of the tour against Victoria at the Olympic Park in Melbourne on 11th June. Victoria's side included Cook, Abonyi and Hammy McMeechan, who had also recently played for Australia against Scotland. Charlton put United ahead in front of a crowd of 31,638 before David Sadler scored an own goal to give Victoria a famous draw. The star of the match was Victoria's Slavia Melbourne goalkeeper Viliam Schrojf, who had played for Czechoslovakia in the side that had reached the final of the 1962 World Cup, losing 3–1 to Brazil.

Soccer World adopted a red theme in honour of Manchester United's visit which was sponsored by tobacco manufacturer W.D. & H.O. Wills

The fifth match of the tour saw Manchester United beat New South Wales 3–1 at the Royal Agricultural Showground in Sydney, watched by 36,599. The match was particularly special for Baartz, still earning praise for his Australian debut against Scotland. The young striker had spent three years at Old Trafford between 1964 and 1966, training alongside the likes of Charlton, Best and Law.

After a few months at United, Baartz had signed a professional contract. 'Originally I went for three months, but I ended up staying for two years,' he said. Baartz seemed destined to play for United's first team but was battling homesickness.

At the time Baartz was there, Manchester was still recovering from the effects of the Second World War, and the weather was always going to be tough for an Australian. Plus, his father had died when he was just 13, his mother did not have a telephone and the only means of communication was via letter. 'I went to Matt Busby and said, "I'm really homesick, I want to go home,"' Baartz said.

Busby's reply was 'But, son, nobody leaves Manchester United. I want you to think about it for a month before I let you go.' At the end of the month, Baartz went back to see Busby, who said, 'You haven't changed your mind, have you?' Baartz told him he had not and headed home.

After the match in Sydney, Busby told the press, 'You saw how Ray Baartz played, and now you know why we wanted to keep him.'

Busby even asked Baartz if he wanted to return to play for Manchester United. 'I said no, I was very happy [in Australia],' Baartz said.

Big crowds attended Manchester United's tour, including against New South Wales in Sydney, when Bobby Charlton had to be quick to get away from pitch invaders

The tour sponsors once were again W.D. & H.O. Wills, who had invested $30,000 in bringing over Scotland and Manchester United. The involvement of the tobacco company was a bonus for the Manchester United players. 'Most of us smoked so we were happy about it – they kept our supplies up!' the goalkeeper Alex Stepney said.

The players who attracted the most interest during the tour were the 'United Trinity' of Charlton, Best and Law. Law had finished as the club's top scorer with 23 goals as they won the First Division. The match programme for the trip predicted that 'Australian fans will be delighted not only with his football, but also with his antics. For Law really lives through a match, and his antics, grimaces, head shakes and other manifestations of his intense emotions never cease to amuse the crowds.'

Few were amused, however, when, during Manchester United's game against a Sydney XI, Law was involved in an incident that saw Australian player Ron Giles leave the field with a broken jaw. 'It was a sheer accident,' the United striker claimed afterwards. 'I never hit him deliberately, we just collided.'

That is not the way that Giles saw it after he ended up in hospital needing an operation. 'Law grabbed me by my shirt and butted his head against my cheek,' was his recollection. When it became public how bad Giles' injury was, the Manchester United players organised a collection that saw the Australian receive $140 as compensation for the time he needed to take off work.

The tour ended in Perth, when Manchester United beat Western Australia 7–0 in a match that saw Law sent off after only half an hour for swearing at the referee. Even this failed to sour the feel-good effect that the visit of such a famous club had created. It had been watched by a total of 191,759 fans.

'It is doubtful if ever in the past any overseas touring team has created greater interest and won more friends,' *Soccer World* wrote. 'Both with their displays on the field and with their open, friendly behaviour off it, the United party have conquered Australia.'

CHAPTER FOUR

Sent to war

Australia's participation in the Vietnam War started when they sent a small team of 30 military advisors in 1962, as part of a commitment to stop the rise of communism in Southeast Asia after World War Two. It was driven by fear that it could land on their shores following growing sympathy for the cause in the country.

In 1965, Australia's involvement was upscaled dramatically in April, a month after 3,500 United States Marines came ashore at Da Nang as the first wave of American combat troops to land in South Vietnam.

Australian Prime Minister Sir Robert Menzies bowed to American pressure and agreed to upgrade its military commitment to help ensure the security of South Vietnam.

South Vietnam was at war with its neighbour North Vietnam after the country had been divided into two following the fall of French Indochina in 1954. A national coalition communist movement called Viet Minh took control of the North, while the United States assumed financial and military support for the South.

Soon, though, an armed movement called the Viet Cong, under the direction of the North, had initiated a guerrilla war in the South. By 1963, there were 40,000 troops fighting in South Vietnam on behalf of the North.

After the Menzies government had made its commitment, Australian troops were soon engaged in significant action in Vietnam. By the beginning of December 1965, only eight months later, there was already dissatisfaction in America, who were calling for extra soldiers from Australia to be sent to support them.

The Australian forces chalked up a notable victory in August 1966 at the Battle of Long Tan. There, despite being heavily outnumbered, they fought off an assault by a much larger Viet Cong unit. A total of 18 Australians died and 24 were wounded, while at least 245 Viet Cong were killed.

In February 1967, though, Australian troops sustained their heaviest casualties in the War to that point. They lost 16 men, and 55 were wounded in a single week. It led to more soldiers being dispatched to the War, despite public support for Australia's involvement starting to wane. Demonstrations against the War across Australia began to increase from a few dozen to thousands marching through the country's main cities.

Australia's involvement in Vietnam rose from a handful of military advisors in 1962 to hundreds of troops, following United States pressure

Australian troops were also having trouble winning over the locals in South Vietnam. The country's Department of Foreign Affairs decided to engage in a bit of soft power by using football, Vietnam's most popular sport, to help get them onside. It was a bold, but dangerous, propaganda stunt, backed by Harold Holt. He had replaced Menzies as prime minister in January 1966 and increased the number of Australian troops sent to South Vietnam.

A tournament called the South Vietnam Independence Cup was to be played in Saigon in November 1967. Teams taking part were set to include Australia, Malaysia, New Zealand, the Philippines, Singapore, South Vietnam and Thailand.

Plans were drawn up in early 1967 to be presented during a visit to Australia and New Zealand of the South Vietnam Prime Minister Nguyen Cao Ky. This came as he sought to build support for the war effort through sporting exchange.

Like Australia, New Zealand had been pressured by the United States government to send troops to Vietnam. New Zealand's involvement in the war was limited compared to the contributions of Australia, and they suffered much fewer casualties. But it still triggered a large anti-Vietnam War movement at home.

A formal invitation to the event was received by the Australian Soccer Federation later in 1967, and by August, the governing body reported that the Department of External Affairs 'supported the tour subject to the security situation'. In the early stages of planning, Australia's participation in the tournament was so secret that *Soccer World* were asked not to publish news of their involvement because it was 'hush-hush', and everything was being managed at 'government level'.

It remains steeped in mystery who at the Australian government officially signed off on sending a group of young footballers into a warzone. 'The matter was discussed up to Cabinet level, but the file on the deliberations was never transferred to the National Archives and is now lost,' said Deakin University historian Roy Hay, whose book *Football and War: Australia and Vietnam 1967– 1972* detailed the tournament.

'I had the late Malcolm Fraser, who was Minister for the Army at the time, on his hands and knees trying to find if there was anything in his files relating to the matter. Fraser was dead against civilian activities in Vietnam and wanted everything done by military people in the chain of command.'

The tournament was to be an 11-day event as part of a six-week tour of Asia by the Australian team. It would be led by a new coach, despite Jozef Venglos being recommended for the post after taking charge for the international series against Scotland. He was overlooked after his greatest supporter, Australian Soccer Federation vice-president Jim Bayutti, retired due to poor health and to concentrate on his construction business.

Venglos stayed in Australia until 1969, before leaving to coach Czechoslovakian club FC VSS Kosice and then his country's under-23 team. He was the assistant coach of Czechoslovakia when they won the European Championship in 1976, and 14 years later, in 1990, was the head coach at the FIFA World Cup in Italy. There, he guided his side to the quarter-finals, where they were eliminated by eventual champions West Germany.

That performance led to Venglos being appointed the first foreign-born manager of a club in the English top flight with Aston Villa, who he managed in 1990 and 1991. After that, he moved around Asia and Europe, managing a variety of club and national teams, including Scottish giants Celtic. Venglos died in 2021 at the age of 84.

Several leading names were mentioned as possible candidates to take over Australia, including former England coach Walter Winterbottom and Jimmy Hill, who had recently left Coventry City after guiding them to the English First Division for the first time in their history. Joe Vlasits, vice-president of the Australian Coaches Federation, had urged a long-term approach. 'It's imperative that for once we look to the future, not just one week,' he told *Soccer World*. 'While the performance of our national team is important, it shouldn't be regarded as the main function of a national coach. After all, how many full internationals does Australia play a year?'

In the end, it was Vlasits, known affectionately to everyone as 'Uncle Joe', who was given the job of coach for the trip to South Vietnam.

Born in Budapest in 1921, Vlasits's brief playing career for Hungarian First Division side Nemzeti Sport Club from Budapest suburb Terezvaros was cut short due to injury. He then accepted a coaching role with the

Hungarian Football Association, having a special interest in developing young players.

Vlasits relocated to Australia from Hungary in 1947 and soon began coaching within the New South Wales State League. This included with Canterbury-Marrickville, where he won the First Division Championship grand final in 1958 and 1960. Vlasits then coached Sydney Prague and St George Budapest in 1961 and 1962, respectively, finishing top of the First Division in each season.

It was part of a well-travelled coaching career in New South Wales, including brief spells with Pan-Hellenic, Bankstown, SSC Yugal and Melita Eagles-Newtown, before he was appointed to lead the national team. Vlasits could certainly never be accused of not embracing the rich ethnic diversity of football in Australia at the time. He was fondly remembered wherever he went.

Shortly before he started his role with Australia, Vlasits had managed the Sydney XI who had played the touring Manchester United team. It was the game where Denis Law had broken the cheekbone of Australian international Ron Giles after headbutting him.

Manchester United's eight-match tour had given Australia's best youngsters the opportunity to test themselves against some of the world's top players and Vlasits a chance to assess their ability. He was convinced that there was enough burgeoning talent in the country to build the nucleus of a good squad. Throughout his coaching career, Vlasits never diverted from his policy of giving youth a chance.

At Canterbury-Marrickville, among the young talents he nurtured was a 15-year-old Johnny Warren alongside childhood friend Johnny Watkiss. Another 17-year-old, goalkeeper Ron Corry, also came through the youth

A 19-man squad managed by Joe Vlasits, sixth left in back row, was chosen to represent Australia in the South Vietnam Independence Cup

scheme at Canterbury. All three were to play crucial roles in Australia qualifying for the 1974 FIFA World Cup.

The average age of the 19-man squad selected by Vlasits for the Asian tour was just 22, and Warren was promoted to captain at the age of only 24. Les Scheinflug and Pat Hughes, who had shared the captaincy duties during Australia's tour of Asia two years earlier, were both missing. Scheinflug was still struggling to recover from the ankle injury he had suffered before that tour started, while Hughes refused to go in a row over money.

The team had been offered only $50 per week to take part, even though all would have to take leave of absence from their jobs to go on the long trip. The 28-year-old Hughes, who had missed the 1967 tour to Asia due to work commitments, claimed he could not afford to play for such low money. Hughes never played international football again and always believed that the Australian Soccer Federation had '"banned"' him because of his stance.

But many of the team that were to prove so successful in later years first flourished on this tour under Uncle Joe.

Among them was the 20-year-old Atti Abonyi, who had made his international debut earlier in the year against Scotland. Abonyi shared a Hungarian background with Vlasits. His family had left Budapest when he was 10 in the wake of the 1956 Hungarian Revolution, the nationwide uprising that was crushed after 12 days by Soviet Union tanks rolling into the country. Thousands of Hungarians were killed, and an estimated quarter of a million fled abroad.

As the Red Army began its brutal assault, Abonyi's father had sneaked out of Hungary into Austria with the promise that he would come back for the rest of his family. 'We didn't know if we would ever see him again,' Abonyi admitted. 'The borders were being closed up again by the time Dad left. Still, there was no other choice. Thousands had already left, and plenty of others were still prepared to take the risk. Some died trying, and plenty went to prison.'

It took Abonyi's father only three weeks to keep good his promise. Having scouted a route out of the country, he decided he needed to return to rescue the rest of the family. 'There ended up being 13 of us,' the youngster remembered. 'My brother and I were the only kids, and while we were obviously scared, I must admit it was all a bit exciting too.'

The group eventually made it to a Red Cross station located in a monastery in Austria, via a November full moon, and wading across a freezing river. All they had of their previous lives was what they could carry on their backs.

The Hungarian Revolution ended a golden period for the country's football team. Between 1950 and 1956, the team played 69 games, recorded 58 victories, 10 draws and suffered only one defeat, in the 1954 World Cup final against West Germany.

Playing on the streets of Budapest before the Soviets took them over, Abonyi was just one of thousands of young boys inspired to play football by the achievements of the likes of Ferenc Puskas, Sandor Kocsis, Nandor Hidegkuti, Zoltan Czibor, Jozsef Bozsik and Gyula Grosics.

The 1956 Olympic Games had been staged in Melbourne and they had made a great impression on Abonyi's father. 'I really had no idea where Australia was,' Atti admitted. 'Dad knew, though, and Australia was his first choice ahead of America, Canada or other European countries.'

The family travelled to Australia on the *Fairsea*, a World War Two escort aircraft carrier before being converted into a migrant ship. Between 1951 and 1969, when it was sent to the ship-breaking yard, it carried thousands of displaced persons to new lives.

The Abonyi family docked in Melbourne on 10th May in 1957, and within a year, Attila had started playing organised football for the first time with St Kilda Juniors. He made the spiritual move to Melbourne Hungaria at the turn of the decade.

The roots of Melbourne Hungaria had started with those 1956 Olympics that had so convinced Abonyi's father that he wanted to relocate his family to Australia. Following the completion of the Games, as many as half of the Hungarian delegation defected. Many chose to stay in Australia. The Hungarian football team had been denied the opportunity to defend the Olympic title they had won in Helsinki four years earlier because of the Soviet Union and were withdrawn on the eve of the tournament. Some members of the football team were among those who settled in Australia and in 1957 founded the Melbourne Hungaria Soccer Club.

Shortly before leaving for the South Vietnam Independence Cup, Abonyi had scored a hat-trick for Melbourne Hungaria as they beat APIA Leichhardt 4–3, including an extra-time winner, in the final of the Australia Cup, before a crowd of 11,185 at Olympic Park Stadium in Melbourne. It completed the double as the team had already lifted the Victorian State League for the first time in the club's history, Abonyi scoring in both of the final matches to ensure they stayed clear of closest rivals Juventus.

It was on a high that Abonyi joined a week-long training camp in North Ryde, a suburb of Sydney, before the Australian squad departed on their Asian tour. It was a chance for those who did not know Vlasits to get acquainted with him. Everyone remarked on his good manners and his heavily accented English, which was often littered with unique phases accompanied by strange facial expressions.

'Uncle Joe was very old-fashioned, even in those days, but I don't think I've met a more honest person,' was how Abonyi remembered him. 'He had so much respect from all the boys – he was like a father figure. He was a tremendous, lovely guy, very hard-working while very old-fashioned in lots of ways – but absolutely brilliant.'

Pastoral care was something that was important to Vlasits, as defender Stan Ackerley recalled. Ackerley had been part of the Australian team beaten 6–1 by North Korea in Phnom Penh in November 1965 but overlooked for the matches against Scotland, before he was recalled for the tour of Asia.

Ackerley combined his football career with working as a labourer, something that concerned Vlasits. 'Uncle Joe knew more about you than you know about yourself,' he said. 'During the day, I worked outside in quite a physical job, labouring with heavy machinery, and when it came to our session Joe said, "Stan, you've had a big busy day today," and I said, "No, Joe, I'm fine!"

'He was a very caring person who knew stuff about you that made you think, *Where has he got that information?* I never heard him say a bad word, even in changing rooms where he should have done at times! But he was such a nice guy, and I had a hell of a lot of time for him.

'As a person, you could not ask for a better coach. Uncle Joe was tremendous. I got on with him like a house on fire. He was the perfect man manager who had this ability to make the players want to do it for him.'

That was to be an important trait, as Vlasits was about to ask his young team to travel into a warzone.

Saigon, thanks to decades of French influence, was known as the 'Paris of the East', but, by 1967, was heavily fortified and more a war garrison than an exotic foreign capital city.

Opinion was divided over whether a team of young Australian sportsmen should be travelling to South Vietnam in the middle of a war. Sydney's *Sun* newspaper labelled the tour an 'improper mission … for a party of lucky young Australians'.

But Andrew Dettre, of *Soccer World*, argued the opposite. 'Australia's role in that war is a fact, whether we like it or not; we [must demonstrate] to the people of Vietnam that Australia is keen to participate in their sporting life, not just their war,' he wrote under his pen name of Paul Dean.

Dettre, however, was less optimistic about Australia's chances of doing well on the pitch in Saigon. On the eve of their departure, under the headline in *Soccer World* 'OUR TEAM GOES TO WAR POORLY ARMED', he blasted the make-up of the squad, the selection of which for the first time had been entrusted to the Australian Coaches Federation, a group founded by Vlasits.

Dettre was also upset that a series of friendlies had been arranged for after the tournament in South Vietnam, rather than as a warm-up to help the team prepare. He warned it was repeating the same mistake that had happened in Cambodia two years earlier, when the team had performed so poorly in the World Cup qualifying games against North Korea.

'It is unlikely that even the toughest US Marines would be thrown into action in Vietnam with more daring and abandon than that soon forced on our Australian soccer team,' Dettre wrote. 'With more intelligent planning, Australia would have started as favourites for the prestige-laden Saigon Tournament. As it is, even a place in the semi-final would be a good result.'

Sharing Dettre's pessimism was Bayutti, whose opinion on everything still seemed to be shared by *Soccer World*, despite his retirement. 'The selection of the squad smacks of politics,' he claimed. 'Every state wanted to get into the act. The result is an unbalanced squad, both in attack and defence. I'm sure all the players will try their hardest for Australia but, frankly, there's not much talent in the squad.'

The party departed from Sydney on 30th October aboard a Pan Am flight, arriving later that day at Saigon's Tan Son Nhut Airport. As they landed, looking out of the window, they were greeted with the sight of warplanes parked almost wing to wing. 'Probably a little bit naive that we were going to a country that was in the middle of war,' Ray Baartz admitted, 'but at no stage did I think that it was going to be dangerous.'

Brian Turner, a 17-year-old selected for New Zealand's squad, remembered his team's flight being given special protection as they approached Saigon. 'We had fighter planes either side of our jet and everyone was quite starstruck,' Turner said. 'As a young boy, I was thinking this is pretty incredible.'

John Holland, reporting for *Soccer World*, described the scene as the Australian party arrived. 'Alighting from the giant airliner, you immediately notice the only persons in sight are servicemen, well armed and apparently representative of several different countries,' he wrote. 'Some are wearing the familiar jungle greens or khaki; others are dressed in neat blues and greys and at all entrances there are a few in the drab faded white of the civilian police force. They are noticeable by their apparent alertness and American-style steel helmets, each marked with its own identification plate and perhaps a badge of rank.

'Those in greens are carrying the latest model automatic carbines, others are welcomed by cumbersome riot guns, or .45 pistols slung off sagging belts in the "Western movie" style.

'Suddenly you become aware that the incessant roar of the constantly incoming and outgoing airliners has been punctuated by a deafening scream, as 500 yards away a flight of Phantom jets tear down the runway at almost unbelievable speed on their way to support an allied action nearby.'

The next shock for the Australian team was their accommodation. The Caravelle Hotel, which everyone called the 'Golden Building', in the centre of Saigon, had been chosen to host all the teams competing in the tournament. In 1964, the Viet Cong had managed to plant a bomb in the hotel, which was used by foreign journalists, and killed several people. The damage was repaired and by 1967 the atmosphere there was described as 'one of relaxed conviviality'.

The hotel may have been many things, but one thing it was definitely not was 'Golden'. 'The place was called the Golden Building,' recalled Abonyi. 'We all thought, *Oh gee, that sounds good*, but … [the hotel] was absolutely atrocious – it was filthy, it was run-down.'

Brian Corrigan had recently been appointed as the team's doctor after returning home to Australia, having held the same role with English First Division club Arsenal. This was his first trip since taking up the role.

'As we walked through the door, I thought, *What a funny thing to do, bringing us in through such a filthy basement*, Corrigan said. 'It turned out to be the main reception area. Our full-back, Stan Ackerley, walked into his room to switch on the light and was thrown right across the room. The light switch had bare wires poking out from it. Abonyi shared his room with a giant lizard.'

Things did not improve when the party gathered in the hotel's dining room. 'On a large plate was a small slice of something I presumed to be greasy Spam,' said Corrigan. '"Is there nothing else?" "No," snarled the surly hotel owner. "That is all you can get because you are issued with football coupons and there are no more left for this meal."'

On another occasion, the hotel staff brought out dinner which the Australian players thought was steak. When they asked for some more, they were informed that it was not steak, but dog. They never asked for meat again.

The Australians were lucky to have Corrigan, who was to play a major role in the team's preparations for the next 29 years. He had travelled back home from England brimming with ideas about how sportsmen and women in Australia could prepare better for major events.

In Cambodia, for the World Cup matches against North Korea, the whole team had suffered stomach upsets. In Saigon, Corrigan banned the team from local water or using ice. Bottled drinks were not necessarily the answer as most of them had a black rim of grease around the top. He recommended beer as one way of hydrating. 'We didn't need much convincing,' Corry, the team's goalkeeper, said.

The New Zealand team, who were managed by former Test cricketer Jack Cowie, were less fortunate. They had travelled to Vietnam without a doctor. Cowie had told his players that there was no need to avoid the local ice. One by one, the squad began complaining of stomach problems. They had to play one of their games during the tournament with only 10 fit players, and David Taylor, at 16, the youngest member of the party, became so ill they had to leave him in the French hospital there when they returned home.

In fact, they thought they were leaving him there to die.

It was Corrigan who probably saved Taylor's life. 'It was coming out black at both ends,' Taylor recalled more than 50 years later. 'If you've ever seen [the film] *The Exorcist*, it was just like that. I had no self-control; the bed was a complete mess. The air was filled with this really putrid smell. Someone called in the Australian doctor, who said I had to go to hospital immediately.'

Taylor was so bad that New Zealand's Hungarian-born coach Juan Schwanner warned the party that they were unlikely to see the schoolboy again. 'He was pretty close to death; that's what Schwanner told us all,' Turner, Taylor's teenage teammate, who was sharing a room with him, said.

Before leaving to return home, Turner visited his teammate, to say goodbye, he feared. It was another unforgettably shocking moment – and not just for his horror at seeing how gaunt and dishevelled Taylor had become since being admitted to hospital. Taylor was having to share his hospital room with a young Vietnamese boy blown up in the War.

'People were lying on the floor with no legs, half an arm, blown away by bombs – it was just incredible for a young boy to see,' Turner said. 'All of that was there – and we were there to think about football. It was crazy.'

Fortunately, Taylor did recover and left Saigon after three weeks in the hospital. He went on to play a total of 47 times for New Zealand.

The day after the squad's arrival in Saigon, the Australians were given a security briefing by members of the Australian Embassy, who were based in the Caravelle Hotel. 'Just after we arrived, they showed us pictures of kids that had been ripped apart with claymore mines,' Ray Richards, another young player on the tour being groomed for the future, recalled of the Embassy briefing.

Claymore mines were weapons Viet Cong insurgents used to remotely detonate explosives.

Among the other advice offered was to be careful of people on bicycles, especially if they had women on the back, because of fears they would shoot at anyone they thought was American. They were also warned that anti-personnel mines may have been planted on fields, and no training was to take place before the pitch had been combed for explosive devices.

'When we got outside the Embassy, it seemed all of Saigon was riding around on bikes with women on the back, and there were people looking under our bus with mirrors to check if any mines had been planted,' Corrigan said. 'Most of the team had been quite blasé about being in a warzone. Now they had suddenly gone quiet.'

Once in Saigon, the Australians had been surprised to discover that South Korea and Hong Kong were entries to the tournament, and that the Philippines had dropped out. The addition of South Korea was particularly significant. Besides being one of the strongest teams in the region, they were America's main ally in Asia. They had committed thousands of troops to the Vietnam War, many more than Australia and New Zealand. Its troops were feared for their ruthlessness, and it was rumoured they had routinely murdered innocent farmers.

The plan to have all eight teams staying in the Golden Building hotel appeared an ill-conceived one from the start as it presented a tempting target for the Viet Cong. On the first night the Australians stayed there, two members of the Viet Cong were arrested close to the hotel carrying explosives. After being tortured, they admitted their plan was to 'blow up South Koreans'. The South Korean team were staying on the floor below the Australians. At the time, the assassination attempt was covered up to avoid spreading panic.

Gary Wilkins makes friends during Australia's trip to Saigon, conceived as a goodwill gesture as much as a sporting endeavour

Fears for most of the players staying in the Golden Building hotel were that they would be caught up in an attack on the nearby Presidential Palace that was being incessantly shelled. There were cars sporadically being blown up within earshot, and getting some sleep amid the sound of gunfire that filled the Saigon night was difficult.

'We were sitting down eating in our hotel and there was this big explosion,' Turner, the New Zealand schoolboy, said. 'Apparently, someone had come past, and a bomb had exploded 60 or 70 metres from where we were. It was that close.'

Turner also remembered how he and his teammates would go up to the roof of the Golden Building, which was usually full of journalists, and watch as American fighter planes, framed against a skyline lit up by flares, would fly over the top of them. 'They'd disappear and then you'd hear this big *whooosh*,' he said. 'They had dropped their bombs and carried on. It was probably about a minute or so away from where we were, but they were areas really close to the city – and people were dying.'

At least the Australians had discovered a solution that meant they no longer had to rely on the Golden Building to fulfil their dietary requirements. Tom Patrick, another member of the accompanying party, who worked for Qantas and was responsible for sorting out logistics and planning, had organised for the group to eat at the Australian Army's 'Canberra Club'. The food was several notches above what they had been eating, and Spam was swapped for steak and beer. There was also an opportunity for the players to relax by playing table tennis.

Even after the team returned to Australia, Vlastis was still fuming about the lack of official government support they had received while in Saigon. 'I must express my frank amazement at the lack of interest the Australian Embassy showed in our team,' he said. 'Before our arrival, nobody from the Embassy bothered to make sure that the hotel and food arrangements were right. Consequently, they were not.

'Then, in the first week, nobody from the Embassy came even near us – except the Second Secretary and a security officer. This officer showed us some horror films about the dangers lurking in the streets of Saigon depicting booby traps and amputated limbs, then packed up the film and departed, his job done. Apart from these two visits, we had nobody else from the Embassy in our hotel – and we certainly didn't get an invitation to visit the Embassy. Had it not been for the Australian Army in Saigon, we would have felt pretty lonely indeed.'

Even being under the protection of the Australian Army at the Canberra Club was not without its security threats. The building was surrounded by sandbags and guarded by two armed soldiers, whose task was to ensure that the traffic kept moving, because the fear was that if it stopped, the Viet Cong would use it as an opportunity to throw a bomb. Their orders were to fire once in the air if the traffic did not start immediately, and then shoot the offender if they ignored the warning. 'The air around our haven of relaxation would always be punctuated by the sound of guns going off just behind our ears,' Corrigan said.

Each day would start with the players and soldiers sharing breakfast in the army canteen, before one group went off to train or play a match and the other to fight.

Training sessions were held at the police recreation ground and had to be coordinated around checks for mines.

After one finishing drill, a stray shot soared over a towering wire fence that marked the field's perimeter. The unnamed player – it has been widely claimed by those that were there that it was Richards – set off after his ball, ignoring warning signs with skull and crossbows. 'People came running and screaming from everywhere, telling us that was a field full of landmines,' Abonyi recalled.

Those frantic calls could have saved the player's life. 'As far as I'm concerned, that ball might still be sitting there,' Abonyi said.

After that, the team conducted most of its training on the roof of the hotel, where they were confined to stretching instead of ball work.

Security was a constant fear throughout the trip. But inevitably when a group of young men are thrown together into this type of situation, there were moments of dark humour too.

Every floor at the Caravelle Hotel had guards assigned to protect it. Each morning, the chief security officer attached to Australia visited their floor to make sure everything was okay. His name was Hung, so the team nicknamed him 'Well'. Each morning, he would arrive to be greeted with, 'Well, Hung.' It was no surprise that he was always a bit bemused as to why everyone laughed as they said it. By the end of the trip, he had decided to just smile politely.

The late additions of South Korea and Hong Kong meant that the groups for the tournament were redrawn after the Australian squad had landed in Saigon. They were put alongside old rivals New Zealand, hosts South Vietnam and Singapore in Group A. Hong Kong, Malaysia, South Korea and Thailand were pooled together in Group B.

Vlastis reported that 'the boys, all in good spirits, are determined to take home the trophy.' He admitted that he was 'more concerned with outside factors, such as climate and possible sickness, than our opponents.'

The only functioning stadium left in Saigon was the Cong Hoa Stadium, which, translated, meant 'Republic Stadium' and which had opened in 1931. In October 1965, the Viet Cong had detonated explosives at the stadium. It killed 11 people, including four children, and injured 42.

At the previous year's National Day Tournament at the stadium, contested by South Vietnam, Thailand and Malaysia, the Viet Cong had taken the opportunity to fire mortar bombs during matches into the area of the city where it was located.

This had contributed to the government in Saigon banning large public gatherings. But this was lifted in time for the South Vietnam Independence Cup, where big crowds were expected. The stadium had also been renovated in time for the event, which kicked off on 4th November when the hosts South Vietnam beat Singapore 2–0 in Group A and Malaysia secured a 3–2 victory over Thailand in Group B.

The stadium may have been given a fresh lick of paint, but little attention had been paid to the pitch. After his first inspection, Vlastis claimed the grass was 'far too high – some four inches'. His instinctive reaction was to file a protest, but he decided that it would be more of a disadvantage to the 'very fast and very nippy' South Vietnamese and South Koreans than to Australia. Vlastis was to be proved right.

The pitch soon began to show the effects of staging two matches a day, during a period when Vietnam's monsoon season was ending. All the games

Australia's new captain, Johnny Warren, leads his team out during the opening ceremony

took place on heavy pitches where, it was reported, 'mud came up to our ankles'.

The South Vietnamese crowd were hostile from the start, and the Australians were grateful for the presence of the group of servicemen they had befriended at the Canberra Club and invited along to support them among the 20,000 spectators.

After the fraught build-up, security fears and the problems of eating properly at the Golden Building, it must have been a relief to both the Australia and New Zealand teams to finally get on the pitch on Sunday, 5th November. At the same time the match started, 70 kilometres away, a major offensive, known as the Battle of Loc Ninh, was reaching its conclusion, with American troops claiming a big victory with the death of 850 Viet Cong.

Before the teams were allowed onto the pitch, they were kept in the tunnel for several minutes while a last-minute sweep of the pitch for landmines was conducted.

The Australians came out of the traps flying and were 2–0 up within 15 minutes, thanks to goals from Baartz and new skipper Warren. The New Zealanders fought back, however, and the two teams went in at half-time level at 2–2.

During the interval, Vlastis decided to replace Frank Micic, who had been struggling in the mud and the humid conditions, with another of the newcomers promoted for this trip. Manfred Schaefer had been born in the German town of Pillau, which is now Baltiysk in Russia near Konigsberg, now

Kaliningrad. In the dying days of the Second World War, his family fled westward to Bremen to avoid the advancing Soviet Union Red Army, along with 450,000 other refugees. In 1954, the family emigrated with Manfred, by then aged 11, to Australia.

Schaefer started his football career in 1960 with Blacktown in west Sydney, playing in the Second Division of the New South Wales State League. In 1963, he joined First Division Budapest Club, later renamed St George Budapest, where he played alongside Warren. The team had won the New South Wales State Championship in 1967.

At 24, Schaefer was older than most of the other players given their opportunity by Vlastis in Saigon. He was renowned for his fitness. Schaefer was a milkman when he was not playing football. He used to complete this round each day on foot. It was claimed that he walked up to 40 kilometres a day.

Exaggerated or not, Schaefer was certainly able to physically deal with the difficult conditions in

Australia started their campaign in the South Vietnam Independence Cup against New Zealand

Saigon. *Soccer World* reported that he 'proved a tower of strength, inspired renewed confidence to his shaken teammates, with some characteristically fierce tackles which revitalised the whole team.'

Abonyi restored Australia's lead in the 51st minute before New Zealand equalised again, thanks to an own goal. Fortunately, Abonyi had got the taste for goals and scored twice in the last 15 minutes to give his team a 5–3 victory. All three goalscorers plus Schaefer were to be an important part of Australia's journey to the 1974 World Cup.

There was little opportunity for the Australian team to rest, as they were in action only two days later against South Vietnam. The home team were coached by Karl-Heinz Weigang. He had been appointed to lead South Vietnam in 1966 having coached Sri Lanka's national team for two years before that.

In his first year, Weigang led South Vietnam to win the Merdeka Tournament, Asia's oldest football tournament, held annually to celebrate

Malaysia's independence. He was to spend his entire career working in Asia and Africa and is still referred to as the 'founding father' of Vietnamese football.

In 1967, there was pressure on him to lead his side to another victory in their own tournament and deliver an important propaganda coup. They had been in a training camp for four months during which Weigang had worked on a 'more direct, robust style', with defenders chosen 'for durability to withstand the toughest of opponents'.

Journalists turning up for major sports events love to file a story upon their arrival, talking about a 'ring of steel' to try to convey the level of security. For Australia's match against South Vietnam, no effort was spared to ensure that the Viet Cong would not be able to launch an attack against a match to be attended by Ky, the former prime minister who had visited Australia earlier in the year and was so keen to use sport to help build bridges. Shortly before the tournament started, he had been promoted to vice-president, with special powers over the military.

Soldiers with fixed bayonets were everywhere, barbed wire, snipers in the buildings surrounding the Cong Hoa Stadium and, outside, army personnel carriers. The crowd of 30,000 were almost to a person against the Australians. Again, the visitors' only support came from the small group of soldiers they had spent time with at the Canberra Club.

Things grew even more tense in the 35th minute when Warren put Australia ahead. 'I remember the dead silence that greeted my goal,' Warren wrote in his autobiography, *Sheilas, Wogs and Poofters*. 'There was a full stadium but no noise! I had to look to the referee to just check the goal hadn't been disallowed.'

Once the crowd had digested what had happened, disturbances erupted almost immediately. The security forces discussed firing tear gas into the spectators to calm things down. Australian officials sitting on the bench on the touchline were advised to vacate their pitch-side position and move into the stands.

They were found positions directly behind Ky. 'I thought it would be as good a time as ever, amid all this pandemonium, for someone to assassinate him, then quickly realised if they were aiming at him, they would just as likely shoot me instead,' Corrigan later admitted.

When the referee blew for half-time, Ky headed to South Vietnam's dressing room. He offered the team six months' salary as a bonus if they could win. The offer backfired, however, because the Australians heard about the incentive as they re-entered the pitch for the second half, and it added to their determination to hang on to their lead.

Soccer World were, in particular, full of praise for Schaefer, who had been included in the starting line-up for the match. He 'used his tremendous strength to break up countless attacks,' the reporter Martin Royal wrote.

News Limited journalist Terry Smith piled praise on Warren. 'Australia captain John Warren's courageous play and sense of humour quickly won him the complete loyalty of the other players,' Smith wrote. 'No one who saw it will ever forget the way in which Warren scored the solitary goal that enabled Australia to score a 1–0 win over Vietnam. He drove himself to exhaustion and was walking around in a daze the following day until he was given a whisky and put to bed.'

After the final whistle, the Australian team were ordered to stay in their dressing room until the security forces could disperse the angry crowd. The team were allowed to leave after half an hour but were still greeted with rocks as they boarded the bus. Before it left, everyone on the vehicle was ordered to lay on the floor with their bags covering their heads.

The team made it safely back to their hotel, but the opinion of Royal about Saigon had not been improved, even by two victories in the opening two matches. 'Let's face it: Saigon is not the best place in the world to hold a soccer tournament,' he wrote. 'It's humid and the whole town stinks to high heaven of rotting garbage. The squalor and filth is pretty depressing. Even the larger buildings, most of them built for the French during their rule, are dilapidated and run-down. Saigon, as a matter of fact, is a place you feel like getting out of the moment you arrive.'

Fellow journalist Smith was in full agreement. 'You could not escape the desperate poverty of the place wherever you went in the corrupt, decrepit city of Saigon,' he wrote.

The Australians were there to do a job, though, and were not going to allow themselves to be distracted. They had four days off before their next match saw them defeat Singapore 5–1, with another hat-trick from Abonyi and goals from Baartz and Alan Westwater, his first for Australia. It guaranteed them a place in the semi-finals which, remember, *Soccer World*'s Andrew Dettre believed would have represented a good performance.

The match against Singapore saw Vlastis give an international debut to Corry in goal as a replacement for the German-born Roger Romanowicz. Vlastis had nurtured him at Canterbury-Marrickville several years earlier. He saved a penalty in the second half and was retained for the rest of the tournament. Corry was another to play a prominent role in Australia's qualification for the World Cup seven years later.

There was little time for preparation for the semi-finals against Group B winners Malaysia as, with the exception of South Vietnam, the teams were expected to play the day after completing their group matches. A torrential downpour a few minutes before the opening match, between the hosts and South Korea, made the match 'more like a combination of water polo and water-skiing', *Soccer World* reported. Even with the extra 24 hours'

Ray Baartz, left, scores for Australia in their 5–1 win over Singapore in their final group game

rest, South Vietnam were no match for their opponents, who ran out easy–3–0 winners.

In their semi-final, Australia were on the attack constantly but could not break down the Malaysians. In the end, it took a goal, nine minutes from the end of extra time, from Baartz to seal the victory. The match finished with tear gas drifting across the Cong Hoa Stadium, after fights broke out among spectators in the 30,000-strong crowd. This seemed to have more to do with angry Vietnamese punters upset at losing money they had gambled on Malaysia winning than with hostility towards the Australians. It was a repeat of what had happened two years earlier in Hong Kong, when Australia had beaten a Hong Kong FA XI 3-1 and stones had been thrown at their dressing room after the match.

Even though they had finished another match in the middle of a riot, it was a bus full of happy Australians who headed back to the Golden Building singing *Waltzing Matilda*.

There was a day's rest for both the finalists before they headed back to the Cong Hoa Stadium on 14th November, in front of another sold-out crowd. When they arrived, the Australian team were upset to discover that the soldiers who had supported them throughout the tournament had been denied entry due to it being at full capacity.

Empty seats on the sidelines were soon found for the servicemen following a threat by the Australian team to boycott the final. Among the Australian troops who had attended all five of the matches was Jack Bromley, a former Australian rugby union international serving in Vietnam as a volunteer medical officer.

If the Australian team were expecting the troops to be their only supporters, especially with the South Koreans having their own even larger group of soldiers providing fanatic backing for their team throughout the tournament, then they were in for a pleasant surprise. When they entered the pitch, they were shocked to hear the home fans cheering for *them*. The reputation of South Korea's troops during the war and alleged atrocities meant they were hated in Saigon.

'They didn't like the Koreans, for some reason, the Vietnamese,' said Baartz. 'They sided with our team, whether it was the way we played football, or what it was, I don't know. But we had more crowd support than they did. They turned it all around. It was nice, because we'd gone in as so-called underdogs, but to have people come out and start cheering for us – it was quite funny.'

If, however, the Australians needed any reminding they were still playing in a warzone, the American artillery provided it by launching a series of attacks in the distance, on the Viet Cong, throughout the game. Tensions were even higher than when the Australians had arrived in Vietnam due to the Battle of Dak To, which was going on at the time and included some of the bloodiest and most intense combat of the War. The *thoop thoop thoop* noise of the mortars being launched towards the enemy provided a frightening soundtrack for the biggest match so far in the history of Australian soccer.

Perhaps it was that which was playing on Australian minds as they allowed the South Koreans to take the lead inside the first minute, following a mix-up in front of Corry's goal. Fears of a repeat of the semi-final against Malaysia began to grow as Australia laid siege to the South Korean goal without equalising. Then, in the 26th minute, Billy Vojtek, born in Croatia and whose family had emigrated to Australia when he was 13, scored a fine individual goal.

Vojtek's goal was particularly celebrated enthusiastically by the local girls in the stadium. The 24-year-old Melbourne Croatia striker had become something of a pin-up since his arrival and was often followed by teenagers hoping to get the chance to touch him. 'Billy, Billy,' his local fan club shrieked after the goal. Vojtek was another new addition to the squad for this trip and was to go on to play a role in the 1974 World Cup qualifying campaign.

The Australians remained on top in the second half, and Abonyi made sure their pressure paid off, with strikes in the 52nd and 84th minutes, to put them 3–1 up and finish the tournament's top scorer with eight goals. Abonyi's second goal against South Korea led to chants of 'Uptoli [Australia in Vietnamese] Number One,' from the Vietnamese crowd.

South Korea scored a late goal, but the 3–2 victory ensured that Warren became the first captain of an Australian soccer team to lift an international trophy. The beaten opponents did not attend the presentation and missed seeing Warren thrusting the large Challenge Cup into the humid night air. It was to be the start of an intense rivalry between the two countries that would peak six years later in Hong Kong.

The Australian players do a lap of honour in Saigon to celebrate lifting their first international trophy

As well as receiving $50 a week compensation during the tour, the players, most of whom had jobs at home, were also given a weekly allowance of $10. In the final, they were also playing for an unexpected bonus.

'John Barclay, he was the team manager,' Ackerley revealed later. 'Before the tour, he told us, "We want the tracksuits back." Before the final, he said, "I'm going to take this on my head. You win the final, you get to keep the tracksuits." So, the big reward for going up to Vietnam in a warzone and winning the tournament was actually that they let us keep our tracksuits.'

The Vietnam Football Federation paid the Australian team's airfares and accommodation during the tour. The Australian Soccer Federation requested a $10,000 subsidy from Australia's Department of External Affairs to cover other costs. It was never officially recorded, but is widely suspected, that the money was not paid.

Hay, in his book *Football and War: Australia and Vietnam 1967–1972*, recalled that Noel St Clair Deschamps, the Australian Ambassador to Cambodia in 1965 when the team played North Korea in the World Cup qualifying matches, had recommended the team should tour Southeast Asia annually. He had estimated the Australian team's presence was 'worth at least $100 million in foreign aid'.

Hay wrote, 'He [the Ambassador] had never been aware Australia had possessed such a powerful propaganda and goodwill weapon as its soccer team.'

It continued to rankle with the players for many years after their success in the South Vietnam Independence Cup that their achievement, in a warzone, was never officially recognised by the Australian government.

Warren strongly believed that the team should have been eligible for the Vietnam Logistic and Support Medal. The medal was created in 1993 to recognise those who played a support role in the Vietnam War. Among the 11,500 Australians to whom it has been awarded are crews of supply ships and aircraft, medical personnel, journalists and sponsored entertainers, who spent a day or more in Vietnam.

In 2005, it was claimed that only individuals who were under government or military jurisdiction during their time in Vietnam were eligible for official recognition. The tracksuits were all the team would receive.

'I think we were probably in more danger than any of them,' said Corry of the recognition celebrities and musicians received for visiting troops. 'We were right in it, while the entertainers would be out at the army bases, which were pretty well protected. Someone has said that we should get a medal, but I don't know. It could have been dangerous, but we considered it more of an adventure.'

Ackerley continues to insist that the footballers had been sent there by the politicians in Canberra. 'We were used by the federal government for political purposes, no question about it,' he said. 'We were young and ambitious then, and if we knew what we were getting ourselves into, we would not have agreed to go. We had no say in it. At the request of the government, we were asked to play in the tournament in order to build the morale of the Australian soldiers in Vietnam.

'It was dangerous – no two ways about it. The disappointing thing is that we were never officially thanked for risking our lives. Entertainers, who went there to perform for the troops, were all recognised and given medals, but not us.

'We became the first Australian team to win an international tournament abroad, but we received scant recognition from the Federation for one hell of an achievement. The tournament was special for me personally because I played in every game, but for our victory not to be recognised officially was frustrating, to say the least.'

The memories, though, were worth a dozen awards to the members of that team that travelled to Vietnam. Every year until his death in 2004, Warren would receive a Christmas card from Abonyi: 'Remember the tunnel in Vietnam' – a reference to the Australian team's entrance before that final in 1967. 'I still remember the hairs standing up on the back of my neck,' Warren recalled.

Before the squad departed Vietnam to continue the rest of their Asian tour, they suffered one final stomach-churning episode. The day after the final, it had been arranged they would all fly to Vung Tau, a popular seaside resort on the peninsula of South Vietnam. The squad was to play a goodwill friendly against an Australian Army select, before a barbecue and a few beers. When Corrigan queried whether it was a safe area to travel to, he was reassured by Australian troops it was also where the North Vietnamese went secretly for some rest and recuperation.

The team, not surprisingly, stayed up through the night celebrating their triumph before heading to the airport for the short flight to Vung Tau. When they got there, they were directed to a bullet-ridden de Havilland Caribou, a twin-engine short take-off and landing plane used primarily for tactical airlift missions. They climbed in through the open back of the aircraft, sat against the wall of the plane and strapped themselves in. The higher the Caribou climbed, the more violently it seemed to toss from side to side.

As they approached Vung Tau, the pilot decided to spice the journey up a bit more and buzzed the off-duty soldiers sunbathing on the beach. When his passengers cheered this manoeuvre, the pilot repeated it, causing many of them to be sick.

It was certainly a memorable end to a trip no one would ever forget.

CHAPTER FIVE

Come on you Emus!

The most successful Australian soccer team in history landed back from its Asian tour in Sydney on Tuesday, 28th November, at midnight on Qantas flight 742.

The tired group of players and officials received a welcome like no other. As each player entered the arrivals hall, they were greeted with thunderous applause by the 500 supporters who had gathered to welcome them. This was despite the late hour, which followed much confusion over when they would be arriving. This was caused by delays in the Qantas flight leaving London, which meant they landed nearly 18 hours behind schedule.

A five-piece uniformed band from St George Budapest, the club that Australian captain Johnny Warren played for, was among those waiting. They were accompanied by the club's majorettes and supporters letting off streamers and holding placards and banners celebrating Australia's success in Vietnam.

'This was no ordinary occasion, one felt, this was a very special carnival, a moving rendezvous between people joined together by the almost holy bond by the common love of soccer,' Andrew Dettre wrote in *Soccer World*. 'Many of them must have felt that if ever there was an hour for Australian soccer to hold its head high, this was the hour. It was bedlam – wonderful, colourful, unforgettable bedlam. Players were torn out of the arms of their wives by complete strangers for a warm handshake, an embrace.'

Many bystanders at the airport, though, were bemused as to what was causing such excitement. 'Stunned and bewildered outsiders – pilots, police, porters – could only stand and gape and grin at the sight of this almost pagan ritual, wondering how a small leather ball and its round-about ways could generate all this emotion,' Dettre wrote. 'The hour, indeed, belonged to Australian soccer.'

After leaving Vietnam, Australia had played another five matches in three countries before returning home. They had won them all. They had first travelled to Djakarta, where they beat representative sides in two matches after the Indonesian Football Association had, at the last minute, cancelled the international games due to the unavailability of some of its top players. But a crowd of 35,000, the biggest of the tour, turned up at the Gelora Bung Karno to see Australia beat a Djakarta XI 3–1.

Australia then travelled on to Singapore, where they defeated the home side 6–1 in the Jalan Besar Stadium – an even bigger victory than they had enjoyed in Saigon. On a pitch described by *Soccer World* as being 'fast, Wembley-like turf', Atti Abonyi continued his fine goalscoring form with another two goals. The match took place against civil unrest after the Singapore government decided to devalue its dollar, which until then had been pegged to British sterling.

Australia returned home to a hero's welcome in Sydney after completing an unbeaten tour of Asia

Australia then won 8–1 against a Combined Services XI, composed mainly of former English amateur players, before leaving Singapore for the final match of the tour in Kuala Lumpur. Upon arrival for the international against Malaysia, the Australian team and officials were shocked to find the stadium in darkness. They were then informed that the Malaysian Football Association had decided to cancel the game due to heavy rain.

The match was rearranged for the next day, and it went ahead, despite another torrential downpour. A crowd of only 500 turned up to watch Australia win 4–0. Tommy McColl opened the scoring in the fourth minute before Billy Vojtek scored in the 28th and 47th minutes. Fittingly, it was Abonyi who scored the 38th and final goal of the tour, taking his final personal tally to 13.

Stan Ackerley was the only member of the team to play in every minute of the tour, while Vojtek and midfielder Alan Westwater also appeared in all of the matches. Vojtek finished the second- highest scorer on the tour with eight goals, including the opening goal in the final of the South Vietnam Independence Cup against South Korea.

Vojtek had gone on the tour even though he had just got married, but he was not going to let that stop him. He revealed how he found out that he had been included in the final party of 19 when it was whittled down from the training group of 40. 'The selectors never let on, but we knew that the guys that were given an injection were the ones that would go,' he said. 'Fortunately, I got one. It was the sweetest needle I ever had.'

Ackerley praised the 'great bunch of lads ... young enough to play for Australia for years yet.' Time was to prove him right.

Australia played five more matches on their way home from Saigon, winning them all, including against a Djakarta XI

It was an opinion shared by 'Uncle' Joe Vlasits. 'Our Australian team has huge potential – it improved from match to match,' the coach wrote in an article published in *Soccer World*. 'I am more firmly convinced than ever that after our return to Australia, it is essential to keep this team somehow together for future occasions. If we do, Australia has the nucleus of a fine team for years to come.'

It was a view shared by Dettre, who, upon the team's return, wrote presciently that 'the foundations for a brighter future were laid in the steamy heat of Saigon.'

Dettre, remember, on the eve of the team's departure to Vietnam, had warned that 'our team goes to war poorly armed' and expressed concerns about lack of preparation and experience. *Soccer World* was happy to admit they were wrong in an editorial entitled 'We'll eat this humble, tasty pudding'.

One thing that *Soccer World* got absolutely right was that Australian football's future lay in Asia. As a result of its history, Australia had strong ties with Europe, particularly Britain. Coverage of the English Football League dominated Australian television and newspapers. As the Manchester United tour earlier in 1967 had proved, visits to Australia by England's top clubs were a massive draw.

But *Soccer World* had been calling, since 1960, for Australia to focus on Asia. The idea had the backing of Vivian Chalwin, a former amateur footballer in England with Hull City and Notts County, before moving to Australia. There, he became the chairman of British Oil Engines and also actively involved in the local soccer scene.

Sir Stanley Rous, secretary of the Football Association in England and later the president of FIFA, had recommended Chalwin to the Australian Soccer Federation soon after he arrived in Australia in 1951. Walter Winterbottom, the Football Association director of coaching and former coach of England, was also a close friend. Chalwin had access to all FA coaching material, and he brought over films and literature for use in his coaching programmes in New South Wales.

Chalwin was also the coach of Granville Soccer Club, APIA Leichhardt, the New South Wales Soccer Association and, in 1953, Australia's national team in a six-match series against Hong Kong Chinese XI. Australia won two matches but suffered three defeats, including a heavy 7–1 loss in Brisbane, with one game drawn.

Even with these close ties to the English game, Chalwin had urged seven years before the trip to Vietnam that 'Australian soccer administrators should now realise that close ties with Asian countries would benefit our soccer.'

The call for Australia to join Asia for football purposes was one regularly taken up in *Soccer World* by the Chinese-born Lou Gautier. He rarely missed an opportunity to lobby for Australia to tie itself to the Asian Football Confederation. After returning from Australia's humiliating defeat in the World Cup qualifying matches against North Korea in 1965, he wrote, 'If the recently ended tour of Southeast Asia has proved anything at all – and I think it has proved many things – then it's the fact that for the time being at least, our place is in Asia soccer.

'We are considered part and parcel of the region's soccer life by others – and it's time we did ourselves. Our vocation most definitely lies in the Asian continent and this tour will, I hope, revolutionise our soccer future.'

Vlasits had noted that after the South Vietnam Independence Cup, even Australia's biggest rivals in Oceania were no match for them. 'I am afraid New Zealand, in international soccer, is a good 20 years behind Australia.'

Aligning with Asia was a subject the editors of *Soccer World* were to return to repeatedly in the intervening years.

It was not until 2006, however, that Australia was finally elected to join the Asian Football Confederation. Australia was the strongest team in Oceania but was never given a guarantee of an automatic place in the World Cup. This was because the winner from that region only receives half a place for the main tournament, forcing them to compete in the intercontinental play-offs on a regular basis. By the time they hitched themselves to Asia, Australia had failed seven consecutive times to qualify for the World Cup.

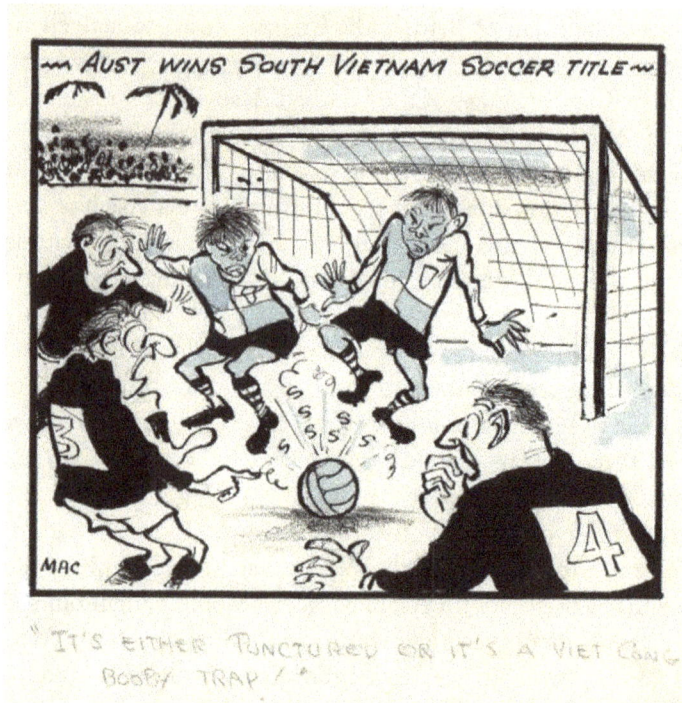

Coverage of the Saigon triumph in the Australian media was minimal, but one cartoonist immortalised their trip to a war zone

It would be wrong to say Australia's triumph in Vietnam had led to an explosion of interest in the national football team. One supporter wrote to Soccer World to complain that coverage in the mainstream media was 'very inadequate for a series of internationals, particularly involving Australia's prestige and in the light of their tremendous success'.

One journalist who did pay attention to the team's achievements was Tony Horstead, who published a regular column on soccer in the *Daily Mirror* in Sydney, under the byline of 'Hotspur'. He did not accompany the team on their visit to Vietnam but wrote about it after the team returned home.

Horstead decided that the newly successful squad needed a punchy name to identify them, just like the rugby league and rugby union teams who were called the 'Kangaroos' and 'Wallabies', respectively. He invited readers to send in suggestions for a nickname and promised a free ticket to the following year's international matches for the winning entry.

A week later, he revealed that 'Emus' was the overwhelming favourite by almost four to one. Other proposed names included Wattles, Jackaroos, Wombats, Bandicoots, Birubieds, Baddwalers, Walleroos, Merinos, Koalas, Woomeras and Sharks.

'The Emu, apart from being part of our national emblem, also has the attribute of being fast and with a mighty kick,' Horstead wrote. 'Whether anyone else in the world knows these facts is doubtful. It will be up to our players, when they play all over the world, to prove they can run faster and kick harder than anyone else.'

Horstead's competition was not popular with all his readers. One wrote, 'What's this bloody silly idea about a name anyway? What's wrong with calling the team Australia?'

Another football fan not supportive of Horstead's attempts at producing a new name was Tommy Dobinson, from Riverwood in Sydney. He wrote to *Soccer World* claiming that 'this kind of nonsense is peculiar to Australian rugby, and I see no reason at all to copy such idiocies.'

Mr Dobinson added, 'Surely that columnist could find something more intelligent to write about; he should leave zoology alone. This type of phoney gimmickry is more suitable for tag wrestling and the roller game than for soccer, where for ages Brazil has been Brazil, England has been England, and no idle, wandering mind has ever suggested that on international tours they be called anything else – except, again, in the world of rugby where with typical grammar-school mentality the British insist on being called the "Lions".'

There was no reference to the 'Emus' when Australia lined up in March 1968 for the start of a three-match home series against Japan. The two countries already knew that they would probably be facing each other in the qualifying tournament for the 1970 World Cup, so it was an ideal opportunity for both to size each other up.

The Japanese team were travelling back from Mexico, where they had held a training camp in preparations for that year's Olympic Games in Mexico City. In contrast, the Australians had not held a single training session since their return from Asia four months earlier.

The Australian Soccer Federation also turned down the request from Vlasits to pick a squad of 25 players. They restricted him to 16 for economic reasons and they met only four days before the opening match. The squad were also missing Abonyi, the top goalscorer on their Asian tour, because he could not get time off work. 'All this despite the many brave words about keeping this team together,' *Soccer World* noted.

The visitors included the country's star player Kunishige Kamamoto, part of Japan's team that had won a bronze medal at the 1966 Asian Games in Bangkok. He scored twice in a 2–2 draw at Sydney Sports Ground before a crowd of 8,646, with McColl and another Scottish-born player, substitute Archie Blue, hitting Australia's goals.

Just 24 hours later, Australia won the next match at Olympic Park in Melbourne 3–1, with Les Scheinflug, Vojtek and Ray Baartz scoring as they came from a goal down. It was the fourth goal scored by Scheinflug in his fifth international, having not played for Australia since captaining them on their Asian tour in 1965, including the two World Cup matches against North Korea. The next match in the series was to mark the end of his international playing career. But it was not the end of Scheinflug's story with the Australian national team.

Even after their success just a few months earlier in Vietnam, there seemed to be little love among many Australian supporters for its soccer team. *Soccer World* reported that Japan's coach, Shunichiro Okano, was 'amazed at the crowd's lack of warmth and feeling towards their national team.

'This was particularly evident in Melbourne,' *Soccer World* wrote, 'where the Australians were not only treated with contempt and icy indifference, but openly abused by sections of the crowd whose only cries of "support" throughout the match were "Go back to Sydney", "Butchers" or "Come on, Japan".'

It showed how football in Australia remained divided along state lines, with the crowd in Melbourne claiming the team was 'stacked with Sydney no-hopers'.

Warren voiced his disgust at the lack of support, which included him being booed when he was substituted during the game in Sydney. 'It would have been better if we had been playing in Vietnam or Korea,' the Australian captain said.

In the final game of the series, at Norwood Oval in Adelaide, Japan reversed the previous match's result. Kamamoto scored twice in the final five minutes as Japan recovered from McColl's 70th- minute goal to win 3–1. After the match, the home crowd carried Kamamoto triumphantly around the ground, perfectly illustrating how little support Australia enjoyed during the series. 'Norwood Oval's crowd was plainly hostile to them, barracking for their downfall and celebrating their doom,' Andrew Dettre wrote in *Soccer World*.

One good thing was that after the failure of the previous year's tour to Asia to make much money, the series with Japan left the Australian Soccer Federation with a profit of $9,000.

Later in the year, Kamamoto finished top scorer at the Olympics with seven goals as Japan won the bronze medal. This included both goals in the third-place play-off against home country Mexico in front of a crowd of 105,000 at the Azteca Stadium.

More than a year was to pass before the Australian team were to take to the international field again, when Greece visited for a three-match series in 1969. The games drew big crowds thanks to the large Greek community in Australia.

The matches were arranged to help Australia fine-tune its preparations for its 1970 World Cup qualifying campaign, and the series got off to a good start. Playing before a crowd of 24,129 at the Sydney Cricket Ground, the venue having been made available unlike in 1967 for Scotland, the home side beat their visitors 1-0 thanks to a penalty in the 60th minute from Abonyi.

Spectators included Gough Whitlam, the leader of the Australian Labor Party. Whitlam was a big sports fan and believed passionately in the government providing support so that Australia could be successful on the world stage. Although it was to be more than three years before he became prime minister, he was to play a leading role in Australia's successful qualifying campaign for the 1974 World Cup.

Curiously, Harold Holt, the prime minister who had backed Australia's visit to Saigon for the South Vietnam Independence Cup in 1967, had disappeared shortly after the team returned home from that tournament. He was never seen again after going swimming off the coast of Victoria on 17th December that year and was presumed dead.

Australia's opening match against Greece also saw the debut of a young English-born striker called Adrian Alston. He had moved to New South Wales to join South Coast United after being recommended to the club by former Blackpool defender Jim Kelly, who had coached Australia in their matches against Everton in 1964. Kelly was returning to the Illawarra-based club in 1967 for a second spell as coach and had persuaded Alston to come with him.

At the time, Alston was playing for Fleetwood Town, a club based on the north-west coast of England, and who competed in the Lancashire Combination. He came from good footballing stock as his brother, Alec, had played over 100 matches for Preston North End, including in the English First Division, alongside the legendary Tom Finney.

Tommy McColl in action in Australia's opening match against Greece in Sydney in 1969 after coming on as a half-time substitute for debutant Adrian Alston

Alston discovered the harder pitches in Australia suited his style better, and he ended his first season at South Coast as joint top scorer with 12 goals in 22 games. Alston had planned only to go to Australia for six months, but he was so successful that he extended his stay and called for his girlfriend to travel over from England to join him.

At that time, eligibility rules were different, so Alston was able to be called up by Vlasits even though he did not have an Australian passport. Alston had joked upon his selection for Australia, 'That's the end of my English career.'

The 20-year-old found his debut tough and was replaced at half-time by McColl, who earned the penalty that won the match. 'I had a very ordinary half of football,' Alston admitted in his autobiography, *Noddy*. 'It was just difficult against a very strong Greek team. I did not see much of the ball and the fact I hardly knew the players I was playing with did not help.

'Vlasits gave me 45 minutes and he was good to me afterwards. He put his arm around me and assured me everything would be okay. "You've done pretty well to shoot up the ladder in one season … you have a long career ahead of you and you will be a star for Australia in years to come," he promised me.'

Vlasits was right and, although Alston did not figure in the rest of the series against Greece, he was to become one of Australia's most important players in the years ahead.

The Greeks did not take defeat well and were much more physical in the second match. Four days later, at the Exhibition Ground in Brisbane, Georgios Dedes scored twice to give Greece a two-goal lead, before Vojtek and Baartz pulled Australia level to earn a 2–2 draw. The match was marred by the Greeks having a player sent off and their coach, Dan Georgiadis, continually being warned by the referee for running onto the pitch.

The Australians were not innocents and knew how to look after themselves, as Manfred Schaefer later admitted. 'One of the opposing midfielders kept kicking Australia's Danny Walsh,' he explained. 'Later, Walsh was flattened from behind and I decided that was enough. I ran nearly the length of the field and landed a right hook on the jaw of the spiteful Greek.

'Muhammad Ali would have been proud of that punch, and everyone at the ground, bar the referee, saw it. But, despite laying out the opponent, I was voted best and fairest player of the match by a panel of soccer writers. I was presented with a beautiful trophy.'

Another crowd of over 24,000 attended the last match in the series at Olympic Park in Melbourne. The Australians were well below the level they had shown in the previous two matches and lost 2–0.

There were now only two months left until Australia travelled to Seoul for the start of their 1970 FIFA World Cup qualifying campaign.

Chapter Six

Cursed

For the second FIFA World Cup qualifying competition in a row, the journey that Australia would need to undertake for the 1970 finals in Mexico would be dictated by geopolitics.

The competition for the 1966 World Cup in England had been blighted by a row over whether Africa should be allowed an automatic place in the tournament, the participation of Apartheid South Africa and the drawing together of North and South Korea.

This time, it was the situation in Rhodesia that shaped things. They had been added to the Asian and Oceania qualifying tournament because, just as had happened with South Africa, members of the Confederation of African Football had shunned them.

The system of racial division operated in Rhodesia was not as elaborate as the one operated in neighbouring South Africa. But it still practised widespread discrimination which reinforced a system of white-only rule. Africans were barred from participating in government and were not allowed to own land.

In November 1965, the Rhodesian government, led by Ian Smith, had announced a unilateral declaration of independence from the United Kingdom, who had annexed the country in September 1923. The territory, formerly known as Southern Rhodesia, had been controlled by the United Kingdom since 1889, when it became part of the British South African Company led by Cecil Rhodes.

In 1966, the United Nations had announced a series of economic sanctions against Rhodesia after they warned the decision to declare itself independent 'constitutes a threat to international peace and security'.

South Africa had been officially suspended by FIFA in 1964, shortly before the qualifying tournament for 1966 was due to begin, following pressure from the Confederation of African Football. Rhodesia, however, were allowed by FIFA to continue playing and moved to a different continent for what would be their debut in World Cup qualifying. It was a decision taken largely as a result, once again, of the view of FIFA president Sir Stanley Rous, who did not believe politics should be allowed in sport.

This was not the only problem that FIFA faced when drawing up the qualifying competition for Asia and Oceania. Besides the fact that North and South Korea needed to be kept apart to avoid a repeat of one of them pulling out, there was the additional problem that the Japanese government did not recognise the regime in Pyongyang.

North Korea had missed the 1964 Olympic Games in Tokyo because a number of its athletes were declared ineligible. As well as having no diplomatic relations with North Korea, the government in Japan also refused to accept the country's demand they be called 'The Democratic Republic of Korea'.

Then, FIFA faced the additional headache that North Korea recognised the sovereignty of the State of Palestine over all of Israel. In 1966, North Korea had started to establish close relations with the Palestine Liberation Organization. North Korea's founder and Supreme Leader Kim Il Sung and Palestine Liberation Organization chairman Yasser Arafat had forged a mutual bond, which included substantial aid being provided to the Palestinians.

On 1st February 1968, at a FIFA meeting in Casablanca, it was announced that eight places were available to teams from Europe, three for South America, one for Africa, one for a team from Asia or Oceania, and one for North and Central America and the Caribbean. It meant a place in the finals for an African representative was guaranteed for the first time, a response to the 1966 boycott. But if Australia were to make it for the first time, it meant they were going to have to take the long road to Mexico.

Australia were paired in the same group as Japan, South Korea and Rhodesia, while New Zealand were drawn against Israel and North Korea. FIFA had ignored a request from the Australian Soccer Federation to put them and New Zealand in the same group. 'Oceania as a separate, autonomous and fully-fledged FIFA Confederation was entitled to its own sub-group, the winner playing off with an Asian team for a berth in Mexico,' Australian Soccer Federation secretary Ian McAndrew told *Soccer World*.

New Zealand had already admitted, upon their return from the South Vietnam Independence Cup the previous November, they were reconsidering whether it was even worth entering the World Cup. 'The performances of the New Zealand team have left a lot to be desired,' New Zealand Football Association promotions director Charlie Dempsey said.

At the same time the World Cup qualifying draw was taking place, the Australian Soccer Federation had received and accepted an invitation to return, later in 1968, to Saigon. Senior officials within the Federation, though, were urging them to rescind the decision. The situation since Australia had returned just a couple of months earlier had worsened considerably. The Viet Cong had launched the Tet Offensive, a major escalation and what turned out to be one of the largest and most important campaigns of the Vietnam War.

'Recent events have proved that no part of South Vietnam, including Saigon, is safe,' an unnamed official told *Soccer World*. 'Exposing the best Australian players to undue danger is totally irresponsible.'

The plan to return to Vietnam was soon dropped.

Discussions about how the World Cup qualifying pool involving Australia, Japan, South Korea and Rhodesia would work was soon underway. FIFA's assistant secretary, Rene Curte, revealed that the governing body was open to the prospect of Australia staging all the matches in the group as part of a tournament. 'If they are convinced that such a tournament can be organised in Australia, FIFA will be pleased to receive the candidature,' Curte said.

Such a proposal hit an immediate problem when it became known that the Australian government would not be willing to grant the Rhodesia team visas to visit the country.

It was then reported that Japan was prepared to host a round-robin tournament, including the one involving Israel and New Zealand. Then, after McAndrew had visited Seoul in May for a meeting of the Asian Football Confederation, a new proposal was put forward.

This would have involved Australia playing New Zealand, Israel meeting Rhodesia and South Korea taking on Japan, with North Korea receiving a bye through to the next round. The ties involving Australia, New Zealand, South Korea and Japan would be on a home-and-away basis, with Israel playing both their matches against Rhodesia at home. A qualifying tournament would then be staged in March 1969, involving the winners of the three ties and North Korea, and would take place in Tel Aviv.

Discussions rumbled on for several months. While some reports suggested all the matches would take place in Israel, another story claimed FIFA were considering forcing the withdrawal of Rhodesia due to its government policies. It was then revealed that the 'McAndrew plan' drawn up at the meeting in Seoul had never actually been presented to FIFA as Israel had later withdrawn its approval.

By the middle of August 1968, there was still no plan in place and all the participating countries had missed a deadline of 31st May to decide which one should stage the qualifying tournament. FIFA secretary general Helmut Kaser was forced to issue a warning. 'As no firm proposal has been received, it seems that FIFA will have to take the initiative,' he wrote in a letter published in *Soccer World*.

Finally, in October, it seemed the deadlock had been broken. FIFA, meeting at its annual Congress in Guadalajara in Mexico, ruled that Australia's group would take place the following October in either Japan or South Korea. They also dictated that North Korea and New Zealand must travel to Israel to play their group. FIFA made it clear that they would not allow any country objecting to play due to political reasons – a clear warning to North Korea.

It was not until the early part of 1969 that it was confirmed that Australia would be travelling to Seoul to meet hosts South Korea, Japan and Rhodesia.

A further twist came when Australia, Japan and South Korea appealed to FIFA for Rhodesia to be excluded from the group on the basis that, as an African country, they should have no role in the Asia and Oceania qualifying process.

Since the draw had been made more than a year earlier, the political situation in Rhodesia had grown worse. In March 1968, only a short time after Rhodesia had been drawn in Australia's World Cup qualifying group, the government executed five Africans for alleged murders in the space of less than a week. This was despite Queen Elizabeth II issuing all the men a reprieve and widespread international condemnation of the sentences.

This was followed on 20th June, the next year, by a referendum being held in the country regarding the adoption of a constitution that would have enshrined political power in the hands of the white minority and established Rhodesia as a republic. Rhodesia's predominantly white electorate overwhelmingly approved both measures.

FIFA still refused to suspend Rhodesia. Instead, they announced a last-minute compromise which meant the winners of the group in Seoul would have to play off against the African country for the right to meet the first-placed country from the other group. Where this play-off would take place remained a mystery after the first choice, Bangkok, had to be dropped when Thailand's government announced they would not grant visas to the Rhodesian team.

By now, Group 2 had been reduced to just two countries after North Korea were expelled by FIFA in June 1969 because of its refusal to play Israel. The team that had been such an unexpected hit at England in 1966, after qualifying at their first attempt, were cast back into the football wilderness.

At the beginning of September, 'Uncle Joe', Joe Vlasits, announced a squad of 22 players for the trip to Seoul. It included 17 players from New South Wales clubs. All the travelling party received vaccinations for smallpox, typhoid and cholera. But plans for a warm-up match against Hong Kong fell through.

The teams from Japan and South Korea, in contrast, had been together for months preparing for this tournament. The Japanese were still riding high off the back of their Olympic bronze medal at Mexico City 1968. They were hit with a major blow, however, when it was announced that their best player, Kunishige Kamamoto, had been stuck down by illness and would not participate.

Australia's team left Sydney on 1st October 1969, nine days before their opening match against Japan at the Dongdaemun Stadium in Seoul. They arrived in the South Korean capital only after long stopovers in Hong Kong and Tokyo. 'I am hopeful, even moderately confident – but not really optimistic,' Vlasits had admitted before leaving.

A plan to start preparing for this qualifying campaign in January had never come to fruition, and the squad had only come together for the three

The Australian team getting ready to take part in the first round of qualifying for the 1970 World Cup

friendlies against Greece in July. 'I wanted the team to play eight or 10 serious matches during the year and all we played was three,' Vlasits said. 'Lack of finance and the enormous distances made it impossible to bring the team together more often. Let's hope this can be done next year, especially if we qualify for Mexico.'

Les Scheinflug, the captain of Australia when they had been so unprepared for the World Cup qualifying matches in Cambodia four years earlier, voiced what Vlasits was probably thinking. 'Lack of preparation would describe it more aptly,' he said. 'You can't go into tough World Cup battles in the haphazard way Australia does.

'The players will get the blame if we don't win in Seoul. This will again be unfair because they are the victims of the archaic system within Australian soccer. You either do something properly, or you don't do it at all.'

At least Scheinflug was going to be in a position to help correct things for the next World Cup qualifying campaign.

All the uncertainty surrounding who they would play, where and when had a 'depressing effect' on Australia's players, Vlasits admitted. He lamented the absence of Rhodesia, claiming that playing six matches instead of four would have suited Australia better 'as our boys are physically stronger than either the Japanese or Koreans, in the long run, and this would have helped us considerably.'

At least Australian captain Johnny Warren sounded a positive note. 'The team has been together, almost to the man, for two years now,' he said on the eve of their departure. 'We all know each other and there is a common bond between the players.'

Warren promised 'we won't be caught unawares as we were in Phnom Penh.'

The Australian party was housed in a three-star hotel called Academy House located less than 10 kilometres from Seoul's city centre and owned by the Christian Academy of Korea. It had no bar; entertainment and music were not allowed. The Australian team had been warned that alcohol had been banned for the three-week trip, but officials accompanying them were relieved to find that they could still order beer from room service at the hotel up until midnight.

Peace had never been declared at the end of the Korea War in 1953, ceasing with an armistice. But, by 1969, there still remained more than 65,000 United States troops stationed in South Korea.

At least there was a sense of tranquillity in Seoul and none of the fear the Australian team had faced in South Vietnam two years previously. The quality of their accommodation was definitely a step up too from what they had experienced in the Golden Building in Saigon. Steak and mushrooms were served each day, while chicken and pork and ice cream and coffee were also available.

The training facilities still left much to be desired, though. The team practised on various pitches around the city, located more than an hour from their hotel, including a baseball field with no goalposts. They were allocated only two training sessions at the Dongdaemun Stadium before their opening match against Japan on 10th October.

Vlasits did provide an early psychological boost for the Australians when, one morning, he had his team assemble early outside the hotel. There, he oversaw a 30-minute session of vigorous calisthenics while he shouted instructions at the top of his voice. It was designed to wake up their Japanese rivals staying in the same complex.

The Australians were using every mind trick in the book to score points against a side already facing a hostile reception in a stadium where, just 24 years earlier, more than 25,000 South Koreans had gathered to celebrate the end of a 35-year Japanese colonial rule.

Before the kick-off, the Australian team walked round the pitch holding the South Korean flag. They were led onto the pitch by the Yohan Technical High School Band playing *Waltzing Matilda*. In the lead-up to the game, teachers from the high school had delivered three cases of apples to the Australian team at their hotel. It was a thank-you for the $500,000 that the Australian government had provided to the school, through the Colombo Plan, to help support the development of South Korea. Pupils were also among the crowd of 3,513 cheering for the Australians during the match and waving flags.

Perhaps it all helped contribute to Australia's 3–1 victory over Japan in the opening match of the round-robin tournament on a freezing day. Scottish-born Tommy McColl put the Australians ahead after only five minutes, before Masashi Watanabe equalised six minutes later. Australia took the lead again in the 68th minute thanks to an own goal from Aritatsu Ogi before Ray Baartz scored the decisive third goal a minute later.

The manner of the performance took even Andrew Dettre by surprise. After all the fears that the team would again enter its World Cup qualifying campaign underprepared, they had started very impressively. 'Australia played much better than anybody here expected,' Dettre wrote in *Soccer World*.

The importance of the result took on even more significance two days later, when hosts South Korea and Japan drew 2–2. Australia's excellent form continued when they beat South Korea 2–1, with goals from Johnny Watkiss and another from McColl in a match notable for the hostile reception the visitors faced from the 25,000 home fans.

'They drove their team on relentlessly,' *Soccer World* reported. 'At half-time, just after Korea's equaliser, the crowd went berserk. Dozens of bands on the terraces played as spectators sang fiercely patriotic songs and fireworks exploded all over the arena.'

The winner, eight minutes from the end, was scored by McColl, who had once been transferred from Colchester United to Chelsea for £7,500 before emigrating to Australia, and was not greeted well.

'The Australians were pelted with cushions, bottles and rubbish after the game, and had to be escorted to their dressing room by riot police,' *Soccer World* wrote.

Brian Corrigan, the team doctor, later described the 'xenophobic South Korean crowd as the most hostile I have ever seen or heard'.

Vlasits was ecstatic after the final whistle. 'This could have been the greatest victory in Australian soccer history,' he said. 'If we get to Mexico, I think this will be the victory that will be most responsible for our success.'

Dettre noted that Australia had not been intimidated by what they faced. 'They took as much as they dished out in this "Battle of Seoul", which will live long in the memory of the handful of Australians present,' he wrote. 'That the Australians did not wilt under such trying conditions speaks volumes for the confidence which has been instilled in them.

'No praise is high enough for the Australian team which stepped into soccer history tonight. It was a stirring team effort which carried us to victory in what must undoubtedly rate as our greatest international triumph.'

Australia now required only two points from their remaining two matches to move into the next round.

Even though the team was doing well, stories began appearing back home that the position of Vlasits as coach would be under threat if he did not lead the team to the 1970 World Cup finals in Mexico. It was also reported that the Australian Soccer Federation wanted to downgrade the position from a full-time role to part time.

A curious incident also occurred when some members of the Australian team began objecting to the daily 7am training sessions. Rather than dismiss the complaints and tell them to get on with it, Vlasits and team manager John Barclay decided to put the matter to a vote. The vote duly went the way of those who wanted to scrap the early-morning training.

Warren doubted that Frank Arok, the Yugoslavian who was his coach at St George Budapest, would have put up with such insolence. 'I cannot even imagine that he would take this way out of any problem,' he said.

The team had only a day to recover from their bruising encounter against South Korea before they faced Japan again.

On their rest day, members of the South Korean Football Association had visited the Australian team at their headquarters to apologise for the behaviour of the crowd the previous day. As a peace offering, they also presented the Australian team with several baskets of fruit.

Sir Stanley, the president of FIFA, also jetted in to watch the closing matches of the tournament. The Briton, who had served in the First World War as an officer in the Royal Field Artillery, had been head of world football's governing body since 1961. Before becoming the secretary of the Football Association in England, he had been an international referee.

Sir Stanley had refereed the 1934 FA Cup final between Manchester City and Portsmouth at Wembley Stadium. In 1938, he had made a major contribution to the sport by rewriting the Laws of the Game, making them simpler and easier to understand.

Sir Stanley was distinctly unimpressed by the performance of Thai referee Wanchai Suvaree during Australia's return match against Japan, watched by a crowd of less than 1,500. Teruki Miyamoto put the Japanese ahead after only four minutes, before McColl scored again in the 39th minute.

McColl's third consecutive goal of the tournament came after Baartz believed he had already equalised. The Japanese were walking back to the centre circle to restart the match when Suvaree, a captain in the Thai police, noticed the linesman with his flag up and disallowed the goal.

It was reported that Sir Stanley turned to Les Bordacs, the founder and long-term president of St George Budapest and Australia's assistant manager on this trip, and said: 'Refereeing is one of soccer's problems the world over.'

South Korea's 2–0 win over Japan on 16th October kept their hopes of reaching Mexico 1970 alive. They knew a victory over Australia in the final match of the tournament meant they would force a play-off, as goal difference was not used in the qualifiers.

South Korea was coached by Kim Yong-sik. When Korea was ruled by Japan, Kim was the only Korean footballer called up for the 1936 Olympics in Berlin. He contributed to Japan's first-round victory by assisting the winning goal against Sweden. In the quarter-finals, Japan were beaten 8–0 by Italy, the eventual gold medallists.

At the 1948 Olympics in London, Kim played for an independent Korea as player-coach and led them to a 5–3 victory over Mexico in the first round, before they were beaten 12–0 in the quarter-finals by Sweden, who went on to win the gold medal.

Kim had then managed South Korea when they had become only the second Asian country to qualify for the FIFA World Cup finals in Sweden in 1954. They had suffered heavy 9–0 and 7–0 defeats to Hungary and Turkey, respectively. His place in Korean football folklore was already assured, but he was determined to pull off another piece of history.

Kim's team, backed by another capacity crowd of 25,000, were certainly fired up for the game, and Park Soo-Il put them ahead in the 28th minute. Baartz's equaliser in the 58th minute was met with another predictable angry response from the home spectators. 'Already vicious for the entire period leading up to our equaliser, large sections of the fanatic, crazed crowd ran amok, tossing beer bottles and cans on the Australian bench,' Dettre said in his report in *World Soccer*.

Maybe it was this 'animal-like outburst' that put pressure on the Malaysian referee, Patrick Nice, and led to him awarding South Korea a penalty in the 66th minute, described by Dettre as 'the harshest of the year'. Incredibly, Australian goalkeeper Ron Corry saved the penalty from Park Lee-Chun.

Corry pulled off a series of other magnificent stops before Warren thought he had won the game two minutes from the end after beating four defenders to score, only for the referee to disallow it for offside. Warren would later describe it as 'probably the best goal I have ever scored'.

Dettre believed that the referee was anything but Nice and alleged that he had 'physically tried to prevent Australia from winning the tournament ... He wasn't just biased – he was plain cheating and so were his two linesmen, and in all my years of soccer I have never seen a more blatant attempt by a referee to shape a result.'

Whether it was a coincidence or not after performing so poorly in front of the FIFA president, Nice never refereed another international match again.

Celebrations had barely started after the final whistle when Barclay, Australia's team manager, was handed a copy of an official protest filed by the South Korean Football Association to FIFA, alleging that seven of their players had travelled on United Kingdom passports and were, therefore, not eligible. The Koreans claimed that this was against FIFA regulations.

Fortunately, Sir Stanley was on hand to diffuse a potentially disastrous situation. The Australian Soccer Federation confirmed that all the British players had lived in the country for more than 12 months.

Sir Stanley was already sympathetic towards the Australians after what he had seen with the refereeing. 'I can hardly remember a team having to play under such adverse conditions,' he said. 'I wouldn't worry too much about it. If your Immigration Department confirms these chaps are regarded as Australians, that's the end of the matter.' Sir Stanley was as good as his word and the protest never went any further.

The cordiality that South Korea's football chiefs had appeared so keen to foster earlier in the tournament seemed to disappear totally after their team's World Cup elimination. 'Australia is not really an Asian country,' one senior official said bitterly.

Having recovered from that passport scare, the Australians then had to deal with the issue of where they would play Rhodesia for the right to face Israel. The Israelis had cruised through their group with 4–0 and 2–0 victories over New Zealand in Tel Aviv.

Before leaving Seoul to return to Europe, Sir Stanley had revealed in a press conference that they had considered Mexico City to stage the play-off, to assess whether the Mexican government would grant the Rhodesians visas in the event they qualified for the World Cup finals. When questioned what would happen if the Mexicans refused, he warned, 'We may take the World Cup away from Mexico and ask the Germans to stage it.'

Sir Stanley's determination to keep Rhodesia in the World Cup, in the face of international condemnation, was clearly becoming a joke. Dettre revealed that 'Rous had walked into the conference with a little school map in his hand and was either hedging or was totally embarrassed.'

If Mexico would not stage the play-off, Portugal had offered to host it in Mozambique, which it continued to govern as a colony. When Dettre asked Sir Stanley whether it was fair that Rhodesia was playing in the Asia and Oceania qualifying tournament, he replied sarcastically, 'It's strange that you only wake up now in Australia and discover that Rhodesia is an African country.' This ignored Australia's earlier complaints about Rhodesia's participation.

Dettre summed up what most people were thinking when he wrote, 'The whole bloody mess is simply unbelievable.'

The hope continued that once the government in Mexico officially announced that it would not grant visas to Rhodesia, then FIFA would cave into international pressure and expel the Africans from the World Cup. Instead, they pushed on with the controversial plan to host the play-off in Mozambique.

FIFA claimed the reason Mexico had been discounted was not because of the visa issue but due to the fact they could not find a suitable stadium to host the matches less than a year before it was due to host football's biggest tournament. 'FIFA's frantic efforts to accommodate Rhodesia would be laughable if they weren't so tragic,' *Soccer World* wrote.

In the same *Soccer World* article, it was noted that the Australian Soccer Federation would need $25,000 to fund the 'safari' to Mozambique, and there were fears that some of the country's players would not be able to get the time off work to take part.

Support for Australian protests about having to travel to Mozambique to play Rhodesia and then, if they won that, face a two-legged tie against Israel, came from an unexpected source. *L'Equipe*, the prestigious French sports newspaper, wrote: 'FIFA has gone too far with Australia. Winning a three-nation tournament in Seoul should have been enough for Australia to qualify for Mexico. No other country will have travelled as much as Australia and played so many qualifying games. Australia has every right to complain.'

Soccer World reader Ronald Rider, from Haberfield in Sydney, wanted his country's Federation to stand up to the world governing body. 'If Australian soccer had any pride, it would tell FIFA where to get off and immediately disassociate itself with the world body,' he wrote in a letter published by the newspaper. 'FIFA hasn't stopped hindering Australia's World Cup progress, so what have we got to gain by remaining a member of this incompetent organisation … Tell the Zurich gnomes to jump in the lake.'

Johnny Warren led a confident Australian team to Mozambique for their World Cup play-off against Rhodesia

FIFA refused to back down and Australia had to accept the fact that it would have just three weeks to get ready to travel to Mozambique's capital, Lourenco Marques, to take on their controversial African opponents.

The two-legged tie was to be organised by the Portuguese Football Association, who were optimistic for big crowds. The Australian Soccer Federation, for one, hoped they were right after having to find $28,000, even more than they expected, to pay for the trip.

At least one fear proved unfounded after Australian Soccer Federation secretary Brian Le Fevre, who had replaced McAndrew earlier in the year, rang up each of the players' employers to ensure they were given time off work so they could take part.

The journey to Lourenco Marques, named after the 16th-century Portuguese trader who had colonised Mozambique, proved to be an incredibly fraught one. The squad landed in Johannesburg in Apartheid South Africa, where they were due to transit for the remainder of the trip to their final destination. Upon arrival, they discovered that the airline had cancelled a number of their seats and there was not enough room for everyone to travel.

According to *Soccer World*, the 'eight members of the party who couldn't be squeezed on the small local airliner on the 300-mile journey to Lourenco Marques on Monday arrived here on Tuesday afternoon – after a day's sightseeing in beautiful Johannesburg – without any complaints.'

This was not the true story, as Corrigan revealed many years later. He had been put in charge by Vlasits of those left behind. This included players Adrian Alston, Jim Fraser, David Zeman and Don Sanell. On the day of their flight to Mozambique, Corrigan had led them on a 5am group run through the streets of the South African city.

'I had no idea where we were going, but off we went in the dark,' he wrote in his autobiography, *The Life of Brian*. 'When we arrived back at our hotel a couple of hours later, we were met by distressed members of the hotel management. Worried about our safety, they had called the police. Nobody, but nobody, walked or ran through the area we had nominated at that time of day. The chances of being murdered, especially if you were white, were too great. I wasn't game to tell Joe about that when we finally caught up with him.'

By the time everyone had gathered at the Girassol, Australia's hotel in Lourenco Marques, all the talk about Mozambique being hit by 'World Cup fever' had subsided. Portuguese officials were warning that they were expecting 'small crowds' for the two matches. They predicted a 'crowd of only 10,000 or less', in the 45,000 capacity Salazar Stadium, which had only opened the previous year. Even this figure proved to be wildly optimistic.

The mood in the Australian camp was relaxed and confident, with several pranks played to help keep the mood light. The most memorable was one played by Alan Marnoch, a Scot once on the books of Dunfermline Athletic before he emigrated to Australia as a teenager. The defender was a notable mimic and could do a good impression of Vlasits.

One day, when the players were sitting by the hotel swimming pool, there was a call for four of them to get dressed into official team blazers and ties, and meet Vlasits in the lobby. They were told that they were to accompany him to an official function. They duly arrived suited and booted in the sweltering conditions, when Marnoch walked past and told them the truth.

Soccer World, meanwhile, captured the mood of everyone connected with the Australian team by already looking forward to the two-legged final play-off against Israel, with the winner booking a place at the World Cup finals in Mexico. It seemed nothing had been learnt from four years earlier, when Australia had so badly underestimated North Korea.

Lou Brocic, the Yugoslavian who had coached New Zealand in their two matches against Israel in Tel Aviv, had written an article for *Soccer World* in which he outlined the efforts that Australia's potential opponents had invested in their football programme. 'I warn my Australian friends against complacency,' Brocic, who had coached some of Europe's top clubs, including PSV Eindhoven, Juventus, FC Barcelona and Red Star Belgrade, wrote.

It was a pity that he had not issued a similar warning for the games against Rhodesia.

Unlike the rest of society in Rhodesia, football was not divided along racial lines. The team to face Australia included eight black and three white players. 'We were considered heroes throughout Rhodesia and people recognised us as good players who played for the national team,' the country's biggest star and captain, Bobby Chalmers, said. 'That was the most important thing they looked at.'

The Rhodesians were out to cause a major upset. 'The Australians were so sure of winning, they completely underestimated us,' claimed Chalmers. 'In fact, they had already booked their flights to Israel.'

The Rhodesian team, coached by former Scottish player Danny McLennan, had not played since 1967. A report in the *Sydney Morning Herald* a couple of days before the match noted that the Rhodesia team showed a 'high standard of their fitness, athleticism and ball skills, as well as the influence of Chalmers,' who they wrote was 'their danger man'.

The Australians were clearly concerned by Chalmers because they tried to get him banned on the grounds that as he lived in South Africa, he should not be allowed to play. FIFA, though, ruled that as a Rhodesian citizen born in Bulawayo, who had never played for another country, there was no reason he should not be allowed to take part.

The Australians were forced to replace Warren just an hour before kick-off of the first match on 23rd November, when he was taken ill with a stomach problem. They also dropped Vojtek for disciplinary reasons after he had returned back to the team hotel the previous evening late, following a missed curfew.

Rhodesia were far from outclassed in the opening match, played in pouring rain, and Chalmers put them ahead in the 63rd minute with a long-range effort from 25 yards. Chalmers certainly lived up to his reputation as the leading striker in the South African National Football League, where he scored at the rate of nearly a goal a game throughout his career.

The Australians training in Mozambique's capital Lourenco Marques, before the tie against Rhodesia

Fortunately for the Australians, McColl continued the outstanding form he had showed in the previous round in South Korea. He netted a 68th-minute equaliser in a match watched by a crowd of just 3,540. The majority of the crowd were supporting Rhodesia after a special train carried fans from Bulawayo, while three chartered flights came from the capital, Salisbury.

'This was the worst team we have played against in the World Cup, but we still only draw 1–1,' Australian goalkeeper Corry told a reporter from *Reuters* afterwards. 'We played 300 per cent below our normal form.'

Stan Ackerley, Australia's captain in the absence of Warren, concurred. 'It's the worst team we've ever played against,' he said. 'If we had played like Rhodesia played last night in South Korea, we would have lost each match 10–0.'

Barclay doubled down on the players' analysis of their opponents. 'Now we know how bad they are, they won't stand a chance,' the team manager said.

Few believed that Australia would not win the second leg. 'They were rather arrogant afterwards, saying they would beat us 6–0 in the second leg,' Chalmers said.

In that second leg, four days later, watched by an even smaller crowd of 2,512 in the rain, Rhodesia's goalkeeper, Robin Jordan, had the match of his life as he saved shot after shot from Australia, who had Warren back in their side.

Corrigan described Jordan as a 'tall, gangly, uncoordinated goalkeeper who was either so brilliant or, much more likely, so hopeless that he kept falling over. Every time he did so, he would somehow manage to block one of our shots at goal, often with his feet.'

With no extra time or penalties, it meant a third match was arranged to take place in Lourenco Marques two days later. If they drew with Rhodesia for a third time, then the toss of a coin would decide who progressed to the play-off against Israel.

It was not just the Australians who were growing worried at this stage. The United Kingdom government was once again taking an interest in Australia's attempts at qualifying for the World Cup finals, just as they had done against North Korea in 1965.

London had already appealed unsuccessfully to FIFA to ask that Rhodesia was not allowed to compete in the World Cup. They were now becoming increasingly concerned that the country, which had unilaterally declared independence from the United Kingdom, could actually qualify for Mexico 1970. A flurry of memos was sent from the UK Foreign Office warning of the implications of what this could mean if it happened.

Fortunately, there was help at hand from a higher power – or at least that is what some people believed.

Corrigan and Tommy Patrick, the Qantas employee in charge of team planning and coordination for the Australian team, were talking to the local liaison man in Mozambique, a local journalist called Fernando Fernandes. He was a stringer for United Press International and shared his office with a brothel. Each weekend, hundreds of white South African men would fly in to visit the establishment to use the services of the black women employed there specially to meet the demand.

As the conversation took place at the bar, it is probably safe to assume that beer had been partaken. Fernandes offered to put Corrigan and Patrick in touch with a local witch doctor, who would put a curse on the Rhodesian goalkeeper and the rest of the team.

'It was arranged that I would meet this man at the football stadium at dawn, never my best time, the following morning,' Corrigan wrote in his autobiography. 'Right at dawn, Fernando and I were standing in the appointed place behind the goalposts. Suddenly, without having seen or heard his approach, our man was standing beside us. It was the most eerie feeling. I had felt certain he would be dressed in the exotic tribal garb witch doctors always wear in the movies. Instead, he was immaculately dressed in a Savile Row suit. I felt quite disappointed.

"'Good morning, sir," he said in a beautiful Oxford accent. "I already know your problem and I can fix it." I was most impressed with that for an opener.

"'How will you do that?'

"'Well, I just plant this bag of bones behind the goalpost pointing straight at the goalkeeper's heart." I looked at him quizzically, but he didn't bat an eyelid. "If you are thinking that he has to change ends at half-time, I can tell you now, it will make no difference.'"

A plan to plant a story in the local newspaper about what the Australians had done was vetoed by the witch doctor, but when Corrigan returned to the hotel they were sharing with their Rhodesian opponents, he made sure they heard about it.

Before he had left to return to the hotel, the witch doctor had told Corrigan, 'That will be 50 pounds sterling, please, sir.'

Corrigan told him he would need to see Barclay as he 'handles all those matters'. The team doctor admitted, though, 'knowing that the sum of money was about all the spare cash the team had'.

Thoughts of payment were probably quickly forgotten by Corrigan as, before a crowd of only 1,500 at the Salazar Stadium, Australia finally completed the job they had been expected to do much more easily. Their star was Willie Rutherford, who had arrived in Australia only the year before after playing in Scotland for East Fife and Forfar Athletic.

Rutherford had nearly been sent home from South Korea during the previous qualifying tournament, because of his attitude towards training. After the first match against Rhodesia, he had been one of three players, along with Vojtek and John Perin, an Italian-born midfielder, to have left the hotel and not come back until after the curfew. Rutherford had stayed out even longer than the other two and did not get home until 6am. 'He told Joe Vlasits he had got up early and been for a run along the beach,' said Vojtek.

Injuries had given the 25-year-old Sydney Hakoah striker his opportunity for the third match in Lourenco Marques, and he put Australia ahead in the 12th minute. It was also from his free kick, 10 minutes later, that Rhodesia defender Philemon Tigere headed an own goal past the goalkeeper Jordan.

Then, in the 35th minute, Jordan collided with Baartz and suffered a bad cut to his head. Rhodesia's hero from the first two matches needed to be replaced by substitute goalkeeper Stewart Gilbert. Chalmers pulled a goal back shortly after the half-time break before Warren put the tie beyond Rhodesia with a third goal in the 56th minute to seal a 3–1 victory.

Rhodesia's manager, McLennan, admitted that 'losing Jordan was a big blow'. A coincidence? Or the result of the spell cast by Corrigan's witch doctor?

The Australians were to cross swords again with McLennan further down the line.

They were to meet the witch doctor again much sooner. The extended stay in Mozambique meant that it would be a race against time to get to Tel Aviv for the next round. The next commercial flight to Johannesburg was not due to leave for a couple of days, so alternative transport had to be arranged. After a big night celebrating, the Australian team arrived at the airport early next morning. A tiny one-engine aircraft was waiting for them.

Before the party could squeeze into the plane, the witch doctor appeared next to Barclay, demanding his payment for services rendered. Barclay refused to speak to the impeccably-suited and booted figure next to him. 'You will be sorry, sir, because I can put a spell on this plane,' the witch doctor said.

The players were shouting at Barclay to pay up, but he remained unmoved. At this point, there was a flash of lightning that lit up the airport. 'You have never in your life seen so many terrified footballers, and we didn't relax until we finally landed in Johannesburg,' Corrigan said.

Over the years, the details about the spell cast by the witch doctor have become conflated, including that Corrigan had met him in the brothel, he had been hired by Warren and that the payment he was demanding was $1,000, not £50.

What cannot be denied is that, for many years, Warren believed the 'spell' cast that morning by the witch doctor at the airport in Lourenco Marques haunted Australian football. After Australia suffered a shock loss to Iran at the Melbourne Cricket Ground in 1997 and failed to qualify for the following year's World Cup in France, Warren publicly claimed 'the curse is still working'.

In 2004, Australian media personality John Safran visited Mozambique and the Salazar Stadium, in a city now rechristened Maputo, to have the curse by the now deceased witch doctor lifted. Safran found another witch doctor, who made him sit in the middle of the pitch while he killed a chicken, with the blood of the dead poultry splattered over him.

The sequence was broadcast on *John Safran vs God*. The following year, Australia beat Uruguay on penalties in a play-off match for the 2006 FIFA World Cup in Germany. It meant they qualified for the tournament for the first time since 1974. A coincidence?

Fears of the 'curse' were for the future, though. In November 1969, the problem Warren and his teammates faced was getting to Tel Aviv in time for the first leg of the final play-off. The final match against Rhodesia had taken place on the Saturday, and they were due to meet Israel the following Wednesday.

Australia needed a replay before they could seal victory over Rhodesia

The Australian Soccer Federation appealed to the Israelis for the game to be put back to Friday, but they refused as they claimed preparations for the tie were too advanced. In the end, FIFA intervened, and a compromise was reached, with the match set for Thursday instead.

The flight turned into a marathon and dangerous affair with the team travelling first from Johannesburg, where they had a six-hour lay-over before flying to Luanda in Angola. A struggle by militants against the Portuguese government, who still ruled the country, had flared up, and it was decided it would be too dangerous for the passengers to disembark the plane. They were forced to sit on the runway for several hours. Once airborne again, the Australian team flew to Lisbon, then to Rome and on to Athens, before arriving in Tel Aviv 38 hours after leaving Mozambique. It was an exhausted party that landed just 24 hours before the biggest match of their lives.

Australia were facing a team that was well drilled and highly motivated under its coach Emmanuel Schaffer. Born in 1923 in Poland, Schaffer had escaped the Nazis by fleeing all the way to Kazakhstan, working in a boot factory and sleeping on a park bench. Out of his entire family – his parents and three sisters – he was the only one to see the end of World War Two.

In 1950, after becoming involved in Polish football for a time, Schaffer relocated to Israel and played there for seven years. In 1958, he moved to Germany to attend a prestigious coaching school, despite his mistrust of Germans. After graduating, Schaffer turned down a number of offers to coach the country as he did not want his son to grow up alongside Germans after they had murdered his family.

Schaffer decided instead to return to Israel, where he was made national coach in 1968. Under him, the team reached the quarter-finals of that year's

Olympic Games in Mexico City. They had drawn 1–1 with Bulgaria and been eliminated only on the toss of a coin. It was still a remarkable achievement as Israel was still in its infancy, having only been established in 1948 following the end of the War. Football was a sport establishing itself too.

Schaffer had taken over a team of mostly undertrained amateurs and honed them into a force to be feared. He was not afraid to call upon Israel's military struggles to help motivate his team. Memories were still fresh of the Six-Day War in June 1967, when Israel had defeated Egypt, Jordan and Syria and occupied the Sinai Peninsula, the Gaza Strip, the West Bank, East Jerusalem and the Golan Heights. 'We have the best army in the world, we have the best engineers in the world,' Schaffer told his players. 'There's no reason why we shouldn't have great footballers too.'

Up-and-coming youngster Giora Spiegel told of how Schaffer tapped into his players' mentality. 'He liked to draw a parallel between our army and soccer,' said Spiegel. 'Our country has the image of a nation always at war. Since the genocide, we have always had to fight. That's what he told the young players. He understood that this typical Israeli character could be applied to the field.'

To prepare for this World Cup qualifying campaign, Schaffer had had his team training up to four days a week in a kibbutz. In contrast, it was a battered and tired Australian squad who arrived with time for just one light training session before the match. Baartz, identified by Schaffer as Australia's key man, was among those missing due to injury.

Vlasits tried to lift his troops, with even those declared fit enough to play nursing injuries after the three bruising matches against Rhodesia. 'This is possibly the only chance in the career of most of you and me to reach the World Cup finals,' he told them. 'By the time the 1974 series comes around, many of you will have retired. So, let's make Mexico now. And we can do it, giving Australian soccer the greatest moment in its history.'

The progress to the brink of World Cup qualification had captured the imagination of the public back in Australia. Early ticket sales suggested that for the second leg of the tie, due to be held in Sydney 10 days after the match in Tel Aviv on 4th December, there could be a crowd of 30,000.

The Ramat Gan Stadium in Tel Aviv was rocking with a capacity crowd of 41,899 crammed inside. After the amount of travelling the Australians had done, it was no surprise that Israel looked sharper and fitter. They took the lead in the 18th minute when a shot from Israel captain Mordechai Spiegler took a deflection over Australian defender Zeman and beat goalkeeper Corry.

Only seven minutes later, Israel were awarded a penalty following a handball by Manfred Schaeffer. But just as he had done in the previous qualifying tournament against South Korea, Corry pulled off a brilliant save. He parried

Spiegel's spot kick and then saved the follow-up. The Sydney United keeper pulled off several other crucial saves in the second half.

Johnny Warren's Australian team returned in hopeful mood from the first leg of the final World Cup qualifying tie against Israel in Tel Aviv

Even though Australia had suffered their first defeat in eight World Cup qualifying matches, they would still go home with their dream of reaching Mexico 1970 very much alive.

Just as when they had returned from their Asia Tour two years earlier, hundreds of Australian football fans turned up at the airport in Sydney to welcome home their team. Then, inexplicably, instead of staying together to get ready for the second leg, they were allowed to go home.

This was despite a plea from Vlasits to keep them together until it was all over. While the Israelis went straight into a training camp to prepare, Australia only got fully back together two days before the match. 'What happens when I do get them together?' Vlasits said. 'The three inter-state players don't show up and Alan Marnoch and Don Sandell could not get time off work. How on earth can I get the team ready in so short a time?'

This short-sightedness, combined with the threat of losing his job, must have stuck in the throat of Vlasits when he read the welcome notes in the matchday programme, where Australian Soccer Federation president Sir William Walkley wrote: 'I pay tribute to the players in the Australian squad, so

I praise our national coach Mr. Joe Vlasits for his contribution. Without his knowledge and ability to extract that little extra from the players, we would undoubtedly have not been so successful.'

There was more anger directed at FIFA on the eve of the match when it was announced that if a replay were required, it would take place in Hong Kong, Israel's choice of venue, after the world governing body had rejected New Zealand, Australia's suggestion.

'It is not surprising that suspicious-minded folk in Australian soccer are convinced this is all part of a cunning FIFA plot to eliminate the Australian team from the World Cup,' David Jack, the *Sydney Sun* soccer correspondent, wrote in the programme. 'Does FIFA hope that Australia will be the first nation ever to drop out of the World Cup through travel exhaustion?'

A crowd of 29,737 were inside the Sydney Sports Ground to watch Australia be led out onto the pitch by Skippy the Bush Kangaroo, star of the eponymous television series, and Ed Devereaux, the actor who played the head ranger in the show. The team was boosted by the return of several players who had missed the match in Tel Aviv, including Baartz, described by Israeli coach Schaffer as 'the biggest threat to our chances'.

There was an unusual guest of honour for Australia's second leg match against Israel in Sydney

For all of the efforts of Baartz and his teammates, they could not break down the Israeli defence, and in the 78th minute, Spiegler scored again to put Israel 2–0 up overall. Johnny Watkiss drew Australia level on the day 10 minutes later, but there was not enough time to score another goal to force a play-off. Australia had travelled more than any other team in World Cup qualifying history, but ultimately fell just short.

In the matchday programme for the second leg against Israel, Sir Stanley had acknowledged Australia's ridiculous schedule when the FIFA president wrote, 'they are surely the most travelled players in this or any other group.'

More than half a century after the campaign, there is still a bad taste in the mouths of the players who were part of that squad. Many believe they were sacrificed by FIFA because of politics.

Willie Rutherford raises his arms in celebration at Australia's equaliser by Johnny Watkiss, on the ground, against Israel, but they still lost 2–1 on aggregate

'Of course, we would have qualified without the extra trip to Mozambique and the third match that could have been avoided,' Ackerley said. 'We would have got to Israel well in advance and prepared better with fresher legs. The long hours in planes did not help us. It was crazy … we had to go around the world to qualify for the World Cup.

'The loss to Israel was devastating. The players had given everything in the pursuit of their dream, and a lot of them even lost their jobs for being away for a long time.'

Each player involved in the World Cup qualifying series later received a cheque for $13.27 for their involvement.

'The team had played in front of hundreds of thousands of people during our qualification odyssey and it had been deemed we deserved less than 15 dollars in return,' Warren wrote in his autobiography, *Sheilas, Wogs and Poofters*. 'It was a disgrace, and we would rather have been paid nothing.'

CHAPTER SEVEN

Don't call me Uncle

A sense of missed opportunity hung over Australian soccer following their failure to qualify for the 1970 FIFA World Cup finals in Mexico, with captain Johnny Warren admitting he and his teammates 'felt cheated and bitter' about what had happened.

In April 1970, the team was invited back to Saigon to take part in the Friendship Cup, in an effort to help boost the morale of a population in South Vietnam that had had to deal with a war that had been going on for nearly 15 years by then.

The United States had begun its unilateral withdrawal of forces, but they still had more than 300,000 troops stationed in South Vietnam, while Australia had nearly 7,000. So, it was no wonder that the Australian team that travelled there had serious reservations.

Joe Vlasits remained in charge of the squad and included a number of new faces, including Jack Reilly, Jimmy Mackay, Peter Wilson, Mike Denton and Garry Manuel, who were all to play important roles in the next World Cup qualifying campaign.

'The team was given a lecture by Australian Embassy officials when we arrived in Saigon and, although it was only to be a short visit, we were allocated 16 permanent soldiers to look after us while we were there,' Warren wrote in *Sheilas, Wogs and Poofters*.

Among advice the party received from the Embassy was 'not to touch the water or the food, not to go out of the hotel at all, to keep away from windows, to stay clear of unattended bicycles in case there was a bomb attached and to be vigilant of packages that appeared to be unattended'.

This visit to South Vietnam is much less celebrated than the one three years earlier but, as Warren noted, 'it was still obviously a very dangerous place to be.'

This trip was much shorter than the previous one, with Australia beating the Kowloon Bus Company, basically Hong Kong's national team, 6–2 at the Cong Hoa Stadium on 25th April, and then the South Vietnamese Army 1–0 the following day. The series was notable for a hat-trick in the opening match from Adrian Alston, his first goals in the gold and green of his adopted country. He then followed up with the winner in the next game.

Both matches were accompanied by the crackling sound of rockets. 'The South Vietnamese actually tried to calm our nerves by explaining that the rockets going off all night were only going out of Saigon, not coming in,' Warren said. 'I'm not sure if this actually reassured us, but the trip went off without a hitch.'

On the way home, Australia beat Western Australia 6–2 in a game held in Perth. It was the last match involving the national team that Vlasits would be in charge of. In June, *Soccer World* had tipped him to be reappointed with 'Zvonimir Rasic of Melbourne and Leo Baumgartner of Ryde' as his two assistants. Shortly after that story, newly elected Australian Soccer Federation president Arthur George announced that 'Uncle' Joe was going to be replaced.

Many of the senior players, particularly Warren, were angry at the decision. 'I felt Joe had been made a scapegoat for our failure to qualify for the 1970 World Cup,' he said. 'He certainly didn't deserve to be blamed, considering we had played eight of our nine matches away from home and still almost made it. But I guess some at the ASF felt someone needed to be held accountable, and they decided it would be Joe.'

Rasic – who everyone called Rale – and Baumgartner were the two candidates considered by George. Baumgartner had been the Austrian, nicknamed 'The Little Professor', whose arrival in 1958 had helped spark the exodus of European players to Australia. The capture of these and other foreign stars, without paying transfer fees, was to result in Australia's suspension from FIFA membership.

The appointment of Rasic on 13th August 1970 was a surprise to most people. He had landed back in Australia in January 1966, following an earlier spell in the country before returning to his native Yugoslavia to complete his mandatory military service. At just 34 years old, he was barely older than some of Australia's players. There was not any chance of him being a pushover, though.

Rasic had been born in Mostar, in what was then Yugoslavia, on 26th December 1935. Yugoslavia was a country made up of Serbs, Croats and Slovenes, created out of conflict, and the world that baby Rasic was born into was not much safer. In 1934, the country's ruler, Alexander I, had been assassinated by a Macedonian freedom fighter. The growing ethnic tension left the country on the verge of a civil war. In addition, the Nazis in Germany, under Adolf Hitler, were becoming increasingly aggressive and had announced plans for rearmament in violation of the Treaty of Versailles, signed at the end of World War One.

Mostar, now part of Bosnia and Herzegovina, situated on the Neretva River near its Old Bridge, and built in the 16th century by Suleiman the Magnificent, is a UNESCO World Heritage Site. Back when Rasic was born, the city was undergoing significant changes, with the council having introduced broad avenues and an urban grid system to improve the city.

Rasic was the second of four children – two boys and two girls – born to Ivan and Stanislava. Ivan was a bookkeeper and Stanislava was a homemaker. But, according to Rasic, he spent most of his early childhood with an uncle, Milan, as his father was often away.

Rasic suffered lots of tragedy early in his life. His uncle was the victim of a 'brutal killing' when he was four and a half years old.

In his autobiography, *The Rale Rasic Story*, published in 2006, he admitted he had few memories of his parents. 'I don't remember at what point they disappeared from my life,' Rasic wrote.

When he was older, Rasic discovered his father was part of the partisan movement established after German, Italian and Hungarian forces invaded Yugoslavia in 1941. He had been killed towards the end of World War Two. Rasic's mother, Stanislava, had passed away in 1945, the year after giving birth to a brother, Dragoslav. She died after being beaten, but Rasic did not find this out until a long time after her death. Fortunately, over time, Rasic was reunited with all his siblings.

Rasic was already in an orphanage in Mostar in 1941 as the German Army advanced on the city. It was decided to relocate the 30 children to a safer place in Belgrade. 'Now, some people have different ideas based on what they have seen in the movies about orphanages,' Rasic wrote in his autobiography. 'They are supposed to be grim, desperate hellholes for the unwanted, misfits and the like. But let me tell you, this was almost paradise on earth for me.'

Besides being given clothes, regular meals and able to take showers with soap, Rasic was introduced to football. The orphanage, called Centralni Lazaret, was on the banks of the Begej River and located opposite the home stadium of OFK Belgrade, winners of five national championships in the 1930s. 'We played "free football" at the orphanage,' he said. 'One versus one, two versus one, three versus three, three versus four.'

Football helped give Rasic a sense of identity. 'We were known by a number in the orphanage,' he said. 'It was a reward if they called you by your real name.'

In the orphanage, Rasic was chosen to share a room with Milan Galic. He was to go on to become one of Yugoslavia's most successful footballers, during a golden period for the sport in the country. Galic was a member of the team that finished as runner-up in the 1960 European Nations' Cup, losing 2–1 in the final to the Soviet Union. Later the same year, Galic scored seven goals at the Olympics in Rome, including the opening goal in the final as Yugoslavia won the gold medal with a 3–1 victory over Denmark.

Subsequently, Galic represented Yugoslavia at the 1962 FIFA World Cup finals in Chile and scored three goals during the tournament, as the team finished in fourth place. In 1965, he was part of the Partizan side that reached the final of the European Cup, where they lost 2–1 to Real Madrid.

In 1949, at the age of 13, Rasic was spotted by Proleter, a club that played in Yugoslavia's Second Division. A talented full-back, in 1953, he was selected for the first team and then the Yugoslavia under-18 team. Rasic then joined First Division side Vojvodina before spells at Spartak Subotica and Borac Banja Luka.

Injuries hampered Rasic at each club, most notably to his knee in a friendly against East German side Dynamo Dresden. 'I had a lot of fluid on my knee, and it took four months to get out of plaster,' he said. 'This was a time when I started to think seriously about my future. Until then, I had never thought my playing career would end. When I returned to playing, I found my speed was slower.'

An opportunity to join French club Grenoble fell through, following a row with an agent, before Rasic had a meeting in 1962 which was to change his life. He met Tiko Jelisavcic, a former opponent, on a short visit home from his job as player-coach with Australian club Yugal in Sydney.

Jelisavcic, later appointed as Australia's first World Cup coach for the ill-fated 1965 campaign, arranged for Rasic to join Footscray JUST, a club established in Victoria by Yugoslav migrants in 1950. Rasic landed in Melbourne in July 1962 and was accompanied by Aleksandar Jagodic, a former player with OFK Belgrade, who was to be appointed as the team's new coach shortly after his arrival.

Rasic's main memory was of how cold it was when they came off the plane. 'I knew all about Australia, every city, because at school we studied the world,' he said. 'I knew all about *sunny* Melbourne until I arrived at the airport. It was worse than Siberia. I turned up in a short-sleeved shirt and shorts. For the first six months, I thought of nothing else but going back to Europe.'

Rasic was left just as shocked at what he discovered when he arrived for training for the first time at his new club. 'I was very disappointed with the facilities as they were then – poor dressing rooms, no showers, and even the spectators were not properly catered for,' he said.

The new arrivals made a swift impact as JUST won the Victorian State League in 1963 and the Dockerty Cup that same year, winning 4–2 against Marabyinong Polonia, a club set up by Poles at the end of World War Two.

Among the innovations introduced by Jagodic was a more continental possession-based football rather than what Rasic described as the 'British style of football, which was to rush around more and get rid of the ball quickly'. Australia's cultural links with Britain, and many of its officials' obsession with English football, was to be a theme of Rasic's spell as national coach and something he often raged against.

After the 1964 season, Rasic decided to return home to Yugoslavia to complete his 18-month national service. It was 'to fulfil a promise', he said. 'It was the greatest human decision I made,' Rasic later claimed. 'I'm so proud. I didn't do it for my country but for the honour of one person, a close friend of my father. I promised him that I would go back to do that, and I did.

'I learnt what the human body is capable of doing for survival while I was in the army. We marched for nine hours over mountains, in temperatures five below freezing. I realised how the mind can overcome such things. And I realised that you could eat bean soup for breakfast. I never, ever, regret joining the army. But I've never had beans since.'

Having finished his duty in July 1965, Rasic decided to resume his playing career in Yugoslavia. He quickly realised, however, that he was missing the edge necessary to play in Europe and that he should return to Australia.

Rasic landed back in Melbourne in January 1966 and returned to Footscray JUST before switching to Yugal, then coached by Vlasits after Jelisavcic had moved to Sydney Hakoah. Rasic was more attracted to coaching by now and was actively looking for the opportunity to take over a team.

In 1967, the year he officially became an Australian citizen, Rasic got his chance when JUST approached him following a disastrous start to the season. They at first resisted his main demand, which was that he would pick the team and not a selection committee, before things became so dire, they gave in.

From the start, Rasic made it clear that any side he coached would have to show discipline. At the first meeting after taking over, he warned former English Football League player Cec Dickson he would not play for JUST again if he ordered a beer. Still, Rasic's coaching debut was very inauspicious as JUST were hammered 7–1 in his first game against Melbourne Hungaria.

Fortunately, Rasic quickly turned JUST's fortunes around, and they avoided relegation. In 1969, they lifted the Victorian State Championship. Rasic's success caught the eye of John Barclay, the official who had managed Australia on their successful tour of Asia in 1967. Barclay asked Rasic to coach the Victoria State side. Among the games Rasic oversaw was a 0–0 draw against the Greek national team and a narrow 1–0 defeat to Romania.

In 1970, Rasic switched to join Melbourne Hungaria but did not stay long before being appointed the new coach of St George Budapest. He was recommended for the job by Frank Arok, another Yugoslavian who had travelled to Australia to pursue his football ambitions. Arok was going home, although he was to return to Australia later and become one of the coaches who tried, unsuccessfully, to replicate Rasic's success in taking the national team to the World Cup.

Rasic had certainly established himself as Australia's most talented young coach in double-quick time. Unlike 'Uncle' Joe, however, he was to be a part-time national coach as the Australian Soccer Federation carried through its threat, first aired during the previous year's World Cup qualifying play-off matches against Israel, to downgrade it from a full-time position. Rasic was offered a three-year contract. He was to be paid $2,000 in the first year and $3,000 in the second and third.

If the Australian Soccer Federation thought Rasic being part time meant he was going to demand anything less than the highest professional standards, they were sorely mistaken. 'For me, it was all about the squad and giving it the best possible chance to succeed,' Rasic wrote in his autobiography. 'There would be no short cuts, no skimping and no excuses. It was my way or forget it.'

Rale Rasic, left, was the surprise choice in August 1970 of Australian Soccer Federation president Arthur George, right, to take over as national coach

George, the man who had appointed Rasic as national coach, had been born Athanasios Theodore Tzortzatos to parents of Greek ancestry before Anglicising his name. A successful lawyer in Sydney, George was knighted in the 1972 Queen's Birthday Honours for services to the Australian-Greek community, universities and sport. Rasic always refused to use the title following a breakdown in their relationship.

But in August 1970, things were all sweetness and light between the two new men at the top of Australian soccer, who shared the common ambition of finally seeing the country qualifying for the World Cup finals.

Rasic was well prepared for the first meeting with George. In his thick Yugoslav accent, he laid out his masterplan, with his main request being that instead of each state having a national selector, he should have the sole right to select the team with 'no interference from anyone'.

The other major request was that, at the end of 1970, the Australian Soccer Federation fund a six-week world tour starting in New Caledonia and then travelling through Asia and Europe before finishing in North America. In the build-up to the tour, Rasic wanted to host regular training camps for the squad to bond together. George had a reputation for being a tough operator and Rasic was surprised when he agreed to everything. He was a 'pushover at the start', Rasic said.

Before the first training camp, Rasic visited his designated choice, the Fox and Hound Motel in Sydney suburb Wahroonga, an Aboriginal word meaning 'our home'. Among the long list of demands he presented to the owners, Ashley and Linda Gerald, was rooms to accommodate up to 26 players at the back of the building from the Pacific Highway and three cooked meals a day.

'And who the fuck is going to pay for all this?' Ashley asked Rasic.

Gerald was instructed to call George, who told him to 'just give him [Rasic] what he wants. He is a tough bastard. We will fix up the bill.'

Rasic's demands continued. They included wanting 'steak to be so big it hangs over the plate, and I want it cooked rare and with the blood oozing out'. When a few players commented that there had been a bit too much blood, Rasic told them: 'Get used to it. That's what I expect from you for the next four years.'

Rasic also made it clear that a few other aspects of the previous regime would not be tolerated. 'I respected Joe Vlasits,' Rasic said. 'I came to Yugal as a guest player for six weeks, and Joe was the coach. He wasn't old, but he was elderly to them. They called him "Uncle". I didn't want anybody to call me "Uncle". I do business, I'm in charge, I must have some title. I studied Joe at the national team and said that can't happen under me.'

Early on during his tenure as Australia's coach, someone bought Rasic a baseball cap that had emblazoned on it, 'THE BOSS'. From then on, that was it. Everyone called Rasic 'The Boss'.

A world tour was organised in 1970 to give Rale Rasic an opportunity to assess the players

Rasic had appointed as his assistant Les Scheinflug, the captain in the World Cup qualifying matches against North Korea in 1965, who had so often been critical of Australia's preparations. Within only a few days of the world tour getting underway at the end of October in 1970, the new management duo was being praised. 'Rarely has a more professional outlook been adopted by any Australia football touring team, let alone a soccer one,' Lou Gautier wrote in *Soccer World*. 'The discipline and team effort has been outstanding and reassuring for the rest of the tour.'

Gautier revealed that 'Rasic's motto is to defend with 11 men and to attack with nine' and urged readers not to read too much into the opening matches. This included 3–1 and 1–0 victories over New Caledonia in Noumea on 23rd and 25th October, respectively. That was followed by a 3–0 win against Hong Kong's Jardine Sports Club, before a crowd of 16,980, on 28th October.

Several players not involved in the 1970 World Cup qualifying campaign were being given the chance to establish themselves on the tour, with Johnny Watkiss, Ray Baartz, Alan Marnoch and Atti Abonyi all having to sit it out due to work commitments.

The new faces included teenager Harry Williams, who in the match in Hong Kong became the first recognised Indigenous player to represent the national team. His first pair of boots had cost $2 from the local Woolworths, and he used to spend two and a half hours travelling through Sydney's suburbs to get to training at St George Budapest.

Mackay, who had made his first appearances in the green and gold during the short trip to Saigon earlier in the year, was another who was to seize his opportunity on the tour. *Soccer World* was full of praise for the 'slender Melbourne Croatia star', even if they were still spelling his surname wrong as McKay.

'If he confirms the form shown in the opening match, he should emerge as one of the stars of the tour and one of the big names of Australian soccer for some years to come,' they wrote.

The tour continued with an easy 9–0 win over Macao – an autonomous region on the south coast of China, across the Pearl River Delta from Hong Kong – on 30th October, before the party travelled on to Iran.

Australia had been expecting to play Iran's national team, but when they turned up in Tehran, it was claimed nothing had been arranged. Instead, a game against local Air Force club Oghab Eagles was organised for 2nd November. Four of the team, including Mackay, had to play in borrowed boots because their luggage had been delayed on the flight from Amsterdam. The match finished 0–0.

Confusion followed over who Australia actually played in the next game, which took place the following day. Rasic claimed, in his autobiography, they took on and beat the full Iran national team, winning 2–1 thanks to a 48th-minute goal from Alston. Most sources, however, list the game as being against Persepolis, who were to lift the Iranian league title the following year.

After a 3–3 draw against a Tehran XI on 6th November, the squad left for Tel Aviv to meet the side that had ended their World Cup hopes a year earlier. Israel were on a high after they had surprised many people with their performance at the World Cup finals in Mexico, which included holding eventual runners-up Italy to a 0–0 draw.

Australia showed what might have been if they had been better prepared and fresher the previous year. Ray Richards scored a 58th-minute goal to give them a 1–0 victory at the National Stadium in Ramat Gan on 10th November, watched by a crowd of 25,000.

Richards was also on the scoresheet the following day as Australia beat Hapoel Haifa 2–1, before heading to Athens for the stiffest test of the tour. In November 1970, football in Greece was enjoying the most successful period in its history. Its national team had narrowly failed to qualify for that year's FIFA World Cup finals, and its top club side, Panathinaikos, had just embarked upon a run which would see them reach the final, at the end of the season, of the European Cup at Wembley Stadium, where they would be beaten by the legendary Ajax side of Johan Cruyff.

Greece selected a much stronger side for the match at the Panathinaikos Stadium on 17th November than the one that had travelled down under the year before. Australia had beaten them 1–0 and drawn 2–2, before losing 2–0 in the final game of a bad-tempered series which had been marred by the bad behaviour of the Greek players and coach. 'We were the huge underdogs,' Rasic admitted in his autobiography. 'Even a draw would be a shock result, for the Greeks had not lost at home for many, many years.'

Rasic made the players train twice a day, with one session being witnessed by the great Hungarian player Ferenc Puskas, the coach at the time of Panathinaikos. He asked Australia's physiotherapist, Peter Van Ryn, what the coach thought he was doing by working at such a high intensity so close to an important match.

At the Panathinaikos Stadium, Alston put Australia ahead after only 11 minutes. Konstantinos Eleftherakis, one of the most sought-after players in Greece at the time and who Real Madrid later tried to sign, equalised in the 21st minute only for Mackay to put Australia back in front almost from the restart. George Blues, another Scotsman who had arrived in Australia via South Africa, put the match beyond Greece with a third in the 77th minute. At the end of the 3–1 victory, Van Ryn said to Puskas: 'Coach crazy, huh!'

It was the finest moment in Australian soccer history so far. Rasic claimed 'it was almost the perfect game for us. I know the victory caused a scene back home, especially in Melbourne among the huge Greek community.'

The Greek coach Lakis Petropoulos picked out Mackay and Alston for special mention, describing them as 'European class' – high praise for players who just a few years earlier had been playing at Airdrie and Fleetwood Town, respectively.

Australia's players celebrate after pulling off a shock 3-1 victory against Greece in Athens in November 1970

Rasic also remembered the match as the first occasion he clashed with Warren, who was captain under him at St George Budapest as well as Australia. At half-time, there was an angry exchange between the two after Rasic criticised Warren for failing to do his job properly when he allowed Eleftherakis to score Greece's equaliser. Warren marked Eleftherakis out of the game in the second half, but Rasic tackled him back at the team's hotel later.

According to his autobiography, Rasic told Warren 'it's either my way or no way at all' and gave him five minutes to think about it. Australia's best-known player quickly returned to confirm 'it's your way, Rale.' The controversy over who should captain Australia was one that was to continue all the way up to the team's first World Cup finals appearance in West Germany in 1974.

Rale Rasic, left, had to make it clear to Johnny Warren, right, who was in charge

Australia drew 1–1 with Greece's B-team at Kavala Stadium on 20th November, before the tour continued to the British Isles. The first match, on 23rd November, saw Australia beat Second Division Luton Town 2–1 at Kenilworth Road in what was the team's first-ever match in England.

Malcolm Macdonald, who at the end of the season was to join Newcastle United for £180,000, put Luton ahead in the 28th minute with a goal that Reilly described as one of the finest he had even seen. 'Manfred Schaefer, who was marking Macdonald, had the ball covered as it came towards us, but he slipped in the mud as he was about to take off for the header,' the goalkeeper said. 'Macdonald was about three feet behind Schaefer and before we knew it, he had jumped four feet into the air and headed the ball into the back of the net.'

Denton equalised for Australia seven minutes later. Only two years earlier, he had been playing in English non-league football, including a spell with Luton's neighbours Bedford Town. 'I just happened to see an article in a magazine called *Soccer Star* that a gentleman called Andrew Dettre was in England to cover the European Cup Final between Man Utd and Benfica and to look for players for a club in Sydney,' Denton said.

'It gave contact details so I thought I would contact him. Much to my surprise, he rang me within a day or two and we had a chat about my career to that point, after which he said he would talk to the club – by this time I knew it was St George Budapest – and who had just had a very poor season. He promised to be in touch but I was still surprised when a few weeks later I received a package in the mail containing a two-year contract and instructions to organise a visit to Australia House.'

Denton scored 42 goals in 44 appearances during his first two seasons in Australia but was surprised when he received a call from Warren congratulating him on being selected for Rasic's world tour. 'I thought he was kidding but the following day I got a telegram from the ASF telling me to report to a tailor in the city to be measured for a blazer and trousers,' Denton said. 'I also had to apply for Australian citizenship, which I did.'

After Denton's equaliser against Luton, victory was settled when Alston hit the winner in the 83rd minute. Alston had been described in the matchday programme as being 'tall and talented' and with a 'power shot'. His performance that night at Kenilworth Road was one that Luton would not forget.

Luton, who had recently appointed popular comedian Eric Morecambe to its board of directors, rolled out the red carpet for their Australian visitors. The club's chairman, Tony Hunt, wrote in his programme notes that it was 'an honour to entertain the Australian national team' and predicted that although 'soccer in Australia has been the Cinderella', it was 'making rapid strides towards gaining its rightful position'.

Peter Wilson challenges for the ball in Australia's match against English Division Two side Luton Town

It was, unfortunately, a different matter two days later when, much to Rasic's anger, Division One Manchester City fielded a reserve side against Australia, However, a team containing future well-known names, such as Willie Donachie, Colin Barrett and Ian Bowyer, was still good enough to win 2–0 at Maine Road. A bonus for Rasic was that he became acquainted with Manchester City's coach, Joe Mercer, who would prove to be a valuable contact later.

This British Isles portion of the tour ended with another defeat, this time 1–0 to a League of Ireland XI at Dalymount Park in Dublin on 27th November. This match saw another notable breach of discipline, and one which was to cost Billy Vojtek dearly.

Rasic decided that out of the 18-man party, only 13 would fly to Dublin for the match, with the remainder of the party remaining in London. 'I had been playing pretty well, so I got upset when Rasic told me that I'd play only in the second half in Ireland,' Vojtek said. 'I got more and more angry, and even my roommates agreed it was ridiculous to leave me out for the first half.

'So, I decided not to take my boots to the ground. I simply left them in the hotel room because I was so angry. I'll never forget the scene in the dressing room. Rasic asked me why I wasn't changing, and I told him I'd forgotten my boots. "Out of the room! Get out!" Rasic yelled, and I was left watching in the grandstand, freezing in the cold. I was so ashamed, I almost walked back to the hotel. I was ashamed to see the others. I now realise, of course, that Rasic had every right to rest me during the first half, or even not to use me at all.'

Rasic suspended Vojtek for the next match and fined him a week's wages. In the end, Vojtek ended up pawning his Australian tracksuit to pay the fine. Vojtek's relationship with Rasic was never the same again.

He claimed that Rasic had later promised him that he would be included in the squad for West Germany 1974, despite missing the play-off victory in Hong Kong against South Korea. He left him out, however. 'I had nightmares for days, no kidding,' Vojtek said many years later. 'You dream about it all your life. I was so close, yet so far away.'

Other players on that tour also found out what happened if they did not obey Rasic's strict disciplinary code. After the second match in Tehran, the Irish-born John Doyle and Scottish-born Dave Keddie failed to observe the team curfew and were caught when Rasic leapt out from behind the sofa in the hotel lobby to catch them. Neither of them were picked for Australia again after the conclusion of the tour.

As Warren had discovered already, you risked upsetting Rasic at your peril. 'I've given up a few good players to achieve a happy harmonious team,' Rasic said. 'In order to get a good team spirit, I would take such a decision any time. Happiness among the players can mean half a team's success.'

By the time Australia arrived in Mexico for the friendly against their national side on 2nd December, they had been on the road for more than six weeks. The match was held at the Azteca Stadium, where just six months earlier, Brazil, inspired by Pele, had produced some of the most memorable football in history to lift the World Cup for the third time with a 4–1 victory over Italy.

Australia played Mexico in the Azecta Stadium only six months after it hosted the 1970 World Cup final

Australia struggled to adjust to the heat and high altitude, and were comprehensively beaten 3–0. 'We could not breathe freely, and the ball travelled fast and played funny tricks in the thin air,' recalled defender Col Curran.

Richards was sent off for throwing the ball into the face of Mexico captain Gustavo Pena. As he walked off the pitch, Richards was pelted with cushions and oranges. He responded by picking up one of the oranges and hurling it back into the crowd.

It did not, however, detract from a tour Rasic called an 'incredible success'. Under their new, inspiring and innovative young coach, it felt like Australian soccer was standing on the edge of something truly special.

CHAPTER EIGHT

Birth of the Socceroos

How and when Australia's football team was nicknamed the 'Socceroos' remains a hotly debated topic. As we discovered in chapter 5, Tony Horstead, the soccer writer for the *Daily Mirror* in Sydney, had run a competition for his readers to choose a punchy name for the team after they returned from South Vietnam in 1967.

The big winner was the 'Emus', which was chosen by a margin of four to one by readers over the Jackaroos, Wombats, Bandicoots, Birubieds, Baddwalers, Walleroos, Merinos, Koalas, Woomeras and Sharks. But it failed to catch on in the same way the 'Kangaroos' and 'Wallabies' had done for Australia's rugby league and rugby union teams, respectively.

The 'Emus' does not appear to have been used again – even by Horstead in his regular column, which he penned under the pseudonym 'Hotspur'. Over the years, however, Horstead has still been credited as coming up with the nickname 'Socceroos' after that successful visit to Saigon.

Johnny Warren, meanwhile, claimed in his autobiography, *Sheilas, Wogs and Poofters*, that it was in 1971, prior to another tour to Vietnam in 1972, that Horstead first used the term.

After spending hours trawling through old paperwork and press cuttings, the definitive answer is that the first mention of the 'Socceroos' was on 3rd May 1972, at what *Soccer World* called a 'glittering affair' in Sydney at City Tattersalls Club, known to everyone as 'Tatts'. The club has been part of the fabric of Sydney since it was founded by a group of bookmakers in 1895, and has grown into one of the largest and most prestigious registered clubs in Australia.

The occasion was the announcement of a new $100,000 war chest, funded by a group of sponsors to help Australia prepare for its campaign to reach the 1974 FIFA World Cup finals in West Germany. 'Everybody was there, as they say, and some more, to see the launching of Socceroo,' Andrew Dettre wrote in *Soccer World*.

Among those in attendance was Australian Soccer Federation president Arthur George, less than a month away from being knighted as a 'Sir', who delivered the 'first address, an eloquent one, as usual', according to Dettre. George announced that Travelodge, News Limited, Pepsi Cola and Philips had agreed to help provide support as Australia tried to make it third time lucky in qualifying for the World Cup.

Dettre's story, under the headline 'Road to Germany now paved with pots of gold', was accompanied by a line drawing of the campaign logo. It consisted of a kangaroo wearing football boots surrounded by the legend 'World Cup 1974 Socceroo'.

Dettre's story was published nine days after the launch, meaning Horstead was the quickest to latch onto the new name. In his column for the *Daily Mirror*, part of Rupert Murdoch's News Limited stable of newspapers, the day after the announcement, Horstead wrote: 'The Socceroos will be the best prepared sporting team ever to represent Australia in a major event.'

The Socceroos' nickname was used publicly for the first time for a friendly against Dundee in Adelaide and proved to be an instant hit with supporters

The new logo was used publicly for the first time when Australia played Scottish First Division club Dundee in a friendly on 17th May in Adelaide, the visitors winning 2–1.

In July 1972, *Soccer World* carried a short picture story under the headline 'Socceroo'. A photograph of two young boys holding footballs and wearing the new logo was accompanied by the caption 'Socceroo tee shirts will be all the rage once Australia's World Cup campaign gets under way. However, they are already on sale right now. Have you got yours yet?'

Then, at the end of September, on the eve of Australia leaving for another tour of Asia, there was a third-of-a-page advert in *Soccer World* paid for by News Limited, Pepsi Cola of Australia, Philips Industries and Travelodge Australia – 'Sponsors of Australia's World Soccer Cup Challenge'. The advert was dominated by the football boot-wearing kangaroo, surrounded by the words 'World Cup 1974 Socceroo', and wished the team a 'successful tour of Asia'.

Horstead seemed pleased to finally have a nickname which he could drop in to describe Australia's soccer team. He wrote an article revealing that he was accompanying the team as 'Australia's Socceroos set forth next Thursday on their Asian tour'.

During that same tour, Lou Gautier described in *Soccer World* how hundreds of local Vietnamese youngsters would turn up for training sessions at the Cong Hoa Stadium in Saigon. The sessions would usually end with coach Rale Rasic and some of the players giving them informal coaching, after which they would hand out Socceroo badges.

Gautier wrote presciently: 'The kangaroo emblem is a sensation, and I think that Australia's national team has now won its spurs to be known worldwide as the Socceroos, like the "Wallabies" in rugby union and the "Kangaroos" in league.'

The term Socceroos gradually began to seep into the popular media and soon spread quickly. By the time the team set off for the World Cup finals in May 1974, *Australian Women's Weekly*, the country's biggest-selling magazine, was referring to the 'Socceroos' with no explanation as it had already become so well known.

The launch of the $100,000 fund signalled the continuation of a new sense of professionalism in Australian soccer that had started with the appointment of Rasic two years earlier. But the amateurism, which so infuriated Rasic, was never far away. During the speeches at Tatts, Ian Brusasco, one of the co-managers that had led Australia to Cambodia in 1965 for the World Cup qualifying matches against North Korea, had addressed the VIP audience.

During it, he had paid tribute to Rasic for having guided Australia, in 1969, so close to qualifying for the 1970 World Cup finals, even though it was 'Uncle' Joe Vlasits who had been the team's coach at the time. Perhaps Brusasco was trying to get on Rasic's good side. He had been the leader during the world tour undertaken in 1970, shortly after the head coach's appointment, and the two had clashed on several occasions during it.

Dettre, a long-standing critic of how the sport was administered in the country, was prepared to cut the Australian Soccer Federation some slack following the sponsorship announcement. 'It would have taken more than an ordinary spoilsport not to be impressed by the occasion,' he wrote in *Soccer World*. 'Soccer seems to be on the way to respectability. The consortium's decision to back the World Cup venture means more than all the lolly in the kitty; it also means moral support, four giant-sized bricks towards the edifice of soccer's building image.'

Dettre noted that 'the money has to be spent wisely' but that 'our World Cup venture, if it still fails, will fail because of human errors or shortcomings, not due to the traditional lack of cash.' Rasic and his players may still have been part time, but the Socceroos, as Horstead had noted in the *Daily Mirror*, were going to be better equipped than ever before to take on the world.

Dettre was more optimistic about Australia finally making it to the World Cup finals than he had ever been. 'If everything clicks – and everybody involved does his bit without striving for starring roles – we may make it, too,' he predicted.

Much of that confidence stemmed from the faith that Dettre had in Rasic, whom he had the opportunity to study close up the previous year. When Rasic had replaced Frank Arok as St George Budapest coach in 1970, shortly before being offered the Australia job, he had vowed to end their reputation for underachieving. His main goal was to lift the 1971 New South Wales championship.

Before that, the club was invited to take part in the Tokyo International Cup, a tournament organised in part by St George Budapest president Alex Pongrass; Dettre and Shun-ichiro Okano, who was Japan's coach when they had toured Australia in 1968 and was now preparing his team for the 1970 Asian Games and 1972 Olympics.

Pongrass was a remarkable Hungarian *émigré* who had avoided the Holocaust and, in 1944, joined the Jewish underground. He had saved the lives of thousands of people by helping distribute documents organised by Swedish diplomat Raoul Wallenberg, which placed as many as 100,000 Jews under the protection of Sweden's neutral government.

Pongrass also helped to rescue Jews who had been sentenced to the infamous death march across Hungary, when hundreds of thousands of them had been deported to Austria following Germany's occupation of the country in March 1944 to prevent its government from negotiating an armistice with the Allies.

After many narrow escapes, Pongrass survived unharmed and arrived in Australia in 1950. Once there, he launched a successful engineering business career. In 1958, he had taken over St George Budapest, then facing financial collapse. Under his guidance, the club grew, relocated to a new stadium and became the best-known team in Australia, producing several players for the national team.

The tournament in Japan was another opportunity to help raise the profile of St George Budapest. It pitted the Australian club against Japan's national side, its B-team and Danish team Boldklubben. St George Budapest, whose side included internationals like Warren, Adrian Alston, Atti Abonyi, Harry Williams, Alan Ainslie, Mike Denton and Doug Utjesenovic, beat the Japanese B-team 6–2 in the opening match, before drawing 0–0 with the full team. They then ensured they would lift the trophy with a 3–0 victory in the final match, against the Danes.

Rasic used that last match against Boldklubben to send another strong message that it was 'Rale's way or no way at all'. Alston and Abonyi had pleaded with him to start them both upfront. He acceded to their demands but made it clear who was in charge by substituting them both at half-time, even though they each had scored as St George Budapest raced into a three-goal lead.

'His attention to detail, his ability to keep control of a myriad of issues, was breathtaking,' Dettre wrote. 'Whether it was organising transport for the team to training, planning the daily routine, ensuring kit was ready, or plotting the tactics for the matches … Rasic was in total control.'

The Tokyo triumph added to the already immense pressure on Rasic to win the New South Wales championship. The team's campaign suffered a major setback when Warren got injured. He had been voted Player of the Tournament in Japan, and it seemed nothing could stop him.

'Things couldn't have been any better on the field for me,' he wrote in *Sheilas, Wogs and Poofters*. 'I was captain of my country and captain of my club. I had just come back from a great tour to Japan, the Australian team was already building up for the next World Cup qualifiers and I was scoring my fair share of goals.'

The incident happened in a New South Wales State League match against Sydney Prague, when Warren went to turn and his right knee gave way. Raul Blanco, an Argentinian who had been playing in Australia since 1968, was initially blamed, but Warren later admitted he had not touched him. 'My knee simply collapsed under me,' he said.

Warren made a comeback four weeks later, against Western Suburbs, but aggravated the injury following an early challenge. On his 28th birthday on 17th May 1971, Warren underwent a revolutionary operation conducted by Dick Tooth, a former Australian rugby union captain. At the time, Warren did not know that Tooth, a pioneer of arthroscopic surgery, planned to perform on him the first full knee reconstruction conducted in Australia.

'I had ruptured the anterior cruciate ligament in my knee and so literally had to have a new one screwed into place,' Warren wrote in *Sheilas, Wogs and Poofters*.

The operation was so revolutionary that even Tooth was not that confident of how successful it would be and whether Warren would play again. Warren was told it was 'extremely unlikely', which he admitted left him 'completely devastated'. Those that wrote off Australia's captain, however, would be proved wrong.

Whether or not it was the loss of their talismanic captain, St George Budapest finished second in the league to Sydney Hakoah, one of the oldest ethnic clubs in Australia, having been founded in Sydney in 1939 by Jewish immigrants.

Unlike most of the rest of the world, though, Australia did not operate a first-past-the-post league system, and the champions were crowned via a play-off series, which culminated in a grand final. Hakoah, who finished four points clear of St George Budapest, did not even reach the final, and it was Rasic's team who lifted the title with a 3–2 win over Western Suburbs. Rasic admitted that he found the system strange, 'but I am not going to be silly enough to suggest Hakoah was the true champion of 1971.'

Johnny Warren suffered a serious knee injury in 1971 that left his career in jeopardy

Within 24 hours of St George Budapest's triumph, Rasic announced that he had resigned and joined Marconi-Fairfield, a club founded in 1958 by Italian immigrants and named after the Italian inventor and electrical engineer Guglielmo Marconi, whose wireless company sent the first direct radio message from Britain to Australia.

Warren's injury left Rasic needing to appoint a new captain for Australia's two-match series against the English Football Association. There was disappointment that the squad sent by the FA did not include better-known players, but it did contain Ipswich Town's Mick Mills, later to captain England at the 1982 FIFA World Cup finals, and Sunderland's Dave Watson, who went on to win 65 caps.

Watson, in fact, scored the solitary goals in the 1–0 victories for the FA in Sydney and Melbourne, respectively.

To take over from Warren, Rasic had turned to 23-year-old Peter Wilson. Wilson had been born in Felling, in the north-east of England, and had emigrated to Australia in 1968 after being released by Middlesbrough. He made only one appearance for the Second Division club, playing at right-back in a 1–1 draw against Charlton Athletic at Ayresome Park in February 1968. He had left them at the end of the season and joined local club Gateshead in the Northern Premier League.

After only two appearances for them in the 1968–1969 season, Wilson accepted an invitation to travel to Australia and join South Coast United. They were based in Illawarra, the coastal region in New South Wales, and the same club Alston had joined the previous year.

Alston had accompanied club official Trevis Birch to meet Wilson when he landed in Australia for the first time. 'We met this six-foot tall, blond defender who had long hair down to his shoulders and who was immaculately dressed,' Alston wrote in his autobiography, *Noddy*. 'He had this beautiful brown leather jacket, a black silk shirt and flared black trousers. He was the epitome of the English fashion of the 1960s. Birch said to me, "Bloody hell, look at this."'

Within a year, Wilson had been drafted into the Australia squad that returned to Saigon in 1970 for the Friendship Cup. He had not missed a match since and played every minute of the world tour under Rasic. The coach claimed that he knew instantly who would replace Warren as captain – 'There was never any doubt,' Rasic said. 'I had been watching Peter closely for some time now.'

Rasic described Wilson as an 'imposing figure, a man mountain, a man who never asked for respect but got it anyway. He was a player's man. Peter was such a dominant player in defence and a truly wonderful leader.'

Nevertheless, in a report for *Soccer World* of the first match against the FA at Sydney Sports Ground, Dettre noted, 'They [the FA] won almost all heading duels and even fellows like [Chris] Garland and [Norman] Piper, not tall by Australian standards, easily outjumped Wilson.'

In the second match at Olympic Park in Melbourne, Wilson was at fault for Watson's second goal in two games. 'Despite that mistake, Peter was superb in both games, marshalling his defence and leading by example,' Rasic said. 'A new leader had been born.'

Australia's performances against the FA had been much better than 20 years earlier in 1951, when, in seven matches, they had conceded 55 goals, including 17–0 and 13–1 defeats, and scored just four.

Rasic was such a fan of Wilson's that in 1972 he was one of his first signings for Marconi-Fairfield, although, curiously, Australian teammate Ray Richards remained captain there.

After the hectic schedule of the previous year, 1971 was much more low-key. Australia were due to play in the Oceania Cup tournament in Noumea in New Caledonia but withdrew after a row about expenses. Earlier in the year, the Australian Soccer Federation had also pulled out of the Merdeka Cup competition in Kuala Lumpur after another argument about what financial assistance they would be receiving from the Malaysian organisers.

It meant that besides the games against the Football Association, the only matches were three friendlies against recent rivals Israel. Wilson featured on the front of the programme for the opening game at Lang Park in Brisbane on 11th November. The match finished in a 2–2 draw, with Max Tolson and Alston scoring Australia's goals.

The local *Courier Mail* newspaper was certainly impressed with the performance of the Australians, perhaps getting a bit carried away. 'The Australians played all over Israel, the country with World Cup experience,' Harry Davis wrote. 'The amazingly fit young Australian side outpaced and outmanoeuvred the visitors in all departments. Australia had its share of bad luck, rather than bad play, which resulted in the test finishing at a 2–2 draw instead of a conservative 4–1 or 5–1 in Australia's favour. Australian soccer proved that we are in world class.'

Three days later, at Sydney Sports Ground, Australia won 1–0 thanks to a 12th-minute goal from English-born striker Alan Ainslie. Four years earlier, Ainslie had been part of the Berwick Rangers team that pulled off the biggest shock in Scottish football history when they beat Rangers 1–0 in the Scottish Cup.

The goal against Israel – a 'fierce, dipping shot' – turned out to be his only one for Australia in a physical match where *Soccer World* accused the home side of reverting back 'to the good old days of guts-and-blood type of football'.

The series ended on a disappointing note at Olympic Park in Melbourne on 21st November, with Australia outclassed and losing 3–1. Rasic called it a 'disastrous result'. Monthly magazine *Soccer Scene* described the three-match series as a 'complete flop', a 'financial disappointment' and a 'waste of time as far as the young players were concerned'. It did concede, though, that the matches had provided 'excellent match practice', which was surely the point?

In 1972, Rasic again lifted the New South Wales championship in similar fashion to the previous year. Marconi-Fairfield finished

Goalkeeper Roger Romanowicz dives at the feet of an Israeli forward during Australia's second 1–0 victory in Sydney in 1971

second in the New South Wales State League, to old club St George Budapest, who were being coached by Arok again. But Marconi-Fairfield won the grand final and also claimed victory in the Australian Club Championship, a tournament involving the four leading clubs from New South Wales and Victoria.

Tolson, whom Rasic had signed from South Coast United, along with Wilson, for $9,000, scored the winning goal in the final against St George Budapest.

Rasic was only denied a unique treble when Richards saw a penalty saved in the final of the Federation Cup by goalkeeper Jim Fraser, allowing St George Budapest to win 3–2. It probably helped persuade Rasic to give Fraser a leading role in Australia's 1974 World Cup qualifying campaign.

At Marconi-Fairfield, Rasic was in his element working under administrators who stuck to his demand that they are 'best seen, not heard'.

For all this success at club level, what Rasic really had his eye on in 1972 was building a successful squad to ensure the newly named Socceroos were ready for the next year's World Cup qualifying campaign.

Following the game against Dundee, Australia faced English club Wolverhampton Wanderers in two games in June. They were one of the top sides in the First Division at the time. Shortly before starting their tour to Australia, they had narrowly failed to lift the UEFA Cup, losing 3–2 on aggregate to fellow English club Tottenham Hotspur in the final.

Wolves' team included several well-known names, including Phil Parkes, Derek Dougan and Alan Sunderland. The squad also contained Jim McCalliog, a member of the Scotland team that had played three matches against Australia in 1967 and whom *Soccer World* had been so disparaging about.

The Socceroos recorded their first victory over an English touring side in 1972 when they beat Wolverhampton Wanderers 1-0 in Melbourne

Australia distinguished themselves well, winning the first game 1–0 at Olympic Park in Melbourne with an 84th-minute goal from Abonyi in front of a crowd of 10,269. It was the first time an Australian side had beaten a touring English team. Australia drew the second match, at Sydney Sports Ground, 2–2 after leading twice through Ray Baartz in front of a crowd of 18,885.

These two matches were just the *hors d'oeuvre* for the main course on 17th June at Sydney Sports Ground: a match against Brazilian side Santos led by

Pele. Memories were still fresh in everyone's minds of the 1970 FIFA World Cup finals, where Pele had been at the apex of a Brazilian side that lifted the trophy for a record third time. He had demonstrated his genius with four goals to be awarded Player of the Tournament, and provided some of the greatest moments in history.

With everyone wanting to see Pele play, Santos had become football's first globetrotting team and played dozens of exhibition matches across the world. In 1969, there had even been a momentary ceasefire during a war in Africa so everyone could see Pele play. For 48 hours, Nigeria and Biafra stopped fighting, during which time Santos drew 2–2 with the Super Eagles. Pele had scored both goals and received a standing ovation from the home fans.

Santos became football's equivalent of the Harlem Globetrotters, taking their prize asset around the world in exhibition matches and prestigious friendlies. The word was that Pele's deal with Santos included part of the fee the club received for such games. In an interview with *Sydney Morning Herald* journalist Alan Speers, Pele refused to reveal how much he was worth. 'You never know, the Brazilian government might be listening,' he told Speers.

Concerned that Pele would get injured before his appearance, Australian Soccer Federation chiefs 'apprehensively scanned wire service cables for news about Santos on their Asian tour in the last couple of weeks', according to a report in the *Sydney Morning Herald*.

Santos did not come cheap and demanded only the absolute best treatment. When the squad, including Pele, landed in Sydney two days before the match and discovered they were staying in a Rushcutters Bay motel, where they were expected to share rooms, they threatened to leave. They refused to back down and, following a long debate, it was agreed that each player and official would have their own room.

The next day, the team initially refused to attend a pre-match reception at the home ground of St George Budapest before backing down, with the full party, including Pele, turning up. In fact, Pele ended up staying until 11.30pm and, according to *Soccer World*, charmed

Lessons in boomerang throwing were among the new skills Pele was taught during his visit to Australia

everyone with 'his pleasant, obliging manner', even if he was accompanied by the four bodyguards who travelled everywhere with him.

The next day, a crowd of 31,755 crammed into the Sydney Sports Ground to catch a glimpse of Pele and the other Brazilian stars, including Edu, another member of the country's World Cup-winning squad at Mexico 1970. It was a remarkable attendance because at the same time in the city, Australia's rugby union team were playing France in a Test match at the Sydney Cricket Ground. This, though, was Pele – possibly the most famous person in the world at the time.

Behind the scenes, however, there was a major row going on between the Australian Soccer Federation and Jorge Gutman, the Santos promoter, which nearly meant the match did not happen at all. Gutman claimed that he had been promised Santos's match fee of $37,000 in United States dollars by 10.30am on the day of the match. He told *Soccer World* that no one from the Federation came to see him until two hours later 'and even then, only had part of the money'.

Gutman was adamant that Santos would not be turning up unless he received the balance of $17,000. As this was a Saturday and the banks were closed, this was a major crisis. It was not until 15 minutes before the scheduled kick-off at 3pm that the Santos players even left their motel. After a cheque was refused, a compromise was finally brokered by the Australian Soccer Federation, Brazilian Consular officials and bank representatives. The remaining balance was withdrawn from the gate receipts and handed over to Gutman. It was later revealed that even after Santos's match fee had been deducted, the event had made a profit of $12,823.

The game started 40 minutes late, which led to the match having to be finished under floodlights. A pylon, which included fans who had clambered up it to get a better view, over one of the stands would not work. It meant that one third of the ground – the Santos goal – was in semi-darkness for the last 35 minutes of the game.

Orlando Lele had put Santos ahead in the 32nd minute, with Jimmy Rooney equalising three minutes later. Then Edu scored in the 60th minute. Maybe it was the problem with the floodlights as to the reason the Santos goalkeeper, Cejas, 'hardly saw the shot as it bulged the roof of the net' in the 67th minute, when Baartz pulled Australia level for the second time in a match that finished 2–2.

The *Sydney Morning Herald* report noted that there was disappointment Pele did not score his trademark 'banana kick – that bends around the wall'. But Richards did such a good job marking him that the great Brazilian later picked him out for special praise. In a newspaper in Germany, Pele said during an interview that he had played against all the top players in the world, including

Germany's Franz Beckenbauer and Bobby Moore from England, but the hardest game of his career was against a 'moustachioed individual in Australia called Richards'. Pele particularly appreciated the fact that Richards did not try to deliberately foul or hack him, as happened most places he went.

Rasic had described Richards as 'hard as nails when it came to a 50-50 ball'. But he claimed that he had warned Richards about Pele that 'if you kick him, I'll take you off, and if you don't mark him close enough, I'll take you off as well. I guess I didn't give him much room to move, but I knew he could do it. The bigger the game, the better he played.'

Many years later, Rasic and Richards clashed over how much notice he received about being told he was going to mark Pele. In his autobiography, Rasic wrote he had told Richards he had the job when the referee knocked on Australia's dressing-room door to get ready to go out onto the field, and the player had responded by 'rushing to the toilet to be violently ill'.

Richards denied the claim. 'I was given the task early in the week so I knew what was going on, irrespective of stories you may hear from Rale that when he told me in the dressing room I went straight to the toilets and vomited,' he said after Pele's death in December 2022. 'I didn't, he told me during the week, so I had to get my head around it and myself into the right frame of mind. Earlier on the morning of the match, while I was being driven to a television studio in a noisy Volkswagen, I got a dreadful migraine. That's what made me ill.'

Richards had been born in England and played for the youth team of amateur club Croydon in South London. At 17, he was offered a trial by Football League side Leyton Orient, but boldly decided to emigrate to Australia instead, having received his immigration papers the same week. 'I took a tube journey to Leyton, watched the players train, and then headed home,' Richards said. 'My father asked how I played but my reply was: "I didn't."

'I wanted to go to Australia. I've got no regrets. I achieved more out of the game in Australia than I would have in England.'

Richards joined Latrobe Soccer Club in Brisbane and was still playing for them when he was called up by Australia for the South Vietnam Independence Cup in 1967. After moving to Sydney in 1968, he was appointed captain of Marconi-Fairfield, a role he continued when Rasic joined.

A weapon in Richards's armoury, that the Socceroos often used, was his long throw. His ability to hurl the ball from the touchline to the far post meant a throw-in was nearly as good as a corner for Australia when they got into the opponent's half. Asian crowds, in particular, were always amazed the first time they saw Richards launch one of his throws.

It had become normal practice in these exhibition matches involving Santos for Pele to be substituted a few minutes from the end to avoid being mobbed at the final whistle. Unusually, against Australia he stayed on until the end.

Richards swapped shirts with him and has always refused to sell it 'because I feel it belongs to Australia's history and I think it should stay here.' Following Pele's death, the shirt was put on display at the museum at the Sydney Cricket Ground.

Richards was so proud of the job he had done marking the Brazilian legend that he later drove round in a Mercedes with the number plate 'Pele 1'. In 1990, when the Brazilian returned to Australia to promote his book, *The Pele Albums*, Richards was asked to drive him around in the car.

'I picked him up at the television station and took him to Dymocks book shop to do the book launch and sign for the people buying the book – they all lined up,' Richards said. 'When I pulled up to the kerb with Pele in the back seat, they all swarmed the car. They said: "Pele arrived in his personal Mercedes!" And I was his chauffeur!'

Australia's Ray Richards, right, did such a good job marking Pele that he picked him out as a tougher opponent than Bobby Moore or Franz Beckenbauer

Pele had plenty of words of encouragement about Australia's chances of qualifying for the 1974 World Cup finals. He claimed that compared to the Socceroos, the Asian teams were 'beginners'. He added to *Soccer World*: 'If the Australian team plays as well away from home, it has nothing to fear in the World Cup elimination matches.'

To help fine-tune preparations for the qualifying competition to be held in 1973, the Australian Soccer Federation had arranged another tour of Asia. Before the players departed, they were all ordered to have haircuts. The 'swinging 60s' had seen long hair among young men becoming fashionable. But in Asia, hair below the collar was considered an insult, and the Socceroos were taking no chances that they might offend somebody.

The tour included a third visit in five years to South Vietnam. By 1972, foreign governments were looking to drastically descale their involvement in the Vietnam War. Along with New Zealand, Australia was one of the countries who left South Vietnam that year. The United States' involvement was confined mainly to using its huge air power to assist the South Vietnamese.

Jimmy Rooney, number seven, scores Australia's first equaliser in a 2–2 draw with Santos

The bombs and sound of gunfire, which had marked the previous visits to Saigon in 1967 and 1970, were notable mostly by their absence this time. 'Apart from the faint noises of a couple of explosions at night, the sickening sounds of shells were thankfully missing,' Gautier wrote in *Soccer World*.

The Australians still faced one of their most terrifying moments of their three visits to Saigon. They were playing against a Saigon All-Stars team, made up of South Vietnam's under-23 side, on 14th October at Cong Hoa Stadium when, at the end of the 2–0 victory, hundreds of spectators invaded the pitch and surrounded Australian players and officials. The crowd were apparently upset at the physical approach of the visiting team.

'They attempted to prevent the Australians from leaving the field and started throwing bottles, rocks, iron sticks and even petrol on the players, who foolishly had been instructed to assemble on the touchline where they were sitting ducks,' *Soccer World* reported.

Tom Patrick, the Qantas employee in charge of the Australian team's planning and logistics, had kerosene thrown into his face and suffered intense pain and temporary blindness. Team doctor Brian Corrigan saved Patrick from a life-changing injury by throwing buckets of water into his eyes. 'By now there was incredible fear,' Rasic admitted. 'It was in everyone's eyes, including the toughest of our tough players.'

Soccer World reported: 'Soldiers intervened to disperse the angry mob but lacked the know-how of an experienced riot squad because the 400-odd uniformed men were troops from the field with no experience of how to handle rioting civilians.'

The scene was described as 'total bedlam', and the attack continued even when the players had been escorted back to the dressing room. A fusillade of rocks was launched, breaking several windows and forcing everyone inside to seek shelter wherever they could find it.

After 30 minutes, the team were led to their bus, but still the Vietnamese fans continued to vent their anger. A bottle smashed a window next to Wilson, and only an Australian flag placed across it prevented the fragments of glass going into his eye. 'Personally, I have never been so scared in all my life,' wrote Gautier.

When the Australian team finally made it back to the safety of their hotel, the players called a meeting and voted unanimously that they would refuse to play the following day's international match against South Vietnam. The matter was threatening to escalate into a diplomatic incident, with Malcolm Morrison, Australia's Ambassador in Saigon, getting involved. He addressed the players and told them it would be better if they played. They still refused.

In the end, it was the Socceroos' physiotherapist, Peter Van Ryn, who convinced the team to reverse their decision and play. As a young man during World War Two, Van Ryn had fought in the Dutch resistance before emigrating to Australia in 1950. He had started working with the Australian team on their world tour in 1970, and had become an integral part of the operation.

During a meeting held behind closed doors, Van Ryn stood up and told the players they owed it to themselves to go out and play, show they were not intimidated and demonstrate the spirit and courage Australia was known for all over the world. 'I am not from your country, but I know you guys are doing the wrong thing,' he told them. Following such a passionate rallying call, the team agreed they would fulfil the fixture.

The next day, the party set off under heavy armed escort, and the streets outside Cong Hoa Stadium were cleared by the police, who adopted a high-profile presence. The pitch was ringed with baton-carrying commandos to ensure the crowd of 23,000 remained in the stands. The Australians pulled off a masterful piece of public relations by carrying a Vietnam flag onto the pitch before the match, running round the pitch with it and then waving it in the centre-circle before bowing to the fans. Australian team manager John Barclay also arranged for the public announcer to read out a statement in which they apologised for the 'rough play' the previous day.

Reminders of the war were still present. Before the match, Socceroos goalkeeper Jack Reilly spotted a security official, with what seemed to be an instrument for detecting landmines, paying close attention to an area in the penalty box. 'I think they might have scored early had I been required to leap around in that spot,' Reilly admitted.

Rasic had ordered his team to tone down some of the aggression from the previous day as the match passed off without any incidents and Australia won 1–0, thanks to a 70th-minute goal from striker Branko Buljevic.

Buljevic had begun his career at OFK Belgrade, the club in Yugoslavia whose stadium Rasic used to play football opposite when he was a child in the orphanage. After emigrating to Australia in 1968, he joined Footscray JUST, Rasic's former club. Buljevic had expected to remain for just three months, before returning home to complete his national service. 'But I was young, and I did not want to waste three years of my life, so we decided to stay here,' he said.

Buljevic had made an immediate impact following his call-up by the Socceroos for the Asian tour, which included the return to Saigon. He had scored two goals on his debut against Indonesia on 7th October at Senayan Stadium in Jakarta, the new name for the country's capital, having been officially recognised in 1972. Australia won 4–1 in the tour opener. *Soccer World* hailed Buljevic as the 'brilliant, orthodox winger' Australia had been searching for.

Buljevic had also scored twice in the game against the Saigon All-Stars team, meaning he had been responsible for all three of the Socceroos' on the South Vietnam leg of their tour. The headline on the *Soccer World* story was possibly inappropriate in the circumstances: 'BULJEVIC MORTARS HIT SAIGON WITH DEADLY RESULTS'.

The Asia tour also featured two matches against Australia's potential World Cup opponents the following year.

In Jakarta on 9th October, two days after they had beaten Indonesia, they faced their oldest rivals, New Zealand. The match took place in 36 degrees Celsius, with Australia comfortably winning 3–1. Alan Vest had put New Zealand ahead after seven minutes. Abonyi and Baartz then scored in the 26th and 54th minutes, respectively, before the victory was sealed in the 76th minute with a goal from Warren.

Like everyone else, Warren had feared his career was over and, at the start of 1972, had enrolled on a four-month coaching course run by FIFA in Kuala Lumpur. While there, he was encouraged by the course tutor, German coach Dettmar Cramer, to try to regain his fitness so he could start playing again.

When he got back from Malaysia, Warren resumed playing for St George Budapest and announced that he was fully back when he scored the winning goal in the 3–2 victory in the Federation Cup final against Marconi-Fairfield. Whether he meant to or not, St George Budapest coach Arok had wound up Warren on the eve of the final.

Warren had written a newspaper article congratulating Marconi-Fairfield on beating them in the grand final. Arok claimed Warren had only written it to get in the good books of Rasic, in a bid to regain his place in Australia's team. He also accused Warren of not putting maximum effort in during the grand final, so as to avoid injury and risk missing the Asia tour. Warren was so angry by the accusations that he failed to attend a function to collect his Player of the Year award and did not speak to Arok for nine years.

After leaving Saigon, Australia travelled to Seoul to play two matches at the Dongdaemun Stadium against South Korea, who the Socceroos could face the following year for a place in the 1974 World Cup finals. The first game, on 22nd October, ended in a 1–1 draw, with Tolson's 12th-minute opening goal being cancelled out by Lee Cha-Man in the 65th minute.

The second match, two days later, resulted in a 2–0 victory for the Socceroos, with Baartz and Jim Armstrong, a prolific goalscorer in the Victorian State League since arriving from Scotland in 1966, hitting first-half goals. The matches attracted reasonable attendances of 17,000 and 15,000, respectively, after locals in South Korea had put up 5,000 posters around the city advertising the matches.

The South Korean press saw enough in the Socceroos' performance to pick them as their country's main rivals for a spot at West Germany 1974. 'Australia fielded a stronger team than in 1969,' the *Sports Daily* in Seoul wrote. 'Their forwards were more aggressive and shot more fiercely. The 1972 team is better organised in defence, but lacks real class. Australia, all the same, is the team to beat for the World Cup.'

Peter Wilson, left, captained the Socceroos in every match in 1972, despite Johnny Warren's recovery from injury

The tour concluded on 29th October at the Rizal Memorial Stadium in Manila, with Australia's first international match against the Philippines. The Socceroos won 6–0 against a 'pathetically weak' home side, with Buljevic hitting his sixth goal of the tour and Warren again among the scorers.

It meant Australia ended with six victories from seven matches, the ideal confidence booster for the start of their World Cup qualifying campaign due to start the following March. Warren was back in the team, but the performances of Wilson had been one of the highlights of the tour, and he was now firmly established as the Socceroos' captain.

On the squad's return to Australia, Wilson was voted as the team's best player of the tour. Richards was named as having put in the best individual performance in a match, and Manfred Schaefer elected the most consistent player. Along with top goalscorer Buljevic, they each received a prize of $100. The four players put the money into a central pot to be shared, so each squad member was given $20.

The tour had been another resounding success, but Warren was still not completely happy, despite having seemingly come back from an injury that had ended his career. He admitted in his autobiography that even after two years out of international football, he 'had expected to come straight back in as captain', but this was a different team to the one he had been part of before his injury. 'I discovered that the Socceroos clearly wasn't my team anymore and had very much become the domain of Rale Rasic,' Warren said.

The topic of who should be Australia's captain was the subject of a letter in *Soccer World* at the end of the tour, which asked whether Wilson's native Geordie accent from the north-east of England should not debar him from holding the role.

'Australia's national team should, at all times, have an Australian-born captain,' wrote P. Dailey from Cremorne in New South Wales. 'Peter Wilson is a great player and an inspiration on and off the field, but I genuinely believe that the job should always go to an Aussie.

'He must create a bad impression overseas to hear the captain of Australia speak with such a broad accent. Many of my non-soccer friends commented unfavourably on this aspect of the Australian team when they heard our current Australian skipper interviewed on the radio recently. They claim they could barely understand a word of what he was saying!'

It is certain Rasic would never have allowed such a thing as a player's accent to cloud his thinking, but the topic of the Socceroos' captaincy was one that was not about to go away.

CHAPTER NINE

Walking the tightrope

At the Australian Soccer Federation Annual General Meeting held in Sydney in December 1972, it was announced that a total of $125,000, including the $100,000 sponsorship fund, had been budgeted to help fund the Socceroos' FIFA World Cup finals qualifying bid.

It was also revealed that the Federation had appointed 13 committees to deal with various aspects of the planning for the campaign, including hosting the Asia-Oceania Sub-Group B1 round-robin tournament in March 1973. The tournament would feature the hosts Australia, New Zealand, Iraq and Indonesia.

As for the previous two World Cup qualifying campaigns, geopolitics had played a large part in shaping how they were organised. Australia had been placed in Zone B, which included teams from West Asia and Oceania. Besides Australia, the original draw included Indonesia, India, Iran, Iraq, Kuwait, New Zealand and Syria, who were all due to meet in a single qualifying tournament. Only Tehran was prepared to stage an event featuring eight teams.

Australia, with support from several other countries, lobbied for the group to be halved, with them serving as one of the hosts. It was a proposal that FIFA were willing to entertain, probably to help ease some of the political tensions that would have been caused by a single group.

Iran and Iraq had been in dispute with each other since 1936, due to opposing territorial claims by both countries over the Shatt al-Arab, a transboundary river that runs partly along the Iran-Iraq border. On 30th November 1971, the day before the British withdrew from the Gulf for good after nearly 150 years in the region, Iran seized three strategic islands in the lower Gulf – Abu Musa and the Greater and Lesser Tunbs – owned by the United Arab Emirates. Their seizure led Iraq to sever diplomatic relations with Iran. Scattered border clashes occurred in 1972, after which Iraq expelled some 72,000 Iranians from the country. In April 1974, it led to the Shatt al-Arab conflict, an 11-month dispute which saw more than 1,000 people killed.

There were also tensions in India after a third war against Pakistan in December 1971, which lasted only 13 days and saw the secession of East Pakistan, creating the independent state of Bangladesh.

New Zealand proposed, in the interests of fairness, that each team should meet the other home and away. In the end, FIFA accepted the Australian

Soccer Federation's plan to split the group in half. To help sweeten the deal, at a meeting of the Asian Football Confederation in Bangkok at the end of April 1972, Australian Soccer Federation president Sir Arthur George and general secretary Brian Le Fevre offered to pay full air fares, first-class accommodation and a daily allowance for a party of 24 from each of the competing teams.

Despite the rising tensions between Iraq and Iran, FIFA still placed them in the same group, B2, to be played in Tehran. Within a few days, Iraq was switched with India into the Socceroos' group. In the end, India withdrew from the qualifying competition altogether. 'Iraq's inclusion will make Australia's task of winning immensely harder,' warned *Soccer World*.

Group B2 now included Iran, Kuwait, North Korea and Syria. The winners of the two groups would then meet home and away. Whoever won that tie would then meet the country that emerged as the winners from Zone A in a tournament to be staged in Seoul in May. Group A1 consisted of Hong Kong, Japan and South Vietnam, while Group A2 was made up of hosts South Korea, Israel, Malaysia and Thailand.

In June 1972, Australia announced that it had resigned from the Oceania Football Confederation, with the hope again of officially joining the Asian Football Confederation. *Soccer World*, which had been campaigning for such a move since 1960, was beside itself with excitement. 'We can only rejoice that Australia is no longer a member of that fictitious organisation and hope that the day when Australian soccer can have its place – officially – in Asia is not in the too distant future,' Lou Gautier wrote.

The only problem was that Asia did not want them, with South Korea among the leading opponents. It was not until 2006 that Australia was welcomed into the Asian Football Confederation. In the meantime, Australia did not officially belong to any of FIFA's five Confederations until they rejoined Oceania in 1978.

As far as Socceroos coach Rale Rasic was concerned, all this politics was something for the men in suits to worry about, not him. The Asian tour, at the end of 1972, had confirmed Rasic's belief that he was on the right path. When he announced a group of 22 players who would attend regular training sessions in the early part of 1973, it included all 20 members who had remained undefeated during the trip to Indonesia, South Vietnam, South Korea and the Philippines.

The only additions included Harry Williams, who in 1971 had become the first recognised Indigenous person to play for the national team. He was joined by Ernie Campbell, a 23-year-old Sydney-born striker who had played under Rasic at Marconi-Fairfield. As a 16-year-old, Campbell had impressed First Division club Chelsea enough on their 1965 tour of Australia for them to offer him the opportunity to play in England. But he had moved back home after a year in London.

The squad, made up of 18 players from New South Wales, three from Victoria and one from South Australia, was to meet once a month in an effort to help maintain team spirit. Rasic also wanted to use the meetings as an opportunity to discuss tactics, with the players' physical conditioning to be taken care of by their club coaches.

In another important piece of forward planning, Le Fevre had also arranged with the players' employers for them to have time off. This was a major sacrifice for the companies involved as the Socceroos faced being away for more than 11 weeks if they went all the way in the qualifying competition.

Australia fine-tuned their preparations for the start of the World Cup qualifying competition with a three-match series against Bulgaria in February 1973. The Bulgarian side was made up of second-string players, so the matches were not given full international status.

In the first game on 14th February, at the Sydney Sports Ground, the Socceroos fought from 2–0 down to draw 2–2 thanks to another goal from Branko Buljevic and penalty from Max Tolson. The rest of the series did not go so well, Bulgaria winning 3–1 at the Hindmarsh Stadium in Adelaide on 16th February and 2–0 at Olympic Park in Melbourne on 18th February.

The final match witnessed the debut of goalkeeper Jim Fraser. He had been the understudy to Ron Corry at Sydney Croatia in 1968, but left to join Polonia, spending two years there before transferring to St George Budapest in 1970.

Fraser's career as a goalkeeper had started in 1957 when having just signed for the under-nines at Hurlstone Park, a suburb in Sydney, he turned up for a lift to an away match. 'It turns out there were only two cars, and they didn't think they had enough room for all the kids,' he recalled.

'They weren't sure whether I could play or not, and the coach threw the ball at me. I caught it, so he said, "We'll make you the goalkeeper." That was that. I actually saved a penalty against Marrickville that day … funny how things turn out.'

Even then, Fraser longed for the chance to play in a different position. 'I hated it,' he said. 'I used to cry because they wouldn't play me on the field. We were a good team, so I didn't have a lot of work to do. I'd get bored. After every game I kept saying I wouldn't come back. But I was always there the next week.'

Fraser earned his opportunity for Sydney Croatia when Corry was dropped from the team because of a dispute and then his replacement got injured. 'I went out there and copped nine goals,' Fraser said. 'The funny thing was, Frank Haffey was at the other end, and he was the bloke who had let in nine goals [playing for Scotland] against England a few years earlier. He grabbed me at the end of the game and said, "Listen, son, just forget it. There's 1,500 people here, nobody will remember it in a couple of seasons. I copped nine in an international and they ran me out of the country, so just make sure you stick at it."

'It was good advice because he basically kept me in the game. The twist was, two years later, St George bought me to replace him. It's a tough game.'

It was just before joining St George Budapest that Fraser had received a late call-up in 1969 for Australia's World Cup qualifying matches against Rhodesia and Israel, although he did not play. In 1971, he broke his wrist, but by the time the World Cup qualifying matches were on the horizon, he was in such good form he replaced Jack Reilly.

As the part owner of a security dog business that provided protection for the building industry in Sydney, established after he left the New South Wales Police Force, it should have been easier for Fraser than other members of the team to get time off work. But it was not like that, and his business commitments were to come at a high price for Fraser further down the line.

Rasic was not downhearted by the Socceroos' performances against Bulgaria, and remained confident about their World Cup chances. 'In my mind, I had everything possible to get the team to where I wanted,' he said. 'Everything had been planned almost to the minute. Incredibly, Australian soccer was working together. A unified nation. Even the Australian Soccer Federation had bent over backwards to ensure the best possible preparation.'

Rasic's optimism was shared by his players. 'Even though we were part-timers, we were training like full-time professionals,' Adrian Alston wrote in his autobiography, *Noddy*. 'We had gone to some difficult places in our travels abroad and we developed a high level of togetherness and fearlessness.'

Australia's campaign was set to begin in Auckland on 4th March, after New Zealand Football Association promotions director Charles Dempsey had successfully lobbied for them to stage one match before returning home to complete the rest of Group B1.

Few were expecting New Zealand to cause too many problems. 'Against

Australia, including captain Peter Wilson, right, and goalkeeper Ron Corry, left, depart for their opening 1974 World Cup qualifying match against New Zealand in March 1973

Australia, their World Cup task appears hopeless,' Gautier predicted in *Soccer World* after the Socceroos had beaten them 3–1 during the Asia tour in Jakarta the previous November.

'They have no physical advantage and are far behind where tactics and talent are concerned. The New Zealand player is just not good enough yet to stand a chance against his Aussie counterpart. The full Australian side would beat New Zealand 10 times out of 10, and a big majority of times by a three or four-goal margin.'

Even Rasic wrote off New Zealand and admitted they 'were not expected to put up much of a fight'.

In the end, Australia were grateful for a point at Newmarket Ground. Brian Turner, who as a schoolboy had witnessed so much when he went to Saigon for the South Vietnam Independence Cup in 1967, had put the Kiwis ahead in the 57th minute before a crowd of 12,000.

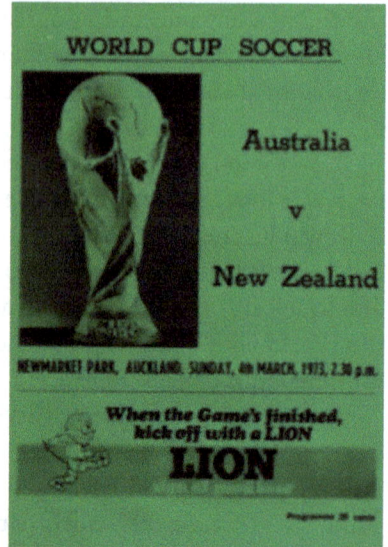

Australia struggled to a 1–1 draw in Auckland, where New Zealand even used the programme to try to gain a psychological advantage

In the matchday programme, the home fans had been urged to create as unfriendly an atmosphere as possible for the Australians. Their neighbours, it was claimed, 'couldn't care less if New Zealand sank under the sea'. The article, written by journalist Trevor Rowse, held nothing back in trying to whip up the local supporters. Among his accusations was that to Australians, New Zealand 'have always been the "Shaky Islands" to them. They rubbish our racehorses, our yachts, our athletes and cricketers and our women.'

It was left to Campbell, one of the two players added to the party that had toured Asia, to come on as a substitute and head home an 85th-minute equaliser to earn a 1–1 draw.

Gautier called it Australia's 'worst-ever performance since the bad old days' and condemned the team's 'kick-and-rush-soccer'. He added: 'The disturbing pattern which has been emerging for many matches now, namely that inane predilection for high balls, came to the fore in Auckland and was a major factor in Australia's disappointing performance. Every ball from the defence and the midfield was booted high up in the air for the forwards.'

New Zealand, under its coach Barrie Truman, who had emigrated there in 1970 having previously worked for the Football Association in England, were much better drilled than anyone expected. Afterwards, Rasic claimed, 'this was like a World Cup final for New Zealand' and acknowledged 'the Kiwis perform like supermen and women whenever they play against Australia.'

Rasic saw only the positives and dismissed the negativity that threatened to derail Australia's World Cup qualifying campaign before it had really begun. Campbell's goal, he insisted, 'highlighted our never-say-die attitude' and was 'pure gold for us'. Rasic was to be proved right.

It meant that the match a week later against Iraq, at the Sydney Sports Ground, assumed even greater importance. There was a fear about the team from Iraq, who were all members of the military and had supposedly been in a secret training camp for several months. Rasic admitted 'the Iraqis were the danger side for us'.

With optimism and interest in Socceroos higher than ever, being beaten in this match could have spelled disaster. 'The Australians know that a defeat against Iraq on Sunday will just about kill their chances of winning the series now that they have dropped a point against New Zealand,' Gautier warned in *Soccer World*.

Just how much soccer had moved up the agenda was demonstrated by the fact that Australia's new prime minister, Gough Whitlam, had written a message for the special souvenir brochure produced for the World Cup qualifying tournament.

Whitlam had led Labor to victory at the 1972 election, after 23 years of continuous coalition government in Australia. His manifesto included numerous socially progressive and reformist policies and initiatives, including the termination of military conscription and the end of Australian involvement in the Vietnam War. Unlike other politicians, Whitlam saw the importance of soccer in Australia and how it had helped immigrants integrate into the country.

'Sport is one of the world's great forces for international amity and understanding,' he wrote in the brochure. 'It brings together people from all cultures and nations. Soccer is the most international of all codes of football, uniting players and supporters from every continent.'

Whitlam was to play an important part in the Socceroos' story, although, at the time, few realised how important.

For the match against Iraq, Rasic had been able to work with his players since they had returned home from Auckland. The mistake of the 1970 World Cup qualifying campaign, when the squad had broken up after landing back from Tel Aviv and reunited again only a couple of days before the vital second leg against Israel, was not to be repeated.

If the Socceroos were terrible against New Zealand, then they were simply terrific against Iraq. The team was strengthened by the return of midfielder Jimmy Mackay, absent for the match in Auckland due to an injury. Gautier

Rale Rasic dismissed any doubts about his team being ready to launch a World Cup challenge after dropping a point in New Zealand

claimed the Socceroos 'had badly missed [his] midfield promptings and grafting'. He was chosen to replace Johnny Warren.

The return of Mackay seemed to add an extra string to Australia's bow, and it was him who provided the free kick in the 49th minute for Ray Richards to put them ahead. Jimmy Rooney, another Scot who had emigrated to Australia in the late 1960s after spells in England with Peterborough United and Scotland with Montrose, also justified his inclusion in the team at the expense of Tolson. He was involved in both of Alston's goals in the 80th and 85th minutes, respectively.

Even a late goal from Iraq could not take the gloss off one of the team's best performances under Rasic. A crowd of 23,762, including Whitlam, went home invigorated after the 3–1 victory and believing this was finally to be Australia's year.

Before the tournament, Rasic had been provided with an 11-page dossier by Lou Brocic. Brocic was a fellow Yugoslavian who had extensive coaching experience across Europe, including with Red

The Socceroos' branding was beginning to appear everywhere

Star Belgrade, Juventus, PSV Eindhoven and Barcelona. Rasic had met him in 1966 after arriving in Australia, where Brocic was coaching South Melbourne Hellas. Brocic had been the man who had warned the Australians not to underestimate Israel in their play-off in the 1970 World Cup qualifying campaign.

The Australian prime minister, Gough Whitlam, showed his support for the Socceroos by turning up in Sydney for the match against Iraq

As well as having worked with some of Europe's best-known clubs, Brocic had also managed several national teams. These included Egypt, New Zealand and Kuwait. He was working as Bahrain's coach when he offered Rasic the intelligence on Iraq. Among the information he had highlighted was that the Iraqis never wore screw-in studs because they were not used to playing on wet pitches.

So, Rasic had the groundsman at the Sydney Sports Ground water the pitch before kick-off and enjoyed watching as the Iraq players 'could barely hold their feet on the slippery surface'.

Only two days later, after their victory against Iraq, the Socceroos returned to Sydney Sports Ground to beat Indonesia 2–1 with goals from Alston and Campbell.

Australia's progress nearly suffered a fatal blow on 16th March, when they blew a 3–1 lead against New Zealand to draw 3–3 in Sydney. Alan Vest, an Englishman who had played non-league football

Ray Richards hugs Jimmy Mackay as he and Manfred Schaefer celebrate Australia's victory over Iraq

before emigrating, put the visitors ahead in the 10th minute – just as he had done in the friendly between the two countries in Jakarta in 1972 – only for Doug Utjesenovic to equalise a few seconds later.

Utjesenovic was another one of the Yugoslavians in the side. He had emigrated in 1969, having also played for OFK Beograd. He originally joined Footscray JUST before transferring to St George Budapest in 1971, to join Rasic. It was a decision that 'changed my life', Utjesenovic later claimed.

Ray Baartz and Buljevic scored in the 19th and 26th minutes, respectively, and the Socceroos looked to be cruising at half-time, much to the joy of the majority of the 14,071 crowd. When Dennis Tindall reduced the deficit five minutes into the second half and Australia failed to take their chances, panic set in. In the 86th minute, home defender Bobby Hogg headed past Corry in the Australian goal to make the score 3–3.

Hogg, yet another Scot who had played for Hibernian, Motherwell and Stenhousemuir before travelling to Sydney to join St George Budapest, was retained for the remaining matches in the qualifying tournament in Australia before suffering a broken leg in a club match. It was an injury he never fully recovered from.

Corry, a stalwart of the Australian squad since the 1967 Asian tour and who had produced so many important saves, including two penalties during the 1970 World Cup qualifying matches, never played for the Socceroos again. He was replaced by Fraser for the rest of the campaign.

Fortunately, the damage caused by the Socceroos yet again failing to beat New Zealand, whose 'task appears hopeless' it had been predicted beforehand, remember, was minimised. That is because Iraq had only drawn 1–1 with Indonesia earlier in the day.

Australia had only two days to get over the disappointment of the match against New Zealand and travel to Melbourne, where the next stage of the tournament was set to take place, to face Iraq for the second time.

The first match, a week earlier, had been notable for the good spirit in which it had been played. Things were different now. Iraq's coach, Gyula Teleki, a former Hungarian international, accused the home team of being a dirty side. 'The Australians play rugby, not soccer,' he told the local media. 'Australian soccer will never progress if it continues to place all emphasis on body contact. Soccer is a skilful game, not karate.'

A crowd of 10,684 at the Olympic Park saw a match where the stakes were high but the quality low. 'The 0–0 draw wasn't pretty, but it was good enough for us,' said Rasic. He dismissed Teleki's complaints about the Socceroos' style of play. 'They gave as much as they got,' he claimed.

Australia now had one match left, while Iraq had a game in hand. On 21st March, Iraq beat Indonesia 3–2 and then, three days later, before the Socceroos' final game at Sydney Sports Ground, thrashed New Zealand 4–0. It meant Australia had to beat Indonesia.

Indonesia had actually been the first team from Asia to compete at the

World Cup finals when, before gaining independence, they had competed at the 1938 tournament in France as the Dutch East Indies. On that occasion they had a straightforward path to the World Cup, as they were initially paired against Japan in the qualifiers, but they withdrew. The United States were then set up as their qualification match, but they too failed to show up, granting the Southeast Asians automatic entry into the finals. That tournament in France was played on a knock-out basis, and the Dutch East Indies were beaten 6–0 in their first match against Hungary in Reims.

Indonesia were considered the weakest of the teams in Group B1 but had taken four points off New Zealand with a 1–1 draw and 1–0 victory. They had suffered several injuries in the match against Iraq and then, against the Socceroos, lost their goalkeeper, Ronny Pasla, in the 24th minute through injury. The previous year, during Santos's tour of Asia, Pasla had become a national hero when he saved a penalty from Pele.

By the time Pasla had to go off, Indonesia were already 2–0 down after Mackay and Atti Abonyi had scored in the third and 23rd minutes, respectively. Mackay added a third five minutes before half-time, and further goals from Abonyi, Richards and Baartz in the second half gave the Socceroos a 6–0 victory.

At the final whistle, Rasic was carried off the pitch on the shoulders of his players. He was realistic enough to know that Australia had only just scraped through. 'While I was happy with the first qualification series, the truth is we played on the edge at times,' Rasic wrote in his autobiography. 'The game

Peter Wilson and Jimmy Mackay, second and third right, are mobbed by fans after Australia's 6-0 victory over Indonesia, while Doug Utjesenovic, left, appears to be trying to smuggle the match ball out

Rale Rasic was carried off the pitch shoulder-high after the Indonesia victory but knew that the Socceroos had ridden their luck

against New Zealand was a real wake-up call. We were almost eliminated at the first hurdle. We were to discover it was sort of a tightrope walk for us.'

The tournament had been considered a success and had been watched by a total of 81,407 spectators, including the match in Auckland. Richards won $100 for being voted Australia's best player during the event. He polled 28 votes to finish ahead of Baartz with 22, Mackay and Hogg with 20 each, and Peter Wilson and Manfred Schaefer 18 each.

The Socceroos had to wait until the end of May to discover who they would meet in the Zone B play-off. It was hosts Iran who came out on top of Group B2, despite losing their final match at the Amjadieh Stadium in Tehran 1-0 to closest rivals Syria.

Iran had qualified for the 1972 Olympic Games in Munich. They had lost their opening two matches 5–0 and 4–0 to Hungary and Denmark, respectively, but had beaten Brazil 1-0 in their final game. The team's star man was Ali Parvin, selected at the end of the 20th century as one of the 17 best Asian players of all time. He had scored the winning goal in Iran's 2–1 victory over Kuwait in the World Cup qualifying tournament, which had proved vital.

Rasic's diligence, which had proved so important in the Socceroos winning their group, was evident again before the two-legged play-off against Iran. He had travelled to Tehran to watch the Group B2 matches and arrived home with photographs of every player and a dossier on each one. These were handed to the Australian players before the match at Sydney Sports Ground on 18th August, with those assigned to mark individual players told to pay special attention.

'By the time they hit town, we knew everything about them,' Rasic said. 'We listed their strengths and weaknesses, best kicking foot, whether they were good in the air or not. In the end, I think we knew more about them than they knew about themselves!'

The level of detail certainly impressed Warren. He had not played any part in the Socceroos' qualifying matches since being dropped after the New Zealand match in Auckland, but was back for the game against Iran. Warren recalled Rasic putting the photographs of their opponents 'up on the wall in the training shed'.

Along with Warren, Col Curran returned at full-back at the expense of Hogg. A blow for Australia was that Schaefer, an integral part of the side, was forced out by a cartilage injury that required an operation.

There was a blow for Iran when Parvin suffered an injury in a warm-up match against a New Zealand provincial side, limping off with a bad cut to his knee that required seven stitches, and was ruled out of the game. Until it was officially confirmed Parvin was missing, Rasic had believed the Iranians were trying to play mind games with the Australians and were 'foxing' when they had announced he would not play.

Australia faced a familiar opponent in the dugout after Iran's appointment as coach of Danny McLennan, who had been in charge of Rhodesia four years earlier when they had given Australia such a scare during the 1970 World Cup qualifying tournament.

McLennan had enjoyed a successful playing career in Scotland and had been a Scottish League Cup winner with East Fife before turning to coaching. In 1961, McLennan applied for the manager's position at Dunfermline but lost out to an emerging Jock Stein, who was later to move to Celtic and become the club's greatest coach.

It was shortly after this that McLennan embarked on a nomadic coaching career that earned him the nickname 'The Explorer'. He managed the Philippines and Mauritius before, in 1965, FIFA president Sir Stanley Rous helped him get the coaching job in Rhodesia. McLennan was so popular in Rhodesia that Pepsi Cola used him in an advertising campaign: 'Drink Pepsi, Danny does …'

He had left Rhodesia following the defeat to Australia in the World Cup play-off, where a witch doctor had been employed by the winners, and he had not coached for four years by the time he turned up in Iran shortly before the first game against the Socceroos.

In an arrangement that Rasic would never have accepted, the power to select the team still rested with Mahmoud Bayati, Iran's coach when they lifted the Asian Cup in 1968 and who had been in charge at the 1972 Olympics.

Within a few days of arriving in Tehran, McLennan realised he had made a terrible mistake accepting the position. Iran had originally been set up as a constitutional monarchy under the Pahlavi dynasty, the country's royal family. But, following the overthrow of the democratically elected prime minister, Mohammad Mosaddegh, in 1953, it had become much more autocratic. The SAVAK, Iran's secret police, closely monitored foreigners in the country, and McLennan quickly became aware his daily movements were under constant scrutiny.

Soccer fever had gripped Sydney in the build-up to the match and all the tickets had been sold. *Soccer World* noted in its preview, written by 'Mike Renwick', that Australia's Minister for Tourism and Recreation, Frank Stewart, was going to be at the match, the second Socceroos game he had attended that year.

What *Soccer World* failed to disclose was that 'Mike Renwick' was the new pen name for Andrew Dettre and that he had started working for Stewart the previous year as his press secretary after leaving the *Daily Telegraph*. 'Renwick' was the name of the street where the newspaper was printed in Sydney suburb Marrickville.

Soccer World readers were left in no doubt how important this match was. 'Let's start this brief preview with what's usually left to the very end: Australia MUST win,' Dettre wrote. 'This second-last hurdle in our path to the final 16 in West Germany must be cleared confidently and convincingly.'

Dettre added, prophetically: 'Australian can do it. In fact, our team may be able to win by two goals – and that should be enough for next week's return match at Tehran.'

Dettre's preview appeared under two logos. The first was the newly released branding for the 1974 FIFA World Cup final, a ball with the three strikes in a background box, with the letters 'WM' – *Weltmeisterschaft*, meaning World Cup – and number 74 below. The second was the increasingly familiar kangaroo wearing football boots and kicking a ball surrounded by 'World Cup 1974 Socceroo'.

As part of its preview, *Soccer World* returned to the contentious issue of the Socceroos' captaincy. They noted that Wilson was set to lead the country for the 19th consecutive match. 'It's odds-on he will again be amongst the outstanding players against Iran because he just doesn't know how to turn in an indifferent performance as leader of the Socceroos,' Gautier wrote. 'A flamboyant figure on and off the field, tall with a mane of long blond hair, Wilson has seldom, if ever, performed poorly for Australia. The accent may be English, but the heart that beats under the green and gold is as Australian as they come.'

It was fitting, therefore, that it was Wilson who should score with a header in the 85th minute – curiously, the third time in this qualifying series they had struck at that stage of the game. It added to the goals in the 43rd minute from Alston and a minute into the second half from Abonyi, to give the Socceroos a 3–0 victory.

A crowd of nearly 30,000 turned up to see the Socceroos beat Iran 3-0

Most of the crowd of 28,881 steamed out of the stadium convinced Australia had done enough. If *Soccer World* thought a two-goal cushion would be enough, then surely three must mean it was signed, sealed and delivered.

The fans may have been ecstatic, but Rasic had been left unimpressed. 'To be honest, we did not play all that well in the first leg,' he wrote in his autobiography. 'Richards, Mackay and Warren were way below their best form, but thankfully Utjesenovic and Curran were brilliant in overlapping down the wings. We should have won by far more, to be honest, but three would be enough ... or so we thought!'

Rasic had also been forced to deal with an unsettling incident before the game. Australian Soccer Federation president Sir Arthur had visited the team at its motel in Wahroonga. According to Curran, Sir Arthur pulled up to the team's training base in his Rolls-Royce and ordered Rasic to cut four members of the 22-man squad for the trip to Tehran.

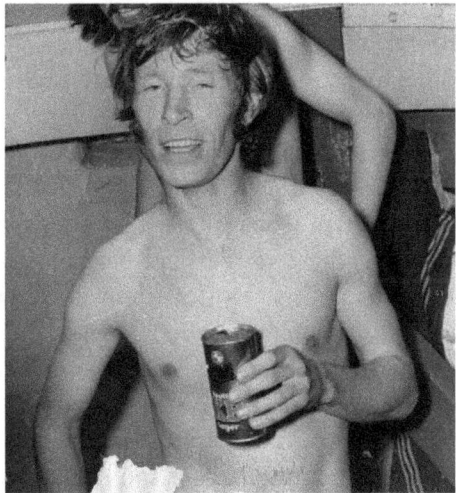

Jimmy Mackay enjoys a beer after the Socceroos' comprehensive victory over Iran

'Rale always stood by us and, of course, he stuck to his guns on this occasion,' Curran said. 'Rale did not want to break up the family and after a big argument Sir Arthur went away in a huff and later was forced to let Rale have his way.'

But Rasic was forced to leave behind his assistant coach, Les Scheinflug, as money was so tight.

The two teams travelled together on the same flight to Tehran, with Rasic ordering his players not to try to engage with their rivals – an instruction Warren ignored. He tried to talk to several of the Iran players, but they were not interested. 'The Iranians were probably thinking it was over for them, but not wanting to give up without a fight either,' Warren concluded.

The truth was that they were probably fearing the reception they were set to receive upon arriving home at Mehrabad International Airport. As dawn broke over Tehran, the arrival of the plane was greeted by thousands of angry Iranian fans hurling missiles towards their own players. The mob were being kept back by cyclone fencing, and riot police were beating protestors on the fingers as they tried to climb over it. 'Everyone was taken aback by the reaction of the home crowd,' Warren said.

The two parties were put on buses and driven out of the back entrance of the airport. On the way, however, they approached a roundabout that had as a centrepiece a huge monument to the shah of Iran, Mohammad Reza, which was to be torn down during the revolution in 1979. More angry Iranian fans had clambered up onto the statue of the shah riding a horse to protest, while others gathered on the roundabout or had parked their cars to try to block the progress of the Iran team.

Both buses and their police escorts drove at speed straight over the roundabout, scattering fans as they sped through the protesters. Dozens of other angry supporters leapt into their cars and started pursuing the Iran and Australia buses.

Several members of the SAVAK were providing security for the Socceroos on their bus. They were 'tough, ruthless and uncaring', according to the team doctor, Brian Corrigan. As the buses sped into the hotel compound, the police blocking the cars that had been trying to follow them at the entrance, the SAVAK officers leapt off the vehicle when it parked and ran into the hotel lobby. They forcibly cleared out everyone standing there. This included relatives of the Iranian team who had been waiting there to welcome their loved ones home. 'We were all wondering what would happen if they were beaten at home,' Warren wrote in his autobiography.

The fans' initial anger soon turned to trying to intimidate the Socceroos. 'Everywhere we went in Tehran, people would hold up four fingers for us to see,' Warren wrote in *Sheilas, Wogs and Poofters*. 'It didn't take us too long to figure out that they were letting us know that we were going to get beaten by four goals. None of us even wanted to contemplate that happening.'

The Australians, by now battle-hardened after having travelled to so many inhospitable venues, were leaving nothing to chance in their preparations. Corrigan had arranged for a large consignment of meat to be flown from Sydney in an attempt to ensure the players' diets were not disrupted. When it arrived, customs officials at the airport refused to wave it through. Instead, they held it for three days, during which time they kept it out in the sun.

When it became public that the Australians had brought in their own food, including vegetables, milk and water, it led to anger in the local media. The topic dominated Rasic's pre-match press conference at the Hotel Intercontinental in Tehran. 'Look, gentlemen, I represent a superior race,' Rasic answered when reporters would not drop the line of questioning. 'In Australia, we eat Australian steak; we don't import US steak like you do.'

The headline in the newspaper the next day was 'The man that wasn't even born in Australia represents a superior race'.

The venue for the match was the Aryamehr Stadium, which had been built and completed in 1971 for the 1974 Asian Games to be staged in Tehran. It had been hoped that those Games would be the forerunner to the city staging the 1984 Olympics, but the political situation towards the end of the 1970s forced Iran to abandon its bid.

The Iranians largely reserved practices on the pitch at the stadium for themselves, and forced the Socceroos to train elsewhere. They were restricted to just one training session on the eve of the match. Warren admitted that it "was 'daunting even with no fans'".

As well as an intimidating home crowd, they would also have to cope with playing at an altitude of over 1,300 metres, which meant that it would be difficult to breathe. On top of this, Tehran was in the middle of a heatwave, with temperatures topping 100 degrees Fahrenheit – 37.8 degrees Celsius. Rasic was concerned that all these factors meant pressure was beginning to build to an unsustainable level. 'Our boys are strong, but just how much intense heat they can take remains to be seen,' he said.

The Iranians also tried to pull a fast one by getting the referee, Pavel Kazakov from the Soviet Union, replaced. They wanted an official from Pakistan appointed instead. At the time, relations between Iran and the Soviet Union were poor as they were close allies of the United States. In contrast, Iran provided financial aid to Pakistan, including in their war against India in 1971. The Australian Soccer Federation complained to FIFA, who claimed they knew nothing about it and that Kazakov would remain in charge.

Kazakov was considered one of Europe's top referees and in May of that year had been the referee for the second leg of the 1973 UEFA Cup final between

England's Liverpool and Germany's Borussia Monchengladbach. He had also been one of the officials at the previous year's Olympic Games in Munich.

The Australian team were caught in a traffic jam on their way to the match on 24th August and, throughout the journey, received abuse from the home fans, including everyone flashing them by now the familiar four-fingered salute. It would have done little to ease the tension that by now was swelling in the stomach of every Socceroos player. Even though Rasic had claimed he had not been happy with their performance in Sydney the previous week, he named an unchanged team.

More than 8,000 miles away in Australia, fans there were settling down to cheer their team on. The Australian Broadcasting Company had arranged to televise the game, which kicked off at 11.30pm Sydney time, live. The slight problem was that in those days, satellite time had to be booked well in advance and there was none available for the national broadcaster to be able to show the whole match. It meant that coverage ceased 25 minutes into the first half and did not resume until 10 minutes into the second half.

Thousands of Socceroos fans must have feared the worst when, in the 14th minute, Iran took the lead. Kazakov, the referee the Australian Soccer Federation had fought so hard to make sure was not replaced, awarded the home side a highly dubious penalty for a handball by Richards. Iran's captain, Parviz Ghelichkhani, coolly sent Australian goalkeeper Fraser the wrong way – the first goal he had conceded since replacing Corry. Richards has never believed that he was guilty of handball. 'The penalty was diabolical,' he said.

Shortly after the satellite coverage to Australia was cut, Iran scored a second goal that no one could doubt. Parvin, one of four changes in the Iranian team beaten in Sydney, set up Ghelichkhani to score again from 25 yards after 31 minutes.

The official crowd figure was 55,997, but estimates of how many people were actually inside the stadium have ranged from 80,000 to 130,000. However many it was, they were like an extra man for the home side. The Australians faced wave after wave of attack from the green-shirted Iranians. Warren admitted in his autobiography that the Socceroos 'were completely rattled' and 'knew we were in big trouble'.

The night before the game, Ghelichkhani had promised the Iranian media he would score two goals in the match. Ghelichkhani was a hero to the fans but was considered a dangerous figure to the shah's regime due to his left-leaning political views. In February 1972, he had been arrested by the SAVAK and held in custody for two months before being released.

He was held captive again and beaten up shortly before the revolution in 1979, and fled the country after Ayatollah Ruhollah Khomeini seized power. He now lives in France, where for many years he edited *Arash*, a political and cultural commentary magazine concentrating mainly on Iranian issues. In 2007, to celebrate the 100th edition of *Arash*, a special event was held in Sydney where Rasic was the guest speaker.

With Ghelichkhani posing a constant threat and Parvin back to provide Iran with much more of a cutting edge, Rasic knew he needed to do something to save the Socceroos' World Cup hopes. 'It was very hot, and the players were complaining they could not breathe,' he revealed. 'The fanatical support, the referee and the conditions were making it almost impossible for us, and I admit I wondered to myself several times whether we would get out of trouble.'

At one stage, Richards was hit by a coin as he prepared to take a throw-in. It was testament to the assailant's strength and accuracy that he managed to launch it over the moat surrounding the pitch and seemed to escape the detection of the dozens of soldiers holding sub-machine guns facing the crowd.

The Australians, unusually wearing white shorts instead of green, were also struggling to make themselves heard to each other. Instructions were being drowned out by the noise created by thousands of vuvuzelas, the plastic horns which were to come to international prominence at the 2010 FIFA World Cup finals in South Africa. They sounded like a swarm of bees and made communication on the pitch almost impossible.

'Nothing could have prepared the Socceroos for the atmosphere in the stadium,' Curran said. 'The noise from the crowd was simply incredible. The sound was distinctly shrill, a sound none of the players had ever heard before, and it had an effect on us.'

Rasic had also been forced to cope with a touchline reporter from Iranian television approaching him after each of the home side's two goals. 'What now, Mr Rasic?' he asked on both occasions. The Socceroos coach needed to summon up all his composure to reply, 'Australia to qualify.'

The plan Rasic produced to ensure that happened was to replace Alston, who had been largely ineffectual during the first half, with Tolson. Tolson was a big strapping centre forward from Wollongong who had spent two years playing in the English Third Division for Workington Town before returning home. But not before having learnt the skill of looking after himself.

'I was on the bench next to Rale in the first half, and I can tell you, if you are on the bench, you would not want to sit beside him,' Tolson said. 'I could tell he was very cranky with the way things were going, but he was a smart guy and in control all the time. He would not let his emotions get the better of him like some coaches do today, so as not to alarm the players. Yet he had a "how are we getting out of this" look on his face and I tell you he was burning inside. At the end of the first half, he grabbed me forcefully by my hair and told me, "Warm up."'

On Rasic's instructions, Tolson ripped into Alston in the dressing room during the interval, calling him a 'Pommy bastard, who didn't deserve to wear the green and gold'. According to Rasic, it 'stirred up the boys'.

More than 50 years later, Tolson's teammates are still in awe of the performance that he put in that day. Tolson may have played only 13 times for the Socceroos, but there is no doubt that without him that day in Tehran, they would not have reached the World Cup finals. 'If we lose this tie, don't come back to the dressing room,' Rasic had told Tolson. The 28-year-old Marconi-Fairfield striker replied, 'Yes, boss.'

Rasic had ordered Tolson to intimidate Iran's goalkeeper, Mansour Rashidi, a replacement for Nasser Hejazi, who was blamed for Australia's goals in the first leg, the first chance he got. Almost immediately, when the second half kicked off, Warren launched a high ball into Iran's penalty area and Tolson bundled Rashidi and two defenders into the net.

In 1965, Dettre had been so offended by this tactic employed by Tolson against the goalkeeper during the infamous 'Battle of Wentworth Park', when South Coast United's match against Pan-Hellenic was abandoned, that he had written an open letter to Tolson in Soccer World. 'You're not charging them; you're putting them out of the game,' he wrote. Now, along with every other Socceroos fan, Dettre was probably cheering.

It was probably only the quick intervention of Rasic that stopped Tolson from being shown an immediate red card. He raced onto the pitch and among the tangle of limbs stamped on Tolson's arm, leading to him screaming, 'What the fuck are you doing?' Rasic ordered Tolson to stay on the ground injured to try to persuade the referee not to send him off.

The unusual intervention worked and by the time the Australian Broadcasting Corporation was able to resume showing the match live, Australia were still holding on to their narrow lead over the two legs.

Tolson followed Rasic's instructions and dropped back to help the defence. He helped neutralise Iran's top striker. 'At one stage I saw him with his hands around the throat of Gholam Hossein Mazloumi,' Rasic recalled. 'He was screaming, "I'm going to fucking kill you!" Needless to say, Mazloumi went missing for the rest of the match.'

Fraser remembered Tolson playing 'like a man possessed' who 'ran all night from box to box'. Corrigan revealed that at half-time Rasic had warned Tolson the Iranian defenders would be 'trying to kick the shit out of him', but that he took them on 'using their own tactics, plus a few of his own, demolishing both of them'.

Another change in the 71st minute saw Rooney replace Warren, and he was ordered to make sure he kept hold of the ball as much as possible. 'In the end, it was probably only our team spirit, goalkeeper Jimmy Fraser and a bit of luck

Australian goalkeeper Jim Fraser repels another Iran attack in Tehran as the Socceroos desperately attempt to hang on to the lead

that saved us,' Warren wrote in his autobiography. 'Jimmy was brilliant and made some tremendous saves to keep us in the match. But the whole team battled to ensure we didn't concede a third goal. It certainly wasn't pretty, and we had our backs to the wall for most of the game.'

Against all the odds, the Socceroos somehow hung on, despite having gone two goals down so early on, and won 3–2 on aggregate. Never had a defeat felt more like a victory. The Iranian team were bereft at the final whistle. Ghelichkhani, his team's best player, was inconsolable. Richards swapped shirts with him, and he accepted the offer only reluctantly. He walked off the pitch with a yellow jersey around his shoulders, having to accept Iran had been knocked out. Four years later, when Iran did qualify for the World Cup finals for the first time, Ghelichkhani was left out of the squad for Argentina because of his political views.

Ironically, the Australians remained upset over the performance of the referee, Kazakov. 'That Russian was a shocker,' Abonyi claimed. 'I am sure that he was paid by the Iranian Football Federation. I saw the gold watch he got before the game, and we heard a story about beautiful girls coming out of his hotel room.'

As they left the pitch after the final whistle, the angry home crowd launched missiles towards the Socceroos. Once the team were on the bus back to the hotel, Iranian fans lined the road to shout, swear and gesticulate at them.

The Socceroos withstood intimidation, questionable refereeing, high altitude and a ferocious home crowd to move to the final stage of World Cup qualifying

At one point, a car drew level with the team bus with an Iranian supporter hanging out of the window. The SAVAK officer at the front of Australia's bus ordered the driver to cut in front of the car to stop it. He jumped off the vehicle, 'grabbed the man and wrenched him out of the car', Corrigan wrote in his autobiography, *The Life of Brian*. 'He then clouted him violently across the head with some sort of waddy before throwing him unconscious and bleeding onto the road. Finally, he ripped the keys from the car's ignition, so no one else could drive, got back in the bus and waved the driver on.'

In the circumstances, the Iranian media were surprisingly magnanimous in their reports the next day. 'We lost because we did not know we were going to face a professional team,' wrote one newspaper. 'We did not know how to play against them.'

There was special praise for Rasic, whom the press in Tehran identified as being the biggest difference between the two sides. 'They are also lucky to have a clever coach,' they wrote. 'If Iran had been coached by Rale Rasic, the result would have been reversed. Rasic not only outwitted our players tactically but also won the war of nerves off the field.'

One of the shah's sons was so impressed with what Rasic's team had achieved that before he left Tehran he gave him an 18-carat gold bracelet.

Rasic was full of praise for his team. 'This is the sign that a team had reached maturity,' he said in the post-match press conference. 'The team has been under tremendous pressure in Teheran, with constant niggling incidents reminding them the stakes were high. The crowd gave great encouragement to Iran and showed obvious hatred for Australia. This, along with the altitude problem, the furnace-like heat, and the fine performance of the Iran team, makes the win in the series incredible.'

It seemed unfair that such a performance still did not mean the Socceroos had qualified for the World Cup finals. They still had a lot of work to do before they could start planning for West Germany 1974.

Once more, Rasic knew they had been close to being eliminated. 'Yet again Australia had managed to dodge another bullet in the race for qualification,' he said. 'It seemed somebody was looking after us.'

CHAPTER TEN

Goal in a million

The Socceroos received a hero's welcome in Sydney when they arrived back from Tehran, but now had to wait more than two months before the final play-off against old rivals South Korea.

The Koreans had emerged victorious in the Zone A qualifying group held in Seoul in May. They had actually finished second in Group A2, behind Australia's 1970 World Cup conquerors, Israel, with one win and two draws.

They had then beaten Group A1 winners Hong Kong 3–1 in the semi-finals, despite falling behind after only five minutes. That set up a rematch with Israel, who had beaten Japan 1–0 after extra time in the other semi-final. The final at the Dongdaemun Stadium had also needed extra time, with teenager Cha Bum-kun scoring the winner in the 109th minute to give South Korea a 1–0 victory.

After arriving home from Iran, Socceroos coach Rale Rasic lifted more silverware as he guided Marconi-Fairfield to a 2–1 win over Sydney Hakoah in the New South Wales Premier League grand final. Rasic admitted that the break away from the Socceroos helped him 'recharge the batteries for what was going to be the biggest moment in the history of Australian soccer'.

Hakoah had been the first club in Australia to employ a full-time coach when they appointed Jackie Gibbons, who had previously played for English First Division club Tottenham Hotspur and later managed Israel's national team.

In the grand final against Marconi, Hakoah's team included one of the Socceroos key players, Jimmy Mackay, whom they had signed at the end of 1972 for $5,000 from Melbourne Croatia. It followed the decision by the Victoria Soccer Federation to ban Croatia, the club Mackay had played for since arriving in Australia in 1965 on a working two-year holiday. He had been persuaded at the airport to join them by former Celtic captain Duncan MacKay.

Croatia's licence was revoked as a result of a pitch invasion during a Victoria State League match in July 1972 against Melbourne Hakoah, which saw fans attack match officials. It followed Croatia's Hugh Gunn being sent off by referee Jimmy Brennan after a series of strong challenges on Bobby Saunders, who formerly played for English club Bournemouth. There were only five policemen there to control the crowd of 1,700, and it needed the players to protect the referee from the angry fans. The game was abandoned.

Croatia was initially suspended for life, but, after an appeal, it was downgraded to a one-year ban. It was the first time this kind of ruling had been handed down in Australian soccer. Croatia applied for readmission to the Victoria Soccer Federation at the conclusion of the 1972 season, but it was rejected, which created further anger in the Australian-Croatian community. Croatia then took the Victoria Soccer Federation to the Supreme Court the following year but lost the case.

Another Socceroo affected by the ban was striker Billy Vojtek, who crossed over to play for Sydney Croatia, while Duncan MacKay missed a season before signing for Perth Azzurri.

It has been claimed that the activities of Croatia's fans were linked to the Ustase, a group of right-wing nationalists committed to destabilising Yugoslavia with the aim of setting up an independent Croatia.

Melbourne Croatia's president at the time was Enver Begovic. Australian soccer then was full of characters with colourful pasts, but none quite as colourful as that of Begovic. He had served as a soldier in both the Ustase Army and the Nazi SS Handschar division during the Second World War.

When the War ended, Begovic claimed he was held as a prisoner of war by the Soviet Union Red Army before escaping to Austria, where he worked for United States intelligence against communist agents. A check by Australian authorities, after Begovic had arrived in 1957, revealed he had served prison time in Austria and Germany for embezzlement and fraud, involving stealing a large sum of money.

Unusually for many of the immigrants from Eastern Europe, when he landed in Australia, Begovic spoke excellent English. Within a year of arriving, he had established a private detective agency in Melbourne. Begovic allegedly later switched political allegiances to work for Yugoslavia and was linked to the case of the 'Croatian Six', where in 1981 six immigrants were convicted of involvement in a conspiracy to bomb two travel agencies, a Serbian community club, a suburban theatre and Sydney water supply pipes. The case has been described as Australia's 'greatest miscarriage of justice' and appeals continue to this day.

It was alleged that Melbourne Croatia's ban was politically motivated, with Tony Kovac, a leading member of the Yugoslavian club Footscray JUST and founding member of the Victoria Soccer Federation, behind the decision.

It demonstrated how soccer in Australia was still split very much along ethnic lines. It made it even more impressive how under Rasic the Socceroos had managed to pull the nation together and gather the public behind them.

The build-up to the game against South Korea in Sydney on 28th October was even more intense than it had been for the Israel play-off four years earlier. Journalists who normally only wrote about rugby league were devoting acres of space to analysing Australia's chances of reaching the 1974 World Cup finals in West Germany.

This was set to be Australia's sixth match against South Korea since the two countries had met for the first time in the final of the South Vietnam Independence Cup in Saigon in 1967, when goals from Vojtek, Atti Abonyi and Johnny Warren had given them a 3–2 victory.

The other four games had all taken place at the Dongdaemun Stadium in Seoul, including two four years earlier in the 1970 World Cup qualifying campaign. Australia had won the first of these 2-1 with a late goal in a match *Soccer World* dubbed the 'Battle of Seoul'. The second ended 1–1 to earn them the tie against Rhodesia.

In 1972, Rasic had the foresight to arrange for two friendlies to be held in Seoul in case the Socceroos were drawn against South Korea in the following year's World Cup qualifying. The first game had finished 1–1, with the Socceroos winning the second 2–0, with Ray Baartz among the goalscorers.

The Australian media were confident about the Socceroos' chances, but Rasic claimed, 'I knew better.' He would not be able to blame lack of planning if they failed as the Australian Soccer

There was unprecedented interest in Australia's final World Cup qualifying tie against South Korea, with the visitors posing for pictures with toy kangaroos

Federation had sanctioned a three-week training camp at the team's regular base in Wahroonga.

Australia's preparations were taking place after the domestic season had finished, and Rasic needed to keep his squad sharp. He was forced to play the New South Wales under-23 team on a weekly basis. Having been on spying missions to watch South Korea, Rasic arranged for the youngsters to play the way he expected the Socceroos' opponents would line up.

Sydney was suffering a heatwave, but Rasic still put the players through hard training sessions morning and afternoon. One afternoon, he heard Mackay turn to fellow Scot Jimmy Rooney and say: 'It would be fucking nice to have a cold beer.' Rasic arranged for two bottles to be sent up and put in the fridge of the room they were sharing.

Rasic had imposed a strict no-alcohol rule and, as tempted as they must have

been to open them, Mackay and Rooney reported to their coach someone had put beer in their room. 'I told them I had given them the beer as a reward for training so hard and they should go back to their room and I would send them another six bottles,' Rasic laughed. It was a small incident but illustrated just how much the players had bought into Rasic's methods and were prepared to follow them.

A major problem was brewing, however. Anger was still simmering among many players involved in the unsuccessful 1970 World Cup qualification campaign at the fact they had travelled the world, with some losing their jobs in the process, and been rewarded so little. They had received a cheque for just $13.27.

Warren had been the captain back then and, although he no longer led the side, remained very influential. He had been trying to reach an agreement with Australian Soccer Federation president Sir Arthur George for several months, only to keep being put off. Things came to a head in the week before the first leg against South Korea. Warren led a delegation of himself, Ray Richards, Manfred Schaefer, Peter Wilson, Baartz and Johnny Watkiss that demanded to see Sir Arthur.

Just as he had before the first match against Iran in August, when he had ordered Rasic unsuccessfully to cut the travelling party to Tehran by four players, Sir Arthur arrived at the Fox and Hound Motel in his Rolls-Royce. He was accompanied by Australian Soccer Federation secretary Brian Le Fevre. In the meeting, Sir Arthur told the players they were not in any position to make financial commitments but promised to 'look after' them.

Warren told Sir Arthur they would need to consult the other players. He ordered them to 'hurry up' as he had another appointment. The delegation returned two hours later and told him the rest of the squad had rejected the promise of the matter being sorted out later. Sir Arthur ordered the players to 'pack their bags' and drove off in his Rolls-Royce.

Warren claimed 'it wasn't simply about the money'. He believed that it was 'also about being treated properly for the effort and loyalty we had given to the game and its administration over a long period of time'.

With just two days before the biggest match in the history of Australian soccer, some players started packing their bags ready to leave the training camp. Shortly afterwards, Le Fevre returned and told them that Sir Arthur wanted to see them again. Having driven round the block, he came back with an offer that would see the players receive a percentage of the television rights if they qualified for the World Cup finals.

After more discussions with their teammates, Warren's delegation accepted Sir Arthur's proposal. A major incident had been narrowly averted.

Rasic admitted that he 'considered it very poor timing because it would affect the players' mental preparation' but understood their position having 'been ripped off so many times in the past by promises of this and that, yet getting nothing or pittance'.

The affair did not improve the deteriorating relationship between the coach and the president of the Australian Soccer Federation. 'I believe Arthur thought I was the ringleader of all of this,' Rasic wrote in his autobiography.

The Australian public were unaware of all this drama happening behind the scenes. A crowd of 32,005 turned up to the Sydney Sports Ground expecting to see the Socceroos take another big step on the road to West Germany 1974. They left disappointed following an abject display, with Australia fortunate to finish the match 0-0 after South Korea dominated. The visitors came close on several occasions to taking a valuable lead back to Seoul, including striker Park Lee-chun hitting the crossbar in the second half.

Warren conceded 'the pay dispute had a lot to do with our average performance'. Rasic called the Socceroos' performance 'shocking', and said that they were 'outplayed in every department'.

The one Australian player to emerge with any credit was the goalkeeper, Jim Fraser. He had been doubtful before the match and ended up playing with a bandage around his stomach. Fraser pulled off a series of vital saves, which meant the Socceroos had something to hang on to for the second leg 13 days later.

South Korean goalkeeper Byun Ho-Young kept a clean sheet as a disappointing Socceroos drew 0-0

'Korea was much, much better than I expected,' admitted Rasic. 'The players were cool and constructive, and their defence was excellent. Our team was shocking. Everything went wrong. The defence and midfield never supported each other. We didn't play well, that's all.'

Rasic still remained optimistic. 'Korea played safe soccer,' he said. 'We will play safe soccer in Seoul, and it will be the Koreans who will be under pressure.'

Following a rest day with their families, the Australian party regathered at their training camp in Wahroonga on the Monday after their horror show against South Korea. Rasic immediately banned all talk of what had happened two days previously. The team spent a week preparing in Australia, before departing for Seoul on 8th November.

Rale Rasic refused to be downhearted after the Socceroos' failure to beat South Korea in Sydney

When they arrived in South Korea's capital via Hong Kong, the Australian party was surprised not to be fast-tracked through immigration control as had happened on previous visits. This time, they were made to stand in a queue for three hours. Rasic was determined to show that this tactic was not going to sap his team's spirit. He ordered the squad to start singing. '[Adrian] Alston and [Ray] Richards fancied themselves as singers and led the boys in a good, old sing-along that had the Korean officials looking on in utter bemusement,' he wrote in his autobiography. 'They must have thought we were stark, raving mad.'

Once through customs, the Australian party was met again by a delegation of supporters from the Yohan Technical High School, whom they had established such good relations with when they had played in Seoul in 1969. The youngsters were holding up a banner that read 'Welcome to the Socceroos' – more proof that the nickname had really caught on. They presented the players with bowls of fruit grown at the school.

The South Koreans still continued, though, to try to undermine the Socceroos' preparations. When the squad turned up at the Dongdaemun Stadium for their appointed training session at the match venue, as allowed under FIFA rules, they found the groundsman locking up. He told them 'No, no. Finished' and claimed that the pitch was too wet for them to train on. The curator changed his mind after he was given a $50 United States note, and reopened the gates.

On the whole, however, the Socceroos received a much friendlier welcome than they had before facing Iran in the second leg of the previous round.

The Australians had once again taken their own food to South Korea, although this time it did not cause the upset it had in Tehran. The steaks, provided by Australian butcher Hall-Kalman Pty Ltd, proved particularly popular. The team were accommodated in the Tokyu and Lee Gardens Hotel, where it was claimed there was only 'praise for the Socceroos, who were a big hit with the waiters, bell boys and lift attendants'.

The charm offensive had continued in the pre-match press conference, where Rasic avoided the mistake he had made in Tehran declaring he 'represented a superior race'. He did not turn down any request for an interview and spoke at length to the local media. Sidney Russell, a journalist for the *Korea Herald*, wrote: 'The Australian team established itself as the friendliest foreign group ever to compete on Korean shores.'

One natural advantage that the hosts did have was the weather. The Socceroos had arrived from a hot Australian spring to a cold South Korean winter, with temperatures below freezing. On the morning of the match at the Dongdaemun Stadium, light snow began falling and left a thin white scattering on the pitch.

The Socceroos were boosted overnight by a telegram from the Australian prime minister, Gough Whitlam. Sent to team manager John Barclay, he said: 'Australian goals in Korea is your current export target. Very best wishes for vital match on Saturday on behalf of Australian people and myself.'

But the Socceroos were soon in deficit following a blistering start from South Korea, who scored twice in the opening stages. Kim Jae-han, who at six foot three inches was unusually tall for a Korean and who Rasic had identified as a potential danger, put them ahead in the 15th minute. It followed a back pass by Doug Utjesenevic that took a bounce off the frozen pitch and deflected off goalkeeper Fraser's chest into the path of Kim.

Then, 12 minutes later, the Socceroos found themselves 2–0 down when Fraser punched a South Korean cross out only for it to deflect off Utjesenevic and into the path of Ko Jae-wook to sweep home. It was a disastrous opening for Rasic, who had made a number of changes from the game in Sydney. These included Schaefer returning from injury to replace Watkiss, and Rooney and Branko Buljevic being picked instead of Warren and Alston.

A curious aspect of the match was that South Korea's coach, Min Byung-dae, had asked for the 32,000 crowd not to applaud if their country scored a goal. It was a bizarre request as in the World Cup matches four years earlier, the Seoul crowd had been so noisy that team doctor Brian Corrigan had called them 'the most hostile I have ever seen or heard'.

Spectators included Park Chung-hee, the army general who had led the military *coup d'état* in 1961 that forced out South Korea's democratically elected government. He had been elected president two years later and ruled the country until his assassination in 1979.

Both goals were greeted by no celebrations, as Min had asked. 'It was a strange move,' Rasic said in his autobiography. 'There was absolute silence in the ground. You could hear a pin drop.'

The quietness is what Fraser remembered most of the match. 'At the ground, I remember a very eerie atmosphere,' he said. 'There was not much noise compared to what we had experienced in Tehran, even though there were about 30,000 people.'

In the silence, Rasic could hear perfectly as Barclay announced: 'We are gone.' It was not what he expected to hear. 'I couldn't believe my ears,' Rasic said. 'Australians prided themselves on never giving up, on fighting to the end, and here was part of the Socceroos family telling me I couldn't win. I saw red … I grabbed him by both his arms and threw him off the bench.'

Almost as soon as Barclay left, Buljevic scored in the 29th minute with a header after full-back Col Curran had beaten two South Koreans and crossed. 'The goal gave us a lot of confidence and after the break we started to attack more,' said Buljevic.

Barclay's pleas to be allowed back onto the Socceroos' bench and into the dressing room at half-time were ignored by Rasic. He relayed to the players what their team manager had said about them. 'They were upset that he did not believe in them,' Rasic said. 'To be honest, I was uncomfortable with what I did to John, but again psychology was playing a huge part. The boys needed a spur. They needed to be lifted and John was the sacrificial lamb.'

Before they left to go out for the second half, Rasic told his players he 'didn't care what the result was' but they must 'not lose this game'.

The tactic worked because just three minutes after the break, Baartz had equalised when he latched on to a long throw-in from Richards. Wilson might even have won it towards the end when he hit the post. The Socceroos had again come close to elimination only to prove that you wrote them off at your peril. 'The Koreans were finished in the second half,' said Baartz.

The South Korea coach, Min, had been one of his country's greatest players. He had represented them at the 1948 Olympics in London, when South Korea had competed as an independent country for the first time after the end of

Ray Baartz celebrates scoring the equaliser to complete the Socceroos' recovery from 2-0 down in Seoul

Japanese colonial rule. Min had also been part of South Korea's team when it reached the 1954 FIFA World Cup finals in Switzerland, losing 9–0 to the great Hungarian team and 7–0 to Turkey, respectively. This did not insulate him from severe criticism from the local media, who did not understand how their team had managed to throw away a two-goal advantage.

Suddenly an incident that had occurred during the Socceroos' trip to Tehran for the previous round took on huge significance. In the build-up to the game against Iran, Rasic had been informed by an Australian journalist accompanying them that a meeting was taking place between the Australian Soccer Federation, FIFA and the South Korean Football Association.

It had been decided by Vic Tutting, representing Australia, FIFA and the South Korean officials, that if the two countries met in the next round and a replay was required, it would take place a week after the game in Seoul. In those days, away goals did not count double, and there were no penalties to decide drawn matches.

Rasic gatecrashed the meeting and demanded that Tutting renegotiate the arrangement, so that a replay would take place in Hong Kong only 72 hours after the second leg. Rasic's theory was that the Socceroos would be able to recover quicker than their South Korean rivals and that would give them a big physical advantage. Following angry scenes, during which the Australian coach refused to leave the room, he finally got his way. Any replay would be held just three days after the second leg in Seoul.

Tutting, the president of the Oceania Football Confederation until he had to step down following Australia's resignation from the continental governing body, was so angry and embarrassed at what happened that when the party got back to Sydney, he demanded that Rasic was fired. That was never going to happen with the Socceroos so close to qualifying for the World Cup. Still, it was another blemish against Rasic's name.

Now, Rasic's insistence on the brief period between the match in Seoul and replay in Hong Kong was looking like a masterstroke. 'I told the players we were virtually on the way home and the Koreans were heading away from home,' he said. 'There was no way they were going to beat us in the third game.'

Baartz thinks the replay had already been won by the time the two teams were on their way to Hong Kong. 'The South Korean team was on the same plane as us going to Hong Kong,' he said. 'We were laughing and joking, and they were all down and despondent because they thought they'd done enough to qualify leading 2–0. We were buoyant, everyone was cracking jokes, and it was a psychological win for us.'

In 1973, Hong Kong was still firmly under British control, having been established as a colony of the British Empire after the Qing dynasty ceded Hong Kong Island in 1841–1842 as a consequence of losing the First Opium War. It meant there would be plenty of support for the Socceroos, with many expatriates living there.

It also meant another change in the weather, this time to almost 100 per cent humidity, which again probably favoured the Australians more than the South Koreans.

There was intense interest in the match, and when the Australians arrived at their base in Hong Kong, the Le Gardens Hotel, dozens of journalists were waiting for them. Rasic had never doubted his Socceroos were destined for West Germany 1974 and told the media: 'We are unstoppable.'

The full Australian squad completed two light training sessions before the match, while Rasic's spies told him that half the South Koreans had to rest to recover from knocks they had received in the previous match. His belief that the Socceroos would recover quicker than their rivals was being fully vindicated.

There was a crowd of 27,284 on 13th November inside the Government Stadium located in So Kon Po, south of Causeway Bay and Victoria Park on Hong Kong Island, for a match where the winner was guaranteed a place in the World Cup finals.

The ground had originally been the burial place for victims of a tragedy at Happy Valley Racecourse in 1918, when a temporary grandstand collapsed, knocking over hot food stalls that set bamboo matting ablaze. In the fire that ensued, nearly 600 people died. The remains were moved in 1953 to another part of the island and the new stadium built.

There was a torrential rainstorm just before the kick-off, but the stadium had excellent drainage and the pitch was soon back in perfect condition. As he walked out for the biggest match of his life, Rasic was handed a small gift. 'Mr Yung was our liaison officer in Hong Kong,' he recounted. 'He said, "Mr Lale Lasic, I'm sure you will win tonight." He handed me a necklace with the number 13 on it. I put it in my tracksuit and did up the zipper.' The number 13 is considered to be especially lucky in Chinese culture.

The Socceroos were dominating the match but were struggling to break through the South Korean defence. Then, in the 70th minute, came the most important goal in Australian soccer history. The Koreans conceded a free kick in their own half. Richards flighted the ball towards the penalty area where, under pressure from substitute Alston, it was headed away by Park Yung-Tae. It fell only as far as Rooney, who cushioned it into the path of his roommate, Mackay.

'The rest seemed to be in slow motion,' Rasic wrote in his autobiography. 'Mackay met the ball with a fierce volley from 30 metres out that sailed into the top left-hand corner of the net, leaving their goalkeeper clutching at thin air. Time stood still for a few seconds both on the field and on our bench … Then the place went crazy.'

The Socceroos rushed to Mackay and lifted him off the ground as they celebrated. Later, they all drunk champagne from the boot that had made all their dreams come true. 'I said to myself, there you are, my son, hit that one,' was Rooney's assessment of his dinky pass to Mackay. 'And didn't he do just that.'

The following week, *Soccer World* published a photograph of South Korean goalkeeper Lee Sae-Yun, recalled for this match after missing the first two games, suspended in mid-air with the blur of the white ball in the top of the net. Under the headline 'GOAL IN A MILLION', the newspaper caption said the keeper had 'dived in vain'. The South Korean press speculated that if coach Min had kept Byun Ho-young, he might have saved it. At five foot ten inches, Byun was an inch taller than Lee.

The truth is that no one would have stopped Mackay's shot.

'An absolute cracker,' said Warren.

'A wonder strike,' claimed Alston.

'For all of us it was the best goal that's ever been,' Rooney insisted.

The following year, the prestigious British publication *Rothmans Football Yearbook* voted the goal one of its six best of the year worldwide. 'A belter, wasn't it?' Mackay said. 'The second I hit it, I knew it was going all the way.'

Mackay's first thoughts after the match were for his wife, Marilyn, the woman he had met after arriving in Australia on a working holiday that had turned into the adventure of a lifetime. She was at home in Melbourne watching on television. 'I wonder what she thought of that shot,' he told reporters. 'She has had to put up with a lot this year with me being away in World Cup camp for almost three months. I think that goal was especially for her.'

The magnitude of what he had done did not hit Mackay until he was back in his hotel room with Rooney. 'We had a can of Carlton Diamond each, sat on our beds, looked up at the ceiling and just thought about it …' he said.

The white blur in the top left-hand corner of the picture is the ball entering South Korea's net after Jimmy Mackay's 25-yard shot had beaten South Korean flailing goalkeeper Lee Sae-Yun

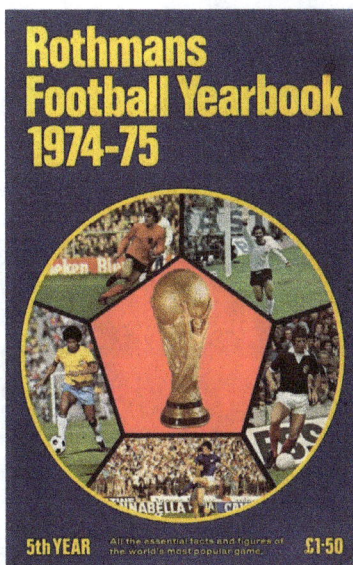

Rasic believed the strike will always have a special place in the folklore of sport in the country. 'There is no way you can deny the goal of Mackay as the greatest in the history of Australian football,' he said.

Mackay was a favourite of Rasic's. 'In the national team, Mackay was the general who directed the pace,' he said. 'He was excellent both in attack and

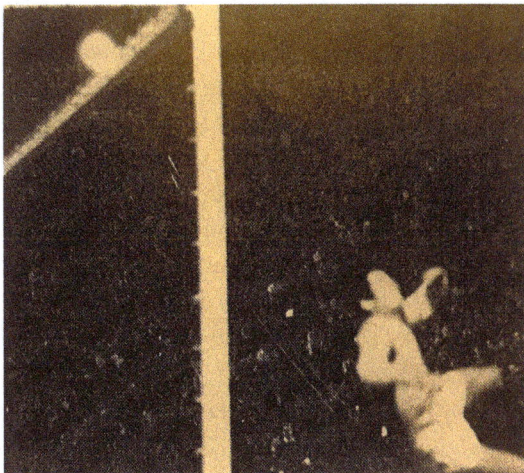

Jimmy Mackay's historic goal was voted one of the six best of the 1973–1974 season by the Rothmans Football Annual in Britain

defence. He was one of the best, if not the best reader of the game that I have dealt with, and he was a giant in big matches.

'I'll never forget Australia's 3-1 win over Greece in Athens in 1970. Not only did Mackay mark Mimis Domazos out of the game, but he also scored our second goal. Against Israel on the same tour, he marked Mordechai Spiegler out of the game yet still managed to be the complete midfield general as well.

'Mackay was certainly one of the most imaginative midfielders ever to play in Australia and one of the best footballers I've seen here. He was a football freak, that's the best way to describe him.'

At least *Soccer World* were spelling Mackay's name correctly now, and Lou Gautier wrote that the goal 'brought fame and glory to Australian soccer'.

Gautier added that 'when Mackay plays, Australia clicks'.

At the final whistle, Rasic, Mackay and the captain, Wilson, were all carried off shoulder-high. Mackay waved the right boot that had scored the winning goal high above his head in celebration. As he was chaired off, Rasic admitted he 'felt he could touch the stars'.

Wilson struggled to take in his journey from a youngster struggling to get a game for Gateshead in the Northern Premier League in England to World Cup captain. 'I feel as though I am walking on a cloud,' he said. 'I keep pinching myself to make sure the whole thing is real.'

There were joyous scenes at the final whistle, with Australia qualifying for the World Cup finals for the first time

Baartz echoed Rasic's belief, expressed after the epic match against Iran in Tehran, that someone was looking after them. 'We just kept battling our way through match after match hoping the gods would be kind to us,' he said. 'Thank heavens they were.'

In the dressing room, Rasic described scenes of 'grown men crying, laughter, songs, yahooing. The champagne flowed. Backslappers came from everywhere.' One of the Socceroos had to be careful during the celebrations, it turned out. Fraser had played with his upper body plastered after the goalkeeper slipped two discs in the week leading up to the game – something he did not reveal until 47 years later. Rasic had asked Fraser, who had played with a bandage around his stomach in the first leg, if he could still play two days before the game and he told him he could.

Among those joining in the revelry was Barclay, the team manager having been restored to the bench after upsetting Rasic in Seoul. Like Mackay, Barclay had been born in Scotland before emigrating and making a new life for himself. He had been an important part of Australia's journey since leading the team on their first trip to South Vietnam in 1967. What made the occasion even more special was that Mackay's historic goal had been scored on Barclay's 46th birthday.

Three days after the match had finished and the team had returned to Sydney, Rasic found the lucky charm containing the number 13 he had been given before the match in his tracksuit as he prepared to wash it. He wore it for the rest of his life.

Rasic deserved a huge amount of credit for having moulded together a team with such a never-say-die spirit who knew exactly what job they were supposed to do. His insistence the replay should take place so soon after Seoul, because the Socceroos were more used to quick turnarounds than their South Korean opponents, may have proved the decisive factor.

That is what Alston, who came on as a 56th-minute substitute in the match in Hong Kong, believed. 'Rale was spot on,' he wrote in his autobiography, *Noddy*. 'Mentally we were stronger because he made us that way since he took over three years earlier. We wanted to get on with it and win the tie. Playing three days later was no big deal for us.'

The match had been broadcast back home by the Australian Broadcasting Corporation – this time without interruptions due to the satellite being booked up – with Martin Royal providing the commentary.

Royal had been the broadcaster's first soccer commentator in 1954 and was the voice of the sport in the country for 30 years, as well as being the leading announcer for royal and ceremonial events.

Originally from England, he had settled in Australia at the end of World War Two after serving in the Royal Navy, where he had twice survived being on ships sunk by the Germans, first by a mine and the second by a U-boat.

In his understated way, Royal called the Socceroos' victory in Hong Kong a 'triumph for Australian soccer'.

In living rooms across the country, celebrations were a lot more raucous. The match had started late Tuesday evening Australian time and finished in the early hours of Wednesday morning. The mood was probably best summed up by *Soccer World*, the one Australian media that had been there every step of the way since the country had begun its bid to qualify for the World Cup in 1965.

'The World Cup agony that has been dragging on since March, briefly infecting Auckland, Sydney, Melbourne, Tehran, Seoul and finally Hong Kong, just had to have a last fling, yanking us well past midnight, glued to our TV sets, chain-smoking, swearing, sighing, praying,' wrote Andrew Dettre under his pen name, Mike Renwick.

'When it was over, not only the players on the pitch, but a whole nation back home embraced. Australia is in the World Cup finals. Let's savour this for a moment. We have reached what often appeared to be a utopistic target, the birthright and privilege of others, not us.

'Our lot, one was inclined to think, was to admire the greats from afar, to hobnob with them occasionally, even take a crack at the Cup, then fail. As we did in 1965 and 1969. But no longer. Thanks to the marvellous 12 boys who hammered the Koreans into the Hong Kong turf, Australian soccer can now hold its head high.'

Suddenly it was not just *Soccer World* that was interested in the Socceroos. 'Wogball' was on the front and back pages of the newspapers in Australia. *The Sun* in Sydney celebrated with 'GREAT SCOT!' and wrote: 'Wee Jim whacks us into the World Cup … and it's bubbly to boot.'

The *Sydney Telegraph* led with 'MUNICH HERE WE COME', with their soccer writer Tom Anderson writing: 'Marvellous, bloody marvellous! Yes, Australian soccer has hit the big time at long last with a magnificent performance.'

Anderson probably especially appreciated the contribution of the Scots in the Socceroos' team. He had been born in East Lothian and played for several clubs in the Scottish and English league before retiring to Australia in 1968. There, he had become a popular journalist and radio host.

'In the past, the Socceroos have been maligned and accused of being a load of second raters and has-beens, but tonight they pulled out all the stops and did Australia proud,' Anderson wrote in his match report from Hong Kong. 'The scenes after the game were unforgettable as the players shed tears of joy and got on their knees and kissed the turf at the scene of their glory.

'All of a sudden, gone were the days when they were described by many as amateurs and mugs. Here was a team that had made the ultimate in football – playing in the elite 16 of world soccer in the greatest sporting competition on earth.'

In the midst of the celebrations, Australian Soccer Federation president Sir Arthur dictated a telegram to be sent to Prime Minister Whitlam. This was in response to the one he had sent before the match in Seoul, stating 'Australian goals in Korea is your current export target'. Sir Arthur answered: 'Produced export target as expected'.

Before continuing their celebrations back at their hotel, the Australians lined up to greet and clap the vanquished South Korean squad as they boarded their bus.

The next day, the South Korean and Hong Kong media joined in the praise for the Socceroos. The *Chosun Ilbo* wrote the Australians' 'fighting spirit and courage have set a magnificent example to Korean sportsmen.'

The *Korea Herald* said: 'Australia deserved their victory with an all-round superiority that demolished Korea's offensive hopes. Korea was lucky to escape with a one-goal defeat.'

The *Korea Times* admitted: 'No team which surrenders a two-goal lead at home deserves to make the final 16.'

Hong Kong's Chinese language newspaper, the *Kung Sheung Evening News*, praised the Socceroos' 'European-style display' and claimed they 'looked as good as several more highly rated teams from Europe and South America seen in Hong Kong.' Richards and Wilson were both hailed by the publication as being 'world class'.

The *South China Morning Post* credited the Socceroos for 'creating one of the big surprises of the sensational build-up to the 1974 World Cup series. Australia in and England out! Who would have believed that?'

The only newspaper that did not seem to give the Socceroos the credit they deserved was Seoul's *Hankook Ilbo*. They claimed 'the match was a nightmare for the 20 million Koreans watching the game on TV' and complained 'the Australians cannot be regarded as Asian – nor as Australians for that matter as their players come from many countries.'

Apart from the sole question raised over the authenticity of the Socceroos' team, the only person to pour cold water on their triumph was Arie Van Gemert, the Dutch official who had refereed the second leg in Seoul and the play-off in Hong Kong.

'The Australian soccer team is not worth a penny,' he said after the match. 'Australia is at least four classes lower than the weakest first division team in Europe. I told the Australians they would not win a match in Germany.'

CHAPTER ELEVEN

Sprechen sie Deutsch?

Criticism of Australia's qualification for the 1974 FIFA World Cup grew, especially as it coincided with England being knocked out of the tournament.

The 1966 World Cup winners had been drawn with Poland and Wales, so qualification for West Germany appeared to be a formality. A three-team group required only four games, and a shorter qualifying campaign starting in November 1972. But a draw with Wales at Wembley Stadium, followed by a 2–0 defeat to Poland in Chorzow, meant England had to win their final game against the Poles in London.

The game, on 13th October, itself belongs in the annals of history as among the most one-sided ever staged. England launched wave after wave of attack but could find no way through in the first half. Before the match, Poland's goalkeeper, Jan Tomaszewski, had been labelled a 'clown' by Derby County manager Brian Clough. He responded by pulling off a series of remarkable saves.

Poland took the lead in the 60th minute and although England equalised six minutes later, they failed to score the winning goal they needed. The game was so one-sided that England had 34 attempts on goal and 26 corners but could still not find a way through.

When he got back from Hong Kong, Rale Rasic fielded several calls from the English media. 'Much was made of the fact that a super football nation like England, who had won the World Cup just eight years earlier, was not in the finals this time and a country known more for the sun, beach, kangaroos, koalas and cricket was,' he wrote in his autobiography.

European football's governing body, UEFA, even discussed the issue at an Executive Committee meeting of how it could be that countries like Australia, Haiti and Zaire could qualify for the World Cup when others like England and Hungary missed out.

The feelings of most of the English press about the qualification of Australia, along with other newcomers Haiti and Zaire, were summed up by an article in *The Times*. They asked why 'nations of little or no football tradition or distinction should be in the final line-up, while the pioneers of the game should be on the outside looking in'.

The Times was supported by West Germany's captain, Franz Beckenbauer. He told the newspaper: 'For me, a World Cup without England is not a real

World Cup at all. For Haiti, Australia and Zaire to be coming and not England does not make sense.'

Distinguished *Sunday Times* football writer Brian Glanville wrote one of the more analytical pieces about the situation in *Soccer World*, under the headline 'Socceroos – but no Lions'. He admitted: 'I don't think the Australians have any right to be in West Germany, but I congratulate them, and I hope they do well. Their achievement in getting there at all is already considerable.'

To back up his claim that the Socceroos did not deserve their place, Glanville quoted the thoughts of Vital Loraux, the Belgian official who had refereed England's ill-fated game against Poland at Wembley Stadium and then Australia's match against South Korea in Sydney later that month. Glanville wrote that Loraux had 'pronounced the standard of the game deplorable, not to be compared with that of the dramatic England-Poland game'. Referees were not fans of the Socceroos, it appeared.

In the article, Glanville proved to be ahead of his time as he called for FIFA to expand the number of teams who qualified for the World Cup from 16 to 32. At the 1982 World Cup in Spain, a total of 24 countries took part in the event, with the number eventually increasing to 32 at France in 1998. For the 2026 FIFA World Cup, to be co-hosted by Canada, Mexico and United States, that figure will be increased again to 48 countries.

When they landed back in Sydney after their dramatic win in the play-off against South Korea, no one cared about the critics, with thousands gathering at Mascot Airport. The goalscorer, Jimmy Mackay, was swamped by dozens of photographers and media. The next day, the front pages of the newspapers were plastered of pictures of Mackay holding his right boot aloft, with his two-year-old son, Malcolm, on his shoulders.

The team were taken to a reception arranged by New South Wales premier Sir Robert Askin. Congratulations from all over the world flooded in. This included from Joao Havelange, already campaigning to replace Sir Stanley Rous as FIFA president at the following year's elections.

Hermann Neuberger and Hermann Joch, president and director of the 1974 World Cup Organising Committee, also sent messages. '"Uncle"' Joe Vlasits wrote a personal '"well done"' note to Rasic, his successor.

Football Associations in Israel, Bulgaria, New Zealand and Iran were also quick to offer their best wishes. The Football Association in England was notable for failing to contact the Australian Soccer Federation. 'Plenty of envious whinging, yes, but no congratulations,' wrote *Soccer World*. 'But is anyone really surprised ...'

A letter written by Ron Volem in Sydney and published in *Soccer World* the week after the Socceroos clinched qualification called on the sport to thank 'the loyal Greeks, Italians, Yugoslavians and other migrants who helped Australian

soccer during club and
national matches. They played
a great role for Australian
soccer because they remained
loyal, to their teams, added
colour to the games by their
cheering and attendances.

'But all some British fans
could do was criticise and
dream about the standard of
soccer in the old country
compared to Australia's. For
crying out loud, instead of
helping Australian soccer by
attending, and adding more

After landing back in Sydney, the Socceroos visited New South Wales premier Sir Robert Askin

life to the game, those bums only sit down and complain about the poor quality
of Aussie soccer.'

Australian soccer had a schizophrenic relationship with English football.
After World War Two, the sport in Australia had been built largely on the
passion and drive of immigrants from Eastern Europe, who did not share the
belief that English football was the be-all and end-all. Many who administered
the game in Australia, however, remained in awe of the fact that football had
been invented and codified in England.

A case in point was the appointment in 1973 by the Australian Soccer
Federation of Eric Worthington as its first director of coaching. For at least two
years before Worthington was given the job, it was widely expected the role
would go to Dettmar Cramer. He had been West Germany's assistant coach
when they finished runners-up at the 1966 World Cup, was highly regarded by
FIFA and made no secret of the fact he was open to working in Australia.

In the end, Australian Soccer Federation president Sir Arthur George chose
Worthington from an all-English shortlist. Worthington had played a handful
of matches in the English Football League with Watford and Bradford City.
He combined that with being a schoolteacher, including a spell at
Loughborough College. Shortly before being appointed by the Australian
Soccer Federation, Worthington had managed the England women's team in
their first match.

Rasic blamed the 'Pommie mafia' for getting Worthington the job and
contributing to the degeneration of his relationship with Sir Arthur. Rasic
should have been bulletproof after guiding the Socceroos to the World Cup
finals for the first time but behind the scenes was already fighting for his job.

Speculation about who would replace Rasic after West Germany 1974 was already appearing in *Soccer World* as early as February, even though he had given no indication he planned to step down.

Rasic blamed Worthington. 'He was always in Arthur's ear about this and that,' he wrote in his autobiography. 'Criticising the Socceroos' style of play and telling him that our football was too defensive. Arthur was taken in by Worthington's smooth talking and glibness.'

As well as being critical of the style of football the Socceroos played under Rasic, Worthington also claimed that the players could not understand their coach's accent and he presented a bad image to the media, particularly on television. 'While Worthington was a quietly spoken person and a good academic, he knew his way around the politics of Australian soccer,' Rasic said. 'He invariably got what he wanted from Arthur George.'

Cramer, meanwhile, the German who many in Australian soccer had been calling to be given the job of director of coaching, was appointed manager of Bundesliga giants Bayern Munich. He led the Bavarian club to consecutive European Cup victories in 1975 and 1976.

Australia had been the 11th of the 16 countries to qualify for the 1974 World Cup. They joined hosts West Germany and defending champions Brazil, along with Argentina, Uruguay, Scotland, Poland, Italy, East Germany, Bulgaria and Holland.

Before the end of 1973, Chile, Haiti, Zaire and Sweden joined them. The final place was decided in February 1974, when Yugoslavia beat Spain 1–0 in a play-off in Frankfurt after the countries had finished level on points and goal difference in their group.

There had been controversy over the qualification of Chile. They had been drawn in a play-off against the Soviet Union. The first leg in Moscow had ended in a 0-0 draw. The match had taken place on 26th September, shortly after a *coup d'état* in Chile saw a military overthrow of the Popular Unity government led by the democratic socialist Salvador Allende as the country's president. Military leader Augusto Pinochet replaced him.

The return leg had been due to take place at the Estadio Nacional in Santiago on 21st November, eight days after the Socceroos' victory over South Korea. The Soviets objected to having to play the match in a stadium where Pinochet had taken opponents, held them captive and then executed them. They called on FIFA to move the game to a neutral venue.

When Francisco Fluxa, president of the Chilean Football Federation, took FIFA delegates to inspect the stadium, the prisoners were hidden and the match was given permission following a cursory 10-minute tour. Prisoners were able to see the delegation through fences in the bowels of the stadium but were unable to alert them of their presence because the soldiers had guns pointed at their heads.

FIFA were appeased but the consequences were clear in the newspaper headlines – 'Come to Santiago or forfeit the game'. The Soviet Union refused to bow to FIFA's demands and declined to travel to Santiago. The world governing body, however, were not prepared to simply award Chile the tie. They insisted the home team would need to take to the field, against no one, and score a goal into an empty net.

The next day, the stands that had previously held political prisoners were sparsely populated with curious spectators to witness the 'ghost match'. They watched the Chilean forwards briefly pass the ball among themselves before captain Francisco 'Chamaco' Valdes apologetically kicked the ball into an empty net. Chile had qualified for the World Cup following an unedifying spectacle that reflected badly on both the new ruling junta and FIFA.

The Socceroos would not have to wait long to find out who they would meet on their World Cup debut. The draw was set for 5th January 1974, in Frankfurt. It took place at 9.30pm local time in HR Sendesaal, a music hall designed by German architect Gerhard Weber and which had been completed 20 years earlier. The draw was televised by Eurovision, shown live in 32 countries and watched by an estimated audience of 800 million people.

Rasic was representing the Socceroos. He was accompanied by Australian Soccer Federation secretary Brian Le Fevre and Tom Patrick, the Qantas employee who had been in charge of travel arrangements for several years stretching back to the 1967 Asian tour, which included the first trip to South Vietnam.

'I've seen some great events in my time but, at this time, this was simply amazing,' Rasic wrote in his autobiography. 'It was breathtaking. I was like a kid in a lolly shop. Of course, the world media was very demanding and almost suffocating. But I didn't care about them for everywhere you looked there was a famous face, a former great player or coach, television and movie stars, officials. And here I was, mixing with them. I was in heaven.'

Before the draw took place, FIFA had announced that the host nation, West Germany, and defending champions Brazil would be seeded and placed into the first position of Groups 1 and 2. The remaining two top-seeded teams, Uruguay and Italy, would be drawn into the first position of Groups 3 and 4.

Pot one consisted of 'Western nations' Scotland and the Netherlands and pot two of 'Eastern Europe', including Bulgaria, East Germany, Poland and Yugoslavia or Spain, who met for the final place the following month. It was decided that South American nations in pot three could not play in the same group during the first stage. That meant Argentina and Chile could not be paired against Brazil and Uruguay. Pot four was the 'Rest of the World', consisting of Australia, Haiti, Zaire and, inexplicably, Sweden.

The 'innocent hand' who made the draws was an 11-year-old boy, Detlef

Lange, a member of the Schoneberger Sangerknaben, a children's choir from Berlin. When the young boy pulled out East Germany in the same Group 1 as West Germany, hush descended over the hall before spontaneous applause broke out over the auditorium.

East Germany owed its origins to the Yalta Conference, held towards the end of World War Two in February 1945. The Allied nations of the United States, the United Kingdom and the Soviet Union agreed on dividing a defeated Nazi Germany into occupation zones, and on dividing Berlin, the German capital, among the Allied powers as well. As West Germany was reorganised and gained independence from its occupiers in

Australia were put into Group 1 alongside hosts West Germany, East Germany and Chile at the draw in Frankfurt

1949, the German Democratic Republic was established in East Germany in October of that year under the control of the Soviet Union.

Given West Germany did not even recognise the GDR as a proper country – the national tabloid *Bild-Zeitung* always referred to the East in inverted commas – the prospect of the two countries meeting for the first time in a full international was a major event. In the circumstances – the fact that Australia, the second-last country to be drawn out of the four pots, were also placed in Group 1 along with contentious qualifiers Chile – it was no surprise that this was largely overlooked.

The German media focused almost exclusively on the meeting between West and East. It was dubbed *Ein Kampf zwischen Brudern* – a 'struggle between brothers'. Was it irony, divine intervention, or merely the playing out of the cards dealt by chance that the schoolchild from the divided city had drawn the two countries together? 'It would mean a 90-minute reunification of Germany,' the press wrote.

The German media covered the fact that their team would be playing Australia when a photographer managed to arrange a shot outside the Olympic Stadium with West Germany and Bayern Munich's star striker Gerd Muller appearing nervously alongside a kangaroo borrowed from the local Hellabrunn Zoo.

Havelange, who later in 1974 succeeded Sir Stanley as FIFA president, subsequently made an unsubstantiated claim that the 1966 and 1974 World

West Germany's star striker Gerd Muller got an early chance to meet a native of Australia when he posed together with a kangaroo from the local zoo

Cups were fixed so that England and West Germany would win the trophy, respectively.

'One Germany would have been bad enough,' Sir Arthur joked following the draw. 'But two? I just can't believe it.'

Rasic, though, claimed to be 'delighted' and that he 'considered it a privilege and an honour to be in the same group as hosts West Germany. I was thinking of how much positive publicity Australian soccer would get. We would be matched against the two German sides and the eyes of the world would be focused on us. How good was that for a nation playing in its first World Cup finals?'

It was announced that the Socceroos would kick off their campaign on 14th June at the Volksparkstadion in Hamburg against East Germany, shortly after West Germany played Chile at the Olympic Stadium in West Berlin. Australia would remain in Hamburg for their next match, four days later, against West Germany. They would conclude Group 1 on 22nd June by relocating to West Berlin to meet Chile.

Rasic was realistic enough to realise that the Socceroos were unlikely to progress further, but he was determined that his team would give the best possible account of themselves. 'Crushing defeats, even against the best in the world, could undo all the good our qualification has achieved,' he warned.

Immediately after the draw, the Socceroos delegation flew to Hamburg to inspect the facilities. Rasic was impressed to discover that during their time in Germany's second-biggest city they would be based at Ochsenzoll, a suburb of

Hamburg and the base for Bundesliga club Hamburger SV. The training ground had 10 football pitches, sauna and spa facilities, medical centre, television room and restaurant. The party then travelled to West Berlin to tour their training base there.

From West Germany they flew to Switzerland, where Rasic had identified setting up a pre-World Cup training base in a place called Birr. He had picked it because it was a small village that would provide peace and the perfect opportunity to fine-tune final preparations. Rasic arranged for the Baeren Hotel to be booked out for the entire Australian party, including 22 players and his support staff.

Rasic, Le Fevre and Patrick continued their tour around Europe by travelling to Austria and Hungary. They had hoped to organise friendlies with each country, but failed as both had their schedules arranged for the next five years. They did manage to secure two warm-up games in Tel Aviv, against old rivals Israel, and a couple of matches against Swiss clubs St Gallen and Bern-based club Young Boys for when they were in training camp. It was also arranged that the Socceroos would stop off in Jakarta on their way to Europe for a match against Indonesia.

Lack of meaningful warm-up matches had been one of Rasic's biggest fears. A proposal to split Australia's squad into 'A' and 'B' teams, and have them compete in the Sydney First Division to ensure they spent the maximum time together before leaving for West Germany, never got off the drawing board.

Rasic was optimistic, though, that an attractive programme of matches could be lined up. 'I hope the Federation can secure six games at home before the team leaves Australia,' he told *Soccer World*. 'However, it is essential we play against teams whose style is similar to those we meet in the finals. We must select our opponents carefully. Every match must be treated as a full-scale rehearsal for our appearance in the finals.'

Rasic had also tentatively raised the prospect of his position as team coach being elevated to a full-time role in the build-up to the World Cup finals. This was swiftly knocked back. Instead, he accepted a new position with Pan-Hellenic, a club based in Sydney suburb Belmore and which had been founded by Greek immigrants in 1957.

As part of an effort to woo Rasic from Marconi-Fairfield, Pan-Hellenic's president, Michael Issakidis, gave him a new Volvo car and a salary of $25,000. Issakidis resigned shortly after appointing Rasic and in 2018 was sentenced to 10 years in prison for his involvement in a $135 million tax evasion case, the largest ever successfully prosecuted in Australia.

The Socceroos' World Cup year started with a series of friendly matches against Hungarian side Ferencvaros, although this was arranged by the New South Wales Federation and not the Australian Soccer Federation.

The team was the most famous and popular in Hungary. Ferencvaros had won the 1964–1965 edition of the Inter-Cities Fairs Cup after defeating Juventus 1–0 in Turin in the final. They also reached the final in the same competition in 1968, when they lost to Leeds United. In 1975, they would reach the final of the European Cup Winners' Cup, losing to Dynamo Kyiv.

It was no surprise that *Soccer World*, with its roots in the Hungarian expatriate community and under Hungarian *émigré* Andrew Dettre, devoted plenty of space to the visit of Ferencvaros, whose two-week tour included two matches against the Socceroos. The first, at Hindmarsh Stadium in Adelaide on 6th February, saw the visitors win 2–1 in front of a crowd of 12,454. It was followed, four days later, by a game at the Sydney Sports Ground, where 15,945 fans watched a goalless draw.

The matches provided an opportunity for Rasic to try out the 4-4-2 formation he planned to use at the World Cup, with a defence of Doug Utjesenovic, Peter Wilson, Manfred Schaefer and Col Curran.

Before the opening match in the series, German journalist Peter Bizer travelled to Australia to do a television feature on the Socceroos, specifically Schaefer, whose upcoming appearance at the World Cup was already creating interest in the land of his birth.

'Nobody in Germany knew the names of any Australian players,' Bizer said. 'Only insiders took notice of the Socceros' 3–1 victory over Greece in 1970. We wanted to produce a story for German television about the Socceroos. We had

A German television crew arrived in Australia in February 1974 to find out more about the Socceroos

read somewhere that there was even a German on the national team who earned his living as a milkman.

'The formidable photographer Anton Czermak – he emigrated from Czechoslovakia to Australia in 1968 – quickly contacted Rale Rasic. What an impressive man Rale was. Just 38 years old. Good-looking, with the manners of a cosmopolitan. Open-minded and cooperative, full of energy and optimism. And immediately likeable with his Bosnian accent. In Germany we call someone like that a "people catcher".

'We filmed a couple of exercise games for our TV report and interviewed trainer Les Scheinflug in his native German language.

'In the eyes of the Australians, soccer did not appear to be the number one sport, as it usually does in the rest of the world. Names like Peter Wilson, Jimmy Mackay, Ray Richards, Attila Abonyi or Manfred Schafer only had a sound for real soccer fans like immigrants from United Kingdom, Germany, Hungary or Italy.'

On the morning before the opening game in Adelaide, the Australian squad were also accompanied by an unexpected guest during a light practice match. British rock star Rod Stewart was performing in the city and staying in the same hotel as the Socceroos, and Bizer recalled how the keen Celtic and Scotland supporter 'suddenly appeared during a training session'.

'Rale Rasic invited him to practise with the team and his talent was immediately evident,' Bizer said. 'It is well known that Stewart wanted to become a professional footballer before his career as a musician.'

Helena Jasinski, a young law student at the University of Adelaide,

Socceroos coach Rale Rasic, left, impressed visiting German journalist Peter Bizer, right, who found him 'full of energy'

appeared in Bizer's film modelling a tee-shirt with the images of 'Tip and Tap', the West Germany 1974 mascots. She also recalled Stewart training with the Socceroos. 'Rod Stewart spent a good three quarters of an hour kicking the soccer ball around with the team, in parklands adjacent to the hotel,' she said.

The following month, on 20th March, at the Sydney Sports Ground, the Socceroos took on an Auckland XI in the last match before Rasic named his preliminary squad for the World Cup. A 0–0 draw did not inspire confidence, with *Soccer World* headlining it as 'ANOTHER "ROO SHOCKER"'. The *Age* in Melbourne claimed that Australia had played 'like a lot of old sheilas'.

The report by Lou Gautier in *Soccer World* noted that before the game, the players' pay demands to take part in the World Cup had been made public. 'Cruel jeers and sarcastic shouts of "You want $8,000 for THAT" echoed around the depressingly empty Sydney Sports Ground as the Socceroos laboriously inched their way to an inglorious 0–0 draw.

'The 2,975 spectators, who all deserve medals for sitting through a pathetically inept performance, let the players know in no uncertain terms what they thought of their financial demands for the World Cup,' Gautier wrote.

Many feared that the Australian Soccer Federation were repeating past mistakes by not preparing adequately for the tests ahead. In an opinion piece next to Gautier's match report, Dettre, under his pen name, Mike Renwick, warned 'Australia's World Cup preparations are in a total shambles'.

He claimed that the Federation 'has tragically failed in ensuring that our team would travel to Germany well braced and seasoned for the toughest tests imaginable'.

CHAPTER TWELVE

Advance Australia Fair

When Rale Rasic announced his preliminary squad of 40 for the FIFA World Cup finals at the end of March 1974, it contained no surprises.

It included almost every member of the previous year's successful qualifying campaign. The notable exception was Ron Corry, who was not named among the four goalkeepers. He had played in the first four of the Socceroos' World Cup matches but was dropped after the 3–3 draw against New Zealand in Sydney.

Jim Fraser, his replacement for the rest of the World Cup matches, was selected along with Jack Reilly, who had not played since the Socceroos' Asian tour of October 1972, and Allan Maher and Jim Milisavljevic, who were both uncapped.

'I had no problem with that,' Corry claimed later. 'I would have thought that I'd be one of the three to go to Germany, but I did not pick the team. I was disappointed but that's football.'

The rest of the preliminary squad were drawn from Australia's under-23 team, although there were no expectations that any of them would be travelling to West Germany 1974.

Soccer World broke down the numbers behind the squad. They noted that 31 of the players were from New South Wales, although nine originally hailed from Victoria and one from Queensland. Of the 40, 16 were originally from Australia, with 24 having been born abroad. Of those born outside Australia, 10 were from Scotland, six from England, five from Yugoslavia, and one each from Germany, Hungary and South Africa.

Soccer World also listed the players' full-time jobs. These included Atti Abonyi as a tailor's cutter, Peter Wilson as a car salesman, Johnny Warren as a public relations officer, Jimmy Mackay as a roof plumber, Jimmy Rooney as a despatch clerk, Col Curran as a driver, Johnny Watkiss as a scrap metal dealer, Harry Williams as a welfare officer and, of course, Manfred Schaffer as a milk vendor.

Undoubtedly, the most exotic occupation of all the players chosen was Fraser, whom *Soccer World* listed as being a 'private enquiry agent'. It led to Wilson dubbing him 'Australia's answer to Philip Marlowe' – the fictional private eye character created by novelist Raymond Chandler.

There continued to be alarm about the lack of matches arranged by the Australian Soccer Federation before the Socceroos left for Europe. On 5th

April, Andrew Dettre, under his pen name, Mike Renwick, wrote a front-page story for *Soccer World* under the headline 'SOCCEROOS ARE BEING LED TO CUP SLAUGHTER!'

Dettre noted that Australia's Group 1 opponents Chile were already in a training camp, and East Germany were playing international friendlies almost every Wednesday in the run-up to the start of the World Cup to prepare themselves. Defending champions Brazil had been together since March, and Poland expected to play eight warm-up matches. Even fellow debutants Haiti had an intensive series of games to prepare themselves, and Zaire had been together for a while to get ready. The Socceroos, meanwhile, were occasionally meeting up on a Wednesday evening for a training session.

'Unbelievably, our officialdom is still totally apathetic and seemingly unaware of the tasks the team must face in less than 80 days,' Dettre wrote. 'Facing either Germany, even with a full preparation, is always a frightening proposition; without any proper preparation, it's sheer suicide.'

Dettre blamed the New South Wales clubs, who were refusing to release their players, and urged Australian Soccer Federation president Sir Arthur George to read them the 'riot act' to avoid the Socceroos 'slow witting its way to a World Cup fiasco'.

Dettre wanted any 'little parochial club official' who 'raises objection' to be outed 'so that we will know at the end of June just who is to be blamed for our pending catastrophe and who should be expurgated from our soccer for good.'

The piece appeared to have been prompted by a chance meeting Dettre had at the airport with Rasic a few days earlier. In his 'Small Talk' column, published in the same edition of *Soccer World*, Dettre claimed that Rasic was 'increasingly pessimistic' about the Socceroos' chances in West Germany and 'readily accepts that even a major disaster is now a possibility'.

Dettre wrote that 'I fear for him' and noted of Rasic that it seemed 'because of the muddle of officialdom in our World Cup preparations he has lost his appetite for a fight.'

With even *Soccer World* having already speculated as to who would replace the coach after the World Cup, Dettre admitted that 'one can only sympathise with Rasic for the botch our administration has created for him: the incredible lack of preparations throughout 1974. But he must now live with the unhappy fact and salvage whatever he can through cool thinking and planning.

'Should the team flop in the Cup, Rasic will be the first crucified, not the little known or totally obscure officials who had all but sabotaged our preparations. So far, after each and every World Cup bid, Australia's national coach vanished from the scene. It would be a pity if Rasic followed them.'

At the last minute, the Australian Soccer Federation managed to arrange for Uruguay to travel to Australia to play two friendlies in Melbourne and Sydney

Rale Rasic's hopes of an intense period of preparation before West Germany 1974 soon disappeared

at the end of April. The South American team had twice lifted the World Cup. The first had been in the inaugural tournament they had staged in 1930 and then again in 1950 when they shocked hosts Brazil.

At the 1970 World Cup in Mexico, Uruguay had reached the semi-finals, losing 3–1 to Brazil, and ultimately finished fourth after West Germany defeated them 1–0 in the third-place play-off. They were among the four seeded teams for West Germany 1974 and considered one of the favourites.

The Uruguay squad to travel to Australia was a mixture of established players and promising youngsters as those playing in Europe were not released by their clubs. The visit to Australia was to mark the end of a four-week tour around Central America and Asia. The team's only defeat in nine matches had been 2–1 to Indonesia in Jakarta.

Even with that setback, Uruguay were likely to be more match ready than the Socceroos, who had not played an international match since that famous night in Hong Kong more than five months previously when Mackay's goal against South Korea had propelled them to the FIFA World Cup finals.

The opening match was scheduled to take place at Olympic Park in Melbourne on 25th April – Anzac Day. The event takes place annually to mark the anniversary of the day when Australian and New Zealand soldiers landed on Gallipoli in 1915 as part of the Allies' invasion during World War One. It is a National Day of Remembrance that commemorates all Australians and New Zealanders who served and died in all wars.

Before the matches against Uruguay, Fraser had informed Rasic that he would not be able to commit to taking part in the World Cup. The business partner of the dog security firm linked to the building trade that Fraser ran had threatened to sue him if he took time off work to prepare for the finals. Fraser feared it could have put in jeopardy the jobs of 150 people.

'Every time I went away the business lost money,' Fraser told SBS Sport in 2018. 'My partner did not understand what football meant to me and kept telling me we were losing money, and it was unfair and if I went to the World Cup the staff could lose their jobs. My wife was under a lot of pressure because she was taking all the calls and my partner even threatened to sue me if I went away again.

'Looking back, I would have loved to change my mind because I desperately wanted to go to Germany. Did the decision affect my life? Of course it did, it's in my mind most days. But I don't think I could have changed my decision.

Goalkeeper Jim Fraser combined playing as a goalkeeper with running a security dog business that required so much time he missed the World Cup finals

'I used to hate it whenever I was asked the question why I was not going. Some English papers even poked fun at me, saying Australia's goalkeeper was staying away from the World Cup to mind his dog. I am still disappointed, but I have come to terms with the fact that I could not have made the decision any other way.'

Fraser's love of dogs later saw him become a professional dog trainer, dealing with behavioural problems for domestic pets through home training programmes. He operated a canine behaviour clinic for the New South Wales Royal Society for the Protection of Cruelty to Animals and was a consultant for Guide Dogs for the Blind. Fraser even co-authored a canine behaviour book, *My Dog*, and wrote *Tales of Wagging Tails – Canine Short Stories*.

Fraser's decision opened the door for Jack Reilly to take over as Australia's number one. Reilly had himself fallen out of favour with Rasic the previous year because of his business commitments in the financial sector. He had told Rasic that he could not guarantee he would be available for training camps and matches unless he was given four weeks' notice.

Reilly had been born in 1943, during World War Two, in Stonehaven, a small town on Scotland's north-east coast. A month before his birth, his father, a paratrooper, was killed in France. It left his mother a widow and him as an only child to support.

Like Fraser, Reilly had not imagined himself ending up as a goalkeeper. He had started playing football as a six-year-old and fancied himself as a winger. The coach of the local team in Stonehaven, an undertaker, was a former goalkeeper and saw promise in Reilly.

Reilly joined Scottish First Division club Hibernian, where the manager was Jock Stein, later to guide Celtic to the 1967 European Cup. The young goalkeeper played only two league matches for Hibernian and eventually moved to the United States to play for Washington Wizards.

Reilly arrived in Australia in 1969, just in time to cash in on the mining boom. He made money on a company called Poseidon, whose shares jumped from 80 cents to more than $200. His interest in the money markets led to Reilly joining First Federation Discount Company, one of the nine authorised dealers controlling liquidity of the Australian financial system. It was a high-pressured job that saw him dealing daily with millions of dollars in trading government bonds and treasury notes.

After arriving in Melbourne, Reilly started playing with the Juventus Club before being drawn in 1972 to St George Budapest in Sydney by Rasic. 'He could read people better than most,' Reilly said. 'He knew what made them tick.'

Reilly spent one season with St George Budapest before he transferred to Melbourne Hakoah in early 1972, for what was an Australian then record fee for a goalkeeper of $6,000.

Reilly's performance in the 0–0 draw against Uruguay on 25th April at Olympic Park in Melbourne, before a crowd of 20,283, delighted Rasic. He admitted afterwards that he had feared the Socceroos could have been completely overwhelmed, having not played in such a high-profile match for so long, by a side ranked among the best in the world. 'The boys were superb and showed what they were capable of against a quality side,' Rasic said.

Rasic claimed he was feeling 'one hundred foot tall', but his happiness was shattered by an incident in the dressing room afterwards that he admitted almost certainly sealed the decision by Sir Arthur to fire him after the World Cup. Following the match, the Australian Soccer Federation president took Bob Hawke, then head of the Australian Council of Trade Unions and a future prime minister, to meet the players.

While he was in the dressing room, Sir Arthur, cigar in mouth, whispered in Rasic's ear and asked him for the names of the 22 players that he had selected for the final squad for the World Cup. When Rasic refused, Sir Arthur demanded he share the names with him. Rasic retaliated by grabbing Sir Arthur by the neck and pushing him out of the dressing room while the players chanted 'Out, out, out.' As he was thrown out of the door, Sir Arthur shouted at Rasic, 'I will sack you.'

Hawke was left standing alone in the changing room. 'Shit, where the hell am I?' he asked. Rasic told him to get out too.

When the Socceroos travelled to Sydney for the next game against Uruguay two days later, Rasic called Sir Arthur to apologise for an incident he admitted he 'regretted' for the rest of his life. The head of the Australian Soccer Federation was not in a forgiving mood. 'When I tell you to do something, you do it,' he told Rasic before slamming the phone down.

When Rasic later looked back on why his relationship with Sir Arthur deteriorated, having started so promisingly when he was appointed Australian coach in 1970, he identified his close relationship with Gough Whitlam as a key factor.

Sir Arthur was very much in the political camp of Liberal, who by 1972 had been part of a coalition government for 23 years. The coalition had followed a series of conservative policies that failed to keep up with how Australia had developed as a result of economic prosperity and immigration. The Liberal-Country Party coalition had won nine consecutive elections, and Robert Menzies had served as Australia's longest-serving prime minister, being in power between 1949 and 1966.

Rasic once described Sir Arthur as a 'brutal' Liberal. He recalled himself being introduced by Sir Arthur to New South Wales Liberal premier Sir Robert Askin as 'the greatest coach and the biggest son of a bitch'. Rasic claimed he shook Sir Robert's hand and replied: 'Pleasure to meet another son of a bitch.' Sir Robert laughed and took it in good spirit, Rasic claimed. Sir Arthur was less impressed and believed he had been made to look a fool.

The Australian Labor Party had appointed Whitlam as its leader following its defeat in the 1966 election. Whitlam was a former barrister who had served as a Royal Australian Air Force navigator during World War Two. Over the six years following his appointment to lead the Labor Party, he developed a series of reformist and socially progressive initiatives and policies. Among the things Whitlam advocated was the end of military conscription and Australian involvement in the Vietnam War, the institution of universal health care and free university education, and the implementation of legal aid programmes.

Like many newcomers to the country, Rasic was inspired by Whitlam's vision of how Australia should look. Everything came together under the slogan 'It's Time', and when Whitlam addressed a political rally at the Sydney Opera House shortly before the election in December 1972, Rasic was one of eight national figures who appeared to offer him their support. Rasic spoke for three minutes at the rally about how good for sport Whitlam would be as prime minister.

Rasic was not a member of the Labor Party but had met Whitlam on several occasions. 'I liked his stature, his sense of humour, his intelligence and his vision,' Rasic wrote in his autobiography.

The Opera House event was televised across Australia, and Rasic's presence was inevitably spotted by Sir Arthur. At the next meeting between the two, Sir Arthur warned Rasic to stop publicly supporting Whitlam. It led to an angry exchange, which ended with Rasic pointing his finger at Sir Arthur and telling him to 'mind his own business'.

Almost everyone below the top officials at the Australian Soccer Federation admired Whitlam because he took an interest in sport, especially soccer. Early initiatives, upon being elected with 49.6 per cent of the vote, included financial support for soccer in Australia. The new government funded an under-23 Socceroos team to visit Indonesia on a friendship trip and also backed an Australian junior championship in 1973.

'Soccer in particular received more attention from the Whitlam government than it did from their predecessors in 72 years,' reported *Soccer World*.

Whitlam's key policies included abandoning what he saw as British colonial relics and replacing them with distinctively Australian symbols. These included Australia abandoning *God Save the Queen* as its national anthem. On Australia Day in 1973, Whitlam announced an 'Australian National Anthem Quest' and invited words and music from the public that might be suitable as Australia's new national anthem. More than 2,500 suggestions for lyrics were received and submitted to the Australia Council for the Arts, and referred to a judging committee.

The committee felt, however, that none of the submissions bettered any of Australia's three unofficial national songs – *Advance Australia Fair*, *Waltzing Matilda* and *Song of Australia*. The government conducted a nationwide poll, which found that 51 per cent of the 60,000 asked preferred *Advance Australia Fair*, 20 per cent wanted *Waltzing Matilda*, and 14 per cent liked *Song of Australia*.

On 9th April 1974, Whitlam announced in Parliament that *Advance Australia Fair* would be the new national anthem and was to be used on all occasions. In truth, it had been the unofficial national anthem for years since it was first performed in public in 1878. The Australian Broadcasting Commission used it to announce its news bulletins until 1952. It was also frequently played at the start or end of official functions and in cinemas. There had even been an unsuccessful campaign before the 1956 Olympic Games, staged in Melbourne, for *Advance Australia Fair* to be played at ceremonies involving Australian gold medallists.

Before the first match against Uruguay in Melbourne, the president of the Victoria branch of the Returned & Services League of Australia, an independent support organisation for people who have served in the Australian military, had defied an order from the federal government for his band to play *Advance Australia Fair*. They instead stuck to *God Save the Queen*.

The band's director admitted 'I did it deliberately. I believe the Australian people haven't yet given the federal government the authority to change our national anthem. It's a fraud.'

For the return match against Uruguay on 27th April at the Sydney Cricket Ground, the crowd included Whitlam. This time, the Socceroos lined up to *Advance Australia Fair*. It remained a matter of great pride to Rasic that it was his multicultural squad, a bunch of immigrants who had put wogball on the map in Australia, who were the first national sports team to officially christen the new national anthem.

It was fitting, bearing in mind the number of Scots in the side, that *Advance Australia Fair* had been written by Glasgow-born composer Peter Dodds McCormick, who had emigrated to Sydney in 1855 at the age of 22.

Rasic was stood next to Whitlam during the playing of the song and noticed tears rolling down the cheeks of the prime minister. 'You hear the national anthem five or six times a day. How come you have these tears?' Rasic asked Whitlam. He replied: 'These moments you have no control over. That's a fascinating feeling and I am proud of it.' 'I understood. From that day on I get tears in my eyes when I hear *Advance Australia Fair*,' said Rasic.

It had already been announced in March that, following consultation between the Australian Foreign Affairs Department in Canberra and the Australian Soccer Federation, *Advance Australia Fair* would be the national anthem played before the Socceroos' matches at the World Cup.

Rasic wanted his players to take pride in the new national anthem and to learn the words. 'I drilled into them the importance of how you look. When the national anthem was on you had to have arms by your side,' he said. 'I made clear, if you are not singing, you don't have to sing, but you stand still.

'Johnny Warren was a very nervous person, but I said "Johnny, 40 seconds for your country. That's your country and you should represent it. The national anthem is a bible for all of us Australians, and you must obey that." Johnny stood still.'

The opening line of *Advance Australia Fair* at that time was 'Australia's sons, let us rejoice', which is something the Socceroos should have been doing after completing a 2–0 victory over Uruguay in their final match on home soil before leaving for the World Cup finals.

In front of an ecstatic crowd of 23,302, goals from Ray Baartz and Peter Ollerton in the 59th and 84th minutes, respectively, gave Australia one of their best wins against the two-time world champions and a side who had reached the World Cup semi-finals just four years earlier.

Baartz's goal was spectacular, a magnificent shot from 25 metres, which showed why Rasic rated him so highly. He had claimed that Baartz was as important to Australia as Pele was to Brazil, Johan Cruyff to the Netherlands and Franz Beckenbauer to West Germany. At 27, Baartz was entering the best form of his life as he prepared for the World Cup.

Col Curran crosses the ball during Australia's 2-0 victory over Uruguay in Sydney in April 1974

After turning down the opportunity to stay in England with Manchester United and returning home, where Baartz joined Sydney Hakoah for a then Australian record of $5,600, he remained at the club for his whole career. He scored 211 goals in 236 matches, a phenomenal figure at any level, and why he was so highly regarded by Rasic.

Baartz had been one of the original team picked for the Asian tour in 1967 and in the seven years since, had played a vital role on many occasions. His performance against Uruguay was one of his best in the green and gold. Baartz was proving unplayable, so the Uruguayans decided to take matters into their own hands.

The first match had been notable for the rough approach the Uruguayans had adopted. This included targeting Manfred Schaefer, a defender considered to be the toughest of all the Socceroos, leading to him being forced off the field and substituted after only 37 minutes following a foul.

The fouls and cynical challenges continued in the second game, including in the first half with Uruguayan Luis Garisto blocking Baartz as he ran into the penalty area. The side of Garisto's hand caught Baartz across the throat in an action that Rasic described as a 'karate chop'.

Baartz admitted that he never

Ray Baartz celebrates scoring the Socceroos' first goal in Sydney against two-time World Cup winners Uruguay

saw the incident coming. 'I was choked,' he said. 'I went down, but after a few minutes' treatment got up and played on.' Baartz reported at half-time he had a sore head but was given a couple of aspirins and went out for the second half to score his stunning goal.

Baartz's goal only made Garisto, nicknamed in his homeland *El Loco*, Spanish slang for crazy, more determined to stop him. A quarter of an hour after Baartz had put the Socceroos ahead, he and Garisto exchanged words. Baartz finished by pointing at the scoreboard to show his rival who was winning and 'he turned round and hit me flat on the chin. Bang!'

Local referee Don Campbell did not see the incident, but the linesman did and drew it to his attention. Socceroos' team doctor Brian Corrigan raced onto the pitch to begin treating Baartz. 'While I was tending to Ray, who was lying very groggy on the ground, I witnessed an astounding incident,' Corrigan wrote in his autobiography, T*he Life of Brian.* 'The Uruguayan captain took their striker Fernando Morena around behind the referee and gave him a swift hard clout on the mouth.'

The bloodied Morena was then paraded in front of Campbell as evidence that Baartz had attacked him first – an act of treachery the official saw through. Campbell was a former Scottish schoolboy international, scoring the winning goal for his country against England at Wembley Stadium in 1951, before emigrating to Australia in 1964. He was officiating only his second international match, having taken charge of the Socceroos' 3–1 defeat to Bulgaria in Adelaide the previous year.

Campbell was being jostled and pushed by the Uruguayan players but managed to extricate himself to send off Garisto. It was the first red card issued in Australia since they had been introduced for international football four years earlier at the 1970 World Cup in Mexico. Garisto refused to leave the pitch and it briefly looked like his teammates may walk off in protest. They were persuaded to continue, although the match ended with more angry protests when Morena had a late goal disallowed for handball.

Concerned players look on as Ray Baartz receives medical treatment after being attacked for the second time in the match against Uruguay

Baartz had initially wanted to continue playing after being felled for the second time by Garisto, but Corrigan ruled this time he was too unwell. The next morning, after waking up, Baartz called Corrigan to tell him that he was suffering from a headache and felt weak down one side of his body. He was rushed to North Shore Hospital in Sydney, where emergency tests revealed that the artery on the right side, which supplied blood to the brain, had been torn by the karate blow and was blocked. Baartz slipped into unconsciousness for two days and at one point doctors were concerned for his life.

When Baartz came round, the doctors at the hospital warned him that another blow to his throat could kill him. His football career was over after 48 appearances for the Socceroos and a record 18 goals. At the time, his wife, Sue, was pregnant with their second child. The fear of what could have been tempered any anger Baartz felt at the end of his career. 'They told me I was unlucky to be hit like that, but so lucky I didn't die,' he said. 'I'm grateful I came out with my faculties intact.'

The Australian Soccer Federation appealed to FIFA for them to ban Garisto from the World Cup. There was no action ever taken against him and he was allowed to travel to West Germany, where Uruguay

The morning after the match, Ray Baartz was rushed to hospital

finished bottom of Group 3, despite being the seeded team. Baartz never received an apology from Garisto for the harm he caused him, but did not hold a grudge. 'The player ... was trying to stop me, but did not mean to do the damage he did,' Baartz said.

CHAPTER THIRTEEN

Why are these kangaroos here?

Rale Rasic had hoped that Ray Baartz would make a miraculous recovery so he could name him in the final Socceroos squad of 22 for the FIFA World Cup finals. He left officially announcing those who would be on the plane to West Germany 1974 until as late as possible, before finally admitting that Baartz would not be fit.

Rasic fought hard, though, with the Australian Soccer Federation to be allowed to add Baartz as a non-playing member of the party that would travel to Europe. The Federation was reluctant at first to give in to the demand as they claimed it would set a precedent if a player got injured in the future. Rasic would not give up. 'I told the suits, "Baartz is not any other player,"' he said. 'I got my way and Baartz came with us to Germany.'

The presence of Baartz was a 'stroke of genius in terms of team morale', Johnny Warren believed. Adrian Alston said 'it was fantastic to see him here. It was very touching.' Alston also admitted 'it must have been very hard for him.'

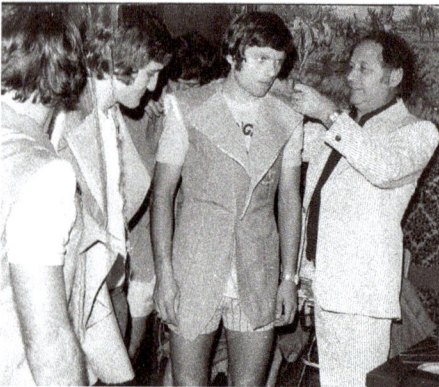

The Socceroos were supplied with made-to-measure suits before West Germany 1974

Australia set off on their World Cup adventure from Sydney on 20th May

Baartz confirmed it was good to be with his old mates but missed the involvement of playing. 'It was extremely tough to watch them go round, and it probably was even harder to take than when I was told in hospital that I should not play again,' he said.

In the background, Warren continued to be upset that he had not been restored to the captaincy. But Rasic had complete faith in Peter Wilson, who had led the Socceroos throughout the successful qualifying campaign. Warren was made vice-captain, but he never appeared to get over the fact he was not chosen to lead out the Socceroos when they made their World Cup debut.

'Even now, I feel I should have been captain, so it's something that I look back on with a great deal of disappointment and regret,' he wrote in his autobiography, *Sheilas, Wogs and Poofters*, published in 2002.

The Australian squad for the 1974 World Cup finals left Sydney on 20th May. They stopped off on the way in Jakarta, where the next day they met Indonesia in a friendly at the Senayan Stadium. Rasic played a full team in a hard-fought match, with goals from Wilson and another defender, Col Curran, in the 77th and 80th minutes, respectively, giving them a 2–1 victory in front of a crowd of 62,000 fans. There was unwelcome news for Curran as, after his goal, he injured his knee ligaments and was left doubtful for the World Cup.

From Jakarta, the Socceroos travelled to Israel for two more warm-up games in a case of role reversal. Four years earlier, Israel had visited Australia for a series of friendly matches as they had prepared for their World Cup finals debut at Mexico 1970.

The Socceroos lost 2-1 to Israel in their final international fixture before the World Cup

The first of the two matches, at Bloomfield Stadium in Jaffa on 28th May, saw the hosts win 2–1, with Australia's consolation goal coming from Jimmy Mackay in the 89th minute after Yehoshua Feigenbaum had scored twice for

Israel. Rasic missed the game as he was in Leipzig watching future opponents East Germany draw 1–1 with England.

The Socceroos were due to meet Israel in a second match in Jerusalem two days later, but the match was called off. When they inspected the pitch, Australian officials discovered there were pieces of broken glass all over it. On the insistence of team doctor Brian Corrigan, Australia refused to take to the field. 'That decision almost caused a riot, but the players' well-being was paramount,' Corrigan said.

Jimmy Mackay gets a ride on a camel during Australia's visit to Israel after a match in Jerusalem was cancelled

On the way to Tel Aviv, the Australian players had been teasing Ray Richards about his dark appearance and big moustache. They warned him that the Israeli security forces might mistake him for a terrorist. Authorities in Israel were still on high alert following the Yom Kippur War the previous October. A surprise attack on Israeli territory by Arab coalition forces had left more than 2,500 Israeli soldiers dead. The Israelis fought back and won, but the situation had considerably increased tensions in the region.

When the Australian party landed, the Israelis did indeed detain Richards as, unfortunately for him, he fitted the description of a suspected terrorist. 'His cause may not have been helped by some of his teammates agreeing with the police that he was the man they were after,' Corrigan admitted. In the end, Richards was released after the Israeli Football Association intervened. Tight security was something the Socceroos would need to get used to when they arrived in West Germany.

After watching East Germany in Leipzig, Rasic drove to Herzogenaurach in Bavaria, where the sportswear company Adidas was based. They gave the Socceroos coach 210 pairs of boots for the players. Adidas even provided a Mercedes large enough to fit all the new kit for Rasic to travel to the Socceroos' training base in Switzerland.

Ray Richards, left, was mistaken for a suspected terrorist in Tel Aviv

The green and gold shirts that Australia would be wearing in the World Cup finals would be unique and, later, considered a design classic. They were supplied by Umbro, the English company who had kitted out both Brazil and England when they had lifted the World Cup in 1958 and 1966, respectively.

The Australian Soccer Federation had a deal with Umbro, who were in league with Adidas at the time. They were the German firm's sole footwear distributor in the United Kingdom while providing textiles expertise in return.

Adidas wanted a presence in the Australian market, and the company's famous three stripes on the national team shirt gave them a profile. The shirt was actually an Umbro airtex jersey, carrying the double-diamond logo with three stripes added down the sleeves. This was in contravention of the rules for the World Cup, which stated that only one type of branding was allowed on each kit element. Special permission was granted to Australia to wear the shirt.

Adidas also supplied the holdalls given to each member of the Socceroos party going to West Germany, each one emblazoned with '1974 AUSTRALIAN WORLD CUP TEAM'.

The squad travelled in style after Sydney tailors Borotex held special fittings so that each member had a made-to-measure suit for their journey to the World Cup.

After the World Cup was finished, Umbro and Adidas used Australia in joint marketing campaigns in the United Kingdom. The Socceroos appeared alongside Scotland, West Germany and the Netherlands, who had contested the final won 2–1 by the hosts. There were pictures of all four teams, with the one of Australia featuring Alston running away from a defender in the Socceroos' opening match against East Germany.

The Socceroos were in distinguished company, with Umbro and Adidas supplying its kit and equipment

Mind you, there were probably questions asked at the headquarters of Adidas when they realised from the picture that Alston was wearing boots manufactured by Japanese company Asics.

'Umbro were again associated with another first, they were the sportswear chosen by Australia to make their initial appearance in the World Cup finals,' it was proclaimed in adverts. 'But then that's hardly surprising since Umbro are already well known "down under" through their factories there.'

For the 2014 World Cup finals in Brazil, the kit worn by the Socceroos was supplied by Nike but paid tribute to the 1974 squad. It featured the return of white socks, and a green collar resembled the uniform worn by Australia in West Germany. Inside the back of the neck of the predominantly yellow jersey was a quote from Wilson: 'We can do the impossible.'

Rasic and Richards already had relationships with Adidas, and their names were used in an advert for the German company that appeared on the back cover of a special World Cup souvenir brochure produced by Andrew Dettre and Lou Gautier for *Soccer World*. The advert said: 'Ray Richards does. So does Rale Rasic and other Australian Soccer team stars. Because they're the fastest, lightest, most flexible boots in the game.'

Rasic and Richards also appeared alongside each other in another advert in the brochure for the sports shop they ran together – a commercial arrangement that would surely not be allowed today. Four-R Sportsworld – named after both their initials – was located at Fairfield in Western Sydney. It promised to offer 'best deals in team strips and soccer equipment', and its suppliers included Bukta, Gordon Banks Boots, Adidas and Gola.

The two ran the company together until 1975 when Richards bought out Rasic. Canterbury Bulldogs rugby league player Steve Want later got involved in the company, which changed its name to Sports Factory and continues to trade online.

Rale Rasic and Ray Richards used the opportunity of the Socceroos' World Cup participation to promote the sports shop they owned together

The *Soccer World* brochure also included adverts for Ampol, the oil company founded by former Australian Soccer Federation president Sir William

Walkley, which had offered so much support to the sport. There was also an advert for Hall-Kalman Pty. Ltd, the meat manufacturer that had provided the steaks Rasic had fed to the Socceroos since becoming coach and which had nearly caused a diplomatic incident in Tehran before the World Cup qualifying match.

There was also a thank-you message from the Australian Soccer Federation, featuring the now familiar Socceroo kangaroo, to the sponsors who had contributed $100,000 to the qualifying campaign.

The unprecedented attention focused on the Socceroos also led to them enjoying the unusual experience of appearing on football stickers that could be put into albums and collected by youngsters around the world.

At the time, there were two companies manufacturing these stickers. FKS Stickers, printed in Spain and distributed in England, had produced the first World Cup album for the 1966 World Cup. Then, for Mexico 1970, Italian company Panini had published the first official FIFA sticker album and followed it up with one for West Germany 1974.

Panini gave more space to the bigger countries than the smaller ones. So, while hosts West Germany, for example, got 14 slots for players, Australia only got six. These included goalkeeper Jim Fraser, who withdrew due to his business commitments, and Baartz, ruled out through injury. Panini did include the player whose goal had got the Socceroos to West Germany 1974 but spelt it 'Jim McKay' – just as *Soccer World* had in the early days of his international career. The other players who featured were Wilson, Manfred Schaefer and Richards.

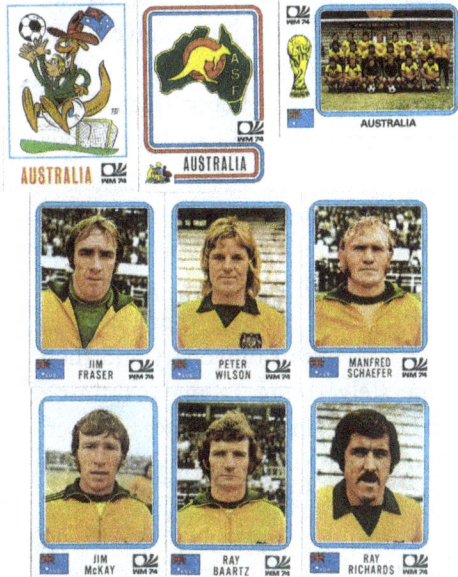

The FKS album, which cost 15 pence to buy in the United Kingdom, with eight stickers in a packet for three pence, was more inclusive and featured 16 players from each of the competing nations. The album actually included 17 teams, since it was not certain at the time of going to press whether Spain or Yugoslavia would qualify, subject to a play-off, so both teams

Panini did not include the full Socceroos squad in its sticker album for West Germany 1974

appeared. FKS managed to spell Mackay correctly, but also included Fraser and Baartz.

Waddington Games also announced that to mark the Socceroos World Cup debut, Subbuteo, the popular tabletop game in which players simulate football by flicking miniature players with their fingers, were releasing a set of the Australian team. Numbered 174 in the Subbuteo catalogue, schoolboys in Britain could buy their own version of the Socceroos for just 50 pence. One slight historical inaccuracy was that Subbuteo always painted Australia wearing yellow socks rather than the white they usually wore at that time.

Rasic arrived at the Baeren Hotel in Birr with his carful of new football boots, ready to meet his players coming from Israel. As instructed, the base had been booked out exclusively for the Socceroos and the small group of support staff accompanying them. That was a shock to Australian Soccer Federation officials and media, who assumed they would be staying in the same hotel, only to have to find alternative accommodation.

To the Socceroos, who had spent the past few years travelling around the world playing in dangerous countries where adequate facilities were at a premium, what they were presented with in Switzerland was a revelation. The pitches were impeccably manicured, there was plenty of basic equipment like goals, nets and balls, dressing rooms had hot water and there was certainly no danger of being blown up during training by treading on a stray landmine.

'Everyone felt fit and inspired during our lead-up games in Switzerland,' said Warren. 'We were given our opportunity to train like professionals and were actually being treated like professionals for the first time in our lives.

'We weren't "sheilas", "wogs" and "poofters" – we were accorded the same respect as the greats of football. That was it. There was no going to work or university and then desperately trying to make training on time. All our attention was focused on improving our skills, our fitness and our overall performance.'

A standout memory of Doug Utjesenovic from the training camp is that it was the first time many players had been offered mineral water to help them rehydrate. 'As typical Aussies, we just drank Coke, and when some of our Anglo-Saxon members in the squad

Jimmy Mackay, Jimmy Rooney, Rale Rasic, Johnny Warren and Doug Utjesenovic pose on a tractor at their training camp in Switzerland

saw people drinking water they sneered and said, "Look at these stupid wogs, drinking mineral water," he said. "But when they tried it they actually liked it."

The Socceroos won all three of their warm-up games in Switzerland. They beat St. Gallen 4–1 in their opening match on 4th June, with Alston hitting a hat-trick with goals in the 69th, 77th and 78th minutes. That was followed two days later with a 2–0 victory over Young Boys with Richards and Abonyi scoring. An additional match was added to the programme on 8th June, when the Socceroos beat Neuchatel Xamax 1–0 thanks to another goal from Richards.

After 10 days of preparing in the peace and tranquillity of a small Swiss Alpine town, it was time for the Socceroos to travel to West Germany to make their debut at the World Cup finals.

The thing that hit everyone as soon as they landed and arrived at Ochsenzoll, the headquarters of Bundesliga club Hamburger SV, was the security. The memories of the horror of what happened at the 1972 Olympic Games in Munich were still fresh in everyone's minds.

Palestinian militants had taken 11 members of the Israeli delegation hostage inside the Olympic Village. The terrorists, who claimed to be part of the Black September movement, were demanding the liberation of Palestinian prisoners held in Israel.

After killing two hostages, they negotiated for a plane to take them out of the country. But a West German police operation to rescue the Israelis went horribly wrong. In the end, all the hostages were killed, along with five of the eight attackers and a Munich police officer. The whole tragedy had played out live on worldwide television and damaged Germany's hopes of presenting a new image after World War Two.

West Germany was also suffering from its own urban guerrillas – the far-left-wing militant Red Army Faction, sometimes known as the Baader-Meinhof Group, who were waging a damaging terror campaign across the country. The Group was engaged in armed resistance against what it claimed was a fascist state and conducted a series of bombings, assassinations, kidnappings, bank robberies and shootouts with police.

The qualification of East Germany and then subsequently being drawn in the same group as West Germany had created an additional major problem for security forces. There remained fears that the communist East would exploit their appearance at the World Cup for ideological and political reasons. A few weeks before the tournament kicked off, West German Chancellor Willy Brandt had been forced to resign after one of his top aides, Gunter Guillaume, was arrested on charges of spying for East Germany.

It was little wonder that everyone involved in security for the World Cup was fearful of what could happen. Dozens of armed guards protected every venue and training facility, many with dogs. A select group of highly trained security officials were assigned to each team and dressed in the same training uniform as the players, with their kit bags containing machine guns instead of boots. Every time they went anywhere, the area was secured and the public were denied the opportunity to meet them.

To the Socceroos, who could normally travel anywhere – even in their own country – in anonymity, it was a big novelty at first. The only downside was that when members of their families came to visit them at Ochsenzoll, they had to undergo a rigorous vetting process that sometimes lasted up to an hour before they were allowed in. Meetings took place in special rooms, and everyone who experienced these meetings imagined that was what it must be like to visit someone in prison.

The West German organisers, though, made no attempt to conceal the identity of the teams as they drove to matches. Mercedes had supplied each of the 16 competing teams with a special bus from its best-selling O 302 vehicle range. The bus for the Socceroos included the 'WM 74' – World Cup 74 – logo, the inscription 'Australien' on the front and sides, and was painted in the national colours green and gold. In addition to the bright exterior, the 1974 World Cup mascots 'Tip and Tap' were on the rear window. The unique livery ensured that wherever the bus went, people would stop by the roadside and wave.

For the first time at a World Cup, each team bus had air conditioning, and the Mercedes vehicles were all equipped with the revolutionary 'Thermo King' system. This was located at the back, on the roof, although instead of a tournament baked in sunshine like Mexico 1970, the 1974 World Cup was plagued by torrential rain. This was despite the fact West German organisers had done extensive computer modelling to try to ensure they picked the best dates.

Inside the bus, there were amenities to keep the players comfortable while travelling to games, some of which would not be appropriate today. Every seat had an individual ashtray. Also, there was a beer tap in the back. Other facilities included an on-board toilet and Blaupunkt stereo with a cassette deck, where the players could listen to the song some of them had recorded before leaving Australia to mark the country's World Cup debut.

The seven-inch vinyl single was called *Sock it to 'Em Socceroos* and was recorded to the tune of *Glory! Glory! Hallelujah!*, written during the American Civil War. The lyrics included '*We are the Aussies and soccer is our game/You can't keep us down under and you don't forget our name*'. On the B-side was the *Socceroos' Supporters Song*. The songs did not trouble the charts.

Ochsenzoll included 10 professional-standard football pitches, accommodation residences, physiotherapy facilities, medical treatment rooms,

Mercedes supplied all 16 teams competing at the World Cup finals with their own personalised bus

staff quarters and a games room with pinball machines and table tennis. The players were amazed when the Adidas boots that Rasic had collected in Herzogenaurach were distributed to them for free. The squad enjoyed being treated so well and the opportunity to devote time to training twice each day.

Boredom was a problem, however, especially with the weather being so poor. One day, striker Max Tolson, whose heroics in Tehran had helped the Socceroos beat Iran over two legs, was playing a casual game of five-a-side in one of the halls and nearly severed his toe when he caught it on the edge of a radiator. It needed to be stitched up and meant Tolson played no part in the World Cup.

'I split my toe in half just before the start of the tournament while we were playing a mini game indoors to kill the time,' Tolson said. 'It was always raining. I hit this metal heater on the wall and that was it. I knew straight away it was the end for me. I was fit and I'm sure I would have got a few minutes here and there, but it was not to be. Watching the boys play from the stands was very frustrating.'

Tolson had already nearly missed travelling to West Germany when on the eve of the team's departure, he contracted mumps. Corrigan, the team doctor, had decided that he should not make the trip, but Rasic overruled him.

One player not troubled by boredom was goalkeeper Jack Reilly, who was continuing to monitor the money markets for his day job as a financial trader. 'We were trading government bonds and treasury notes, and some bank bills,' Reilly recalled. 'And the day before I left for Germany, for six and a half weeks, we were looking at a $2.7 million loss. I said, we had to take it and deal with it. So off I went and two days before our first game against East Germany, I got a call from a dealer saying we had made all our money back and $2.8 million on top of it. The slate was clean. It was a relief.'

To help look after the Socceroos in Hamburg, the local organisers had appointed Uwe Seeler as a liaison officer. To the embarrassment of Rasic, none of the players appeared to realise that he was one of Germany's greatest players. He had played in the West Germany team that had finished runners-up to England in 1966 and third at Mexico 1970. In 72 internationals, he had scored 43 goals. Seeler was a legendary figure in Hamburg, having scored 404 goals for them in 476 games.

Once Rasic told the players who he was, the Socceroos began treating him with the respect he deserved. They also realised what a major figure Seeler was when he appeared alongside Pele at the

Rale Rasic appeared in a major spread in British magazine Radio Times *where he was photographed at home with his family in Sydney*

tournament's opening ceremony. The Brazilian superstar was holding the Jules Rimet Cup, which Brazil had been allowed to keep after winning it three times. Seeler was presenting the new trophy created by Italian sculptor Silvio Gazzaniga.

A big press corps was covering the Socceroos, many of them from Australia. *The Age* soccer writer Laurie Schwab tried to convey to uneducated readers back home just how big the World Cup was. 'It's been estimated that 100 million people – from Santiago to Sofia, from Helsinki to Hobart – will watch the final of the series on TV,' wrote the son of German immigrants, who grew up in Victoria. 'This number rivals even the combined congregations at the world's Christian churches at Christmas.

'The soccer audience is also expected to be bigger than the one which watched man take his first

Peter Wilson told British journalists that 'life is good' in Australia, and pictures of him standing in front of the Pacific Ocean were published to prove it

steps on the moon. All this is not as surprising as it seems. During the World Cup finals, millions of people throughout the world merge themselves into a strange sub-culture. To these people, Beckenbauer means much more than Nixon; they know Johan Cruyff well, but the name Giscard d'Estaing means little to them.'

Schwab had the foresight to see the bigger picture and wrote: 'The full effect of Australia's presence among all this hysteria won't be felt for quite a while, for the greatest impression will be left not on our adults but on our children – especially our junior soccer players.'

There was plenty of interest among the British press, who wanted to interview the players who had moved from England and Scotland to become naturalised Aussies. The London Fleet Street newspapers, in particular, latched onto the Socceroos. 'The English media was there all the time and at that St. Gallen game too,' recalled Alston in his autobiography, *Noddy*. 'England had failed to qualify so they were interested in me and the other "English" players in the squad, like Wilson, Ollerton and Ray Richards.'

The interest should not have been a surprise as just a few years earlier Alston and Peter Ollerton had both been turning out for non-league club Fleetwood Town and were now getting ready to play in the World Cup. In fact, there were more players at West Germany 1974 associated with Fleetwood Town than that year's FA Cup winners, Liverpool, whose only representative was Peter Cormack in the Scotland squad.

Alston had already been linked with a move back to England to play for Division Two club Blackpool, just up the road from his hometown, Preston. He was given the clear impression by the English journalists that his performances had caught the eye of teams there. 'They certainly gave me the idea that I was being looked at by some clubs,' he said. 'You could tell with the way they were interviewing me.'

At the time, Alston was still unsure as to whether he would even start the Socceroos' World Cup matches. He had been on the pitch for the start of nine of Australia's 11 qualifying matches and had scored four goals. But he had only been used as a substitute for the last two matches against South Korea, the game in Seoul and play-off in Hong Kong. Alston claimed he 'was confident' but admitted 'there was always a doubt at the back of your head'.

Rasic was the main subject of a major spread in the World Cup preview issue of the *Radio Times*, published by the British Broadcasting Corporation, and the United Kingdom's biggest-selling magazine. They had sent a reporter to interview him in his family home in Sydney suburb Greenacre before leaving for West Germany.

The journalist, Robert McFarlane, noted that Rasic lived in an 'unspectacular redbrick house like hundreds of others in the same street.

Inside, however, Rasic has transformed his home into a plush teak-veneered thickly-carpeted comfort.'

Rasic proudly told McFarlane, 'I have doubled the value of the house in three years.' The writer continued to gush that 'behind the house, the deep blue water of the rectangular swimming pool shimmers behind the barbecue. It's the good life.'

The article noted that Rasic is 'totally devoted to Australian soccer, to such an extent that he and his attractive 31-year-old wife Barbara have not had a holiday together for seven years.' It also noted that 'there are two children, Daniella (6) and Simon (3), polite, intelligent and under firm European-style parental control.'

Rasic bristled at the suggestion of the reporter that Australia had had an easy path towards qualifying for West Germany 1974 and that it was unfair they had made the World Cup while England were missing.

'Don't kid yourself it's easy to play in Asia,' Rasic told McFarlane. 'Asians are very proud and loyal, and we played 11 matches to qualify - England played only four. We played in temperatures above 100 degrees against Indonesia [in Sydney] and below freezing point in Korea. And the Asians are the equals of anyone in the world in terms of skill. And not all of them are small, you know. The Koreans are tall strong players and very well-drilled.

'We definitely deserve to be in the World Cup more than England because we put in so much preparation. England probably had the easiest draw of all.'

The *Radio Times* also spoke to Wilson, who seemed to be enjoying the attention leading Australia in the World Cup was bringing him. He appeared in a full-page colour picture standing in front of his car, stylishly dressed and wearing a pair of sunglasses with wife Robin by his side and the Pacific Ocean in the background.

'I've made a name here I couldn't have in England ... there I would have probably been a run-of- the-mill club soccer player,' he told the magazine. 'But here I can't go any further. I'm captain of the Australian soccer team. It's the greatest thing that's ever happened to me.

'When I was playing for Middlesbrough I was regularly in the second team and not getting many games in the first team. I suppose that was because in my position they had the club captain and two or three other really strong players.

'So, when a few friends I had in Australia wrote and said the life is good, the soccer is good and the money not bad, I thought I'd give it a go for a couple of years.'

Wilson gave British readers a peek into what they could expect from the Socceroos. 'There's going to be a lot of pressure on the two Germanys to do well and score goals, so we'll play defensively and then counter-attack – obviously if we try to match them for skill, stamina and speed we'll be run off our feet.

'The South Americans will also find it hard in Munich (sic) and I think it will be a European team, possibly Italy or West Germany, who'll take the Cup out.'

Wilson was also interviewed by *Shoot*, Britain's most popular weekly football magazine. The first question was not about the Socceroos but about England's failure to qualify for West Germany 1974. 'Being British by birth, of course, I'm naturally interested in what happens to England, and like many of my colleagues I would have liked England to have been competing in West Germany,' he answered. 'But we are all Australians now, and our country of birth is of secondary importance – it's playing for Australia that counts, and reaching the finals is terrific.'

The German media were, of course, making a beeline for Wilson's defensive partner Schaefer, who they always referred to as 'Der Milchmann' due to his job as a milkman in Sydney. His unusual story enthralled the public in the country of his birth, and he was always given a special wave and cheer when he was recognised.

When the Socceroos played West Germany, star striker Gerd Muller asked Schaefer if he really earned his living as a milkman and was an amateur footballer. Schaefer proudly replied that he had received $4,600 by qualifying for the World Cup. 'That's what I earn a week,' replied Muller.

Being back in the country they had left to start new lives was a strange sensation for Schaefer and the Socceroos' assistant coach, Les Scheinflug,

Manfred Schaefer, right, and Les Scheinflug, left, discussed being back in Germany after leaving many years before

who had finally made it to the World Cup finals having captained Australia in their first campaign, which had ended so badly against North Korea in 1965.

'Before the first game against the GDR, I sat with Manfred Schaefer for a long time in the evening,' Scheinflug said. 'We talked about our roots, about the strange feeling of competing against our home country. The division of the country was rather irrelevant for us. After all, we both grew up in West Germany. I emigrated with my parents in 1955, when I was 17. I could barely speak English and wanted to go back to Germany. In 1961, I went back to my birthplace in Buckeburg in Lower Saxony. But suddenly, I felt homesick for Sydney. It was paradoxical: the feeling of no longer having a home.'

It was a question that Rasic was always asked in interviews, about his foreign legion. 'Australia's World Cup players may come from many nations, but when we are together, we are all Australians,' he told British magazine *Sports World*.

Rasic always warned the international media not to underestimate his Socceroos. 'Ten years ago, Everton came and put eight goals past Australia,' he said. 'They could have gone on scoring all night if they had wished. But I guarantee one thing: not Everton, not Leeds, not even West Germany, could score eight goals against us now.'

Most people remained sceptical and were convinced that Rasic's Socceroos were going to be like kangaroos to the slaughter. According to the bookmakers in London, Australia officially started the 16-team tournament as 250-1 outsiders to win, bigger outsiders than even Zaire and Haiti, the other newcomers.

For all their fascination with Schaefer, the German media were especially unkind about the Socceroos. Tabloid *Bild-Zeitung* brutally summed up what most people there were thinking. 'Why have we got these kangaroos at the World Cup?' they wrote in an editorial. 'How have we ended up with this bunch of no-hopers at the world's greatest tournament?'

Chapter Fourteen

They are robots

There was intense interest in the participation of East Germany, Australia's first World Cup opponents. They had formed a national team in 1951 and been allowed to join FIFA the following year, despite the objections of West Germany.

East Germany had been trying to qualify for the World Cup since Sweden 1958, but West Germany 1974 was the first time they had made it. The team had finished top of Group 4 in the European Zone, one point ahead of Romania, winning five of their six matches.

The East Germans were a well-drilled team and had been together for several years. Their 'amateur' status had allowed many of the players to be members of the country's Olympic team that had competed at the 1972 Games in Munich, where they had won a bronze medal. Along the way, they had beaten hosts West Germany 3–2 in a match watched by a crowd of 80,000 at the Olympic Stadium.

It was the start of a short golden period for football in East Germany. The month before the World Cup started, the country's top club, FC Magdeburg,

The East Germany squad pose for a picture shortly before the start of their debut in the World Cup finals

had lifted the UEFA Cup Winners' Cup. They had beaten Italy's AC Milan 2–0 in the final at the Stadion Feijenoord in Rotterdam. Several members of the Magdeburg team were included in East Germany's World Cup squad, coached by Georg Buschner.

Buschner had the luxury of spending time with his players every week at one of the East German government's Sportschules, a facility for elite competitors that had helped turn the country's athletes into among the best in the world. Since East Germany had made its debut in the Olympic Games as a separate country at Mexico 1968, they had punched way above their weight for a country of 17 million people. In the 1972 Olympics in Munich, they had finished third in the overall medals table, behind only the Soviet Union and United States, with 20 golds.

Yet, despite enthusiasm in East Germany for success in the Olympics in sports like athletics, swimming and weightlifting, football remained the people's game in the 'people's state'. It meant that the sport was accorded a degree of autonomy not afforded to other sports much more tightly controlled.

That independence suited the single-minded Buschner, who was largely allowed to work as he wished. He was mostly permitted to select players purely on their ability rather than having to choose politically-dependable socialist role models. That did not mean the Minister for State Security – better known as the Stasi – did not take a close interest in the team. After the Berlin Wall fell in 1989, state documents revealed that Buschner himself had worked as a Stasi informer.

As one of East Germany's players from the 1974 World Cup later discovered, while a player's ability on the pitch may have been more important than what they believed off it, the Stasi did have its limits.

Striker Hans-Jurgen Kreische was dropped after the tournament and missed being part of East Germany's Olympic gold medal-winning team at Montreal 1976 due to a chance encounter. After beating West Germany 1–0 in the final match of Group 1, Kreische was on a flight to Hanover and found himself sitting next to West Germany's finance minister, Hans Apel.

Apel had been a spectator at the previous evening's game in Hamburg and afterwards was despondent about his country's chances of lifting the World Cup. Kreische, though, reassured his neighbour that 'West Germany will be world champion'.

Apel told Kreische he was talking nonsense and that 'perhaps you're too polite to tell me how bad this team is'. He suggested a bet – five bottles of whisky. It was agreed the bet would only be honoured if Kreische was correct.

West Germany duly lifted the World Cup trophy with a 2–1 victory over the Netherlands, and Apel called East Germany's Ambassador in Bonn. 'I said to him, "You will get five bottles of whisky, and you will transport them please to Herr Kreische,'" Apel said. They were duly delivered to a shocked Kreische, who never believed the bet was serious.

The Stasi were suspicious that there was more to this than just a simple friendly wager and that Apel was trying to help Kreische defect to the West. So, a striker who had scored 25 goals in 50 appearances for East Germany was banned and never played for his country again after 1975. When the Berlin Wall came down in 1989, Apel contacted Kreische and apologised for the irreparable damage he had done to his career.

During his scouting trip to Leipzig the month before to watch East Germany draw 1–1 with England, Socceroos coach Rale Rasic would not have seen Kreische as he was missing through injury, having been an important part of the team for five years.

After that game, Rasic had spent some time with Joe Mercer, whom he had met during Australia's world tour in 1970 when they had played Manchester City. At the time, he had been angry the English First Division club had fielded a reserve side.

Mercer, who had enjoyed remarkable success as coach of City, had been appointed as England's caretaker manager following the dismissal of Sir Alf Ramsey after the 1966 World Cup winners failed to qualify for the World Cup.

Mercer noted that the East Germans seemed to have the ability to run forever and never tired. 'What do you think of the Germans?' Rasic asked him. His reply was simple: 'Son, you want some advice ... park the fucking bus and hope for the fucking best. They are robots.'

Following the collapse of the Berlin Wall, it emerged that East Germany had been running a state-sponsored doping programme for years, with the aim of bolstering its international image through sporting success. The system had been developed following the appointment of former Hitler Youth leader and Nazi Party member Manfred Ewald, who had been made East Germany's sports minister in 1961.

The level of drug use among East Germany's footballers before the 1974 World Cup remains unknown. Football was among those included in a category called 'Sport 1', along with athletics, rowing, swimming and weightlifting, as a discipline that offered the most opportunity for international success. Athletes in all those sports were regularly given performance-enhancing drugs, so it is probably safe to assume that there was some kind of doping programme in place for the World Cup, especially as drugs testing then was so unsophisticated.

Certainly, after their match against them, Socceroos goalkeeper Jack Reilly believed they were fuelled by more than just bratwurst and sauerkraut. His description of them was an 'East German team that ran for 130 minutes in a 90-minute game'.

Australia's right-back Doug Utjesenovic also noticed how strong the East Germans were. 'They were not that impressive technically, but physically they were something else,' he said. 'I remember facing their left-winger who was in the army, and I noticed that each one of his thighs was as big as my two put together.'

When the Stasi files on doping were unlocked in the 1990s, the names of hundreds of top athletes, including many Olympic medallists, were revealed. These were all part of State Plan 14.25, secretly launched around the time of the World Cup in 1974, and which mandated the systemic use of performance-enhancing drugs for East German Olympic aspirants, including some pre-pubescent children.

Of course, at the time of the World Cup, there was no talk of doping, and Buschner put the success of his team down to its togetherness. 'We are a strong, athletic team with tactical discipline,' he said. 'But at the technical level, we are not at the top. There are a few countries ahead of us, like Brazil, England and West Germany. Players like Pele and Bobby Charlton we haven't, but the big thing is our teamwork.'

Even though they had played regularly, including that 1–1 draw with England, little was known about the East Germany team competing at West Germany 1974. They were keen to keep it that way by largely avoiding any media spotlight before the start of the World Cup. They had wanted to prepare for their matches at their normal training base near East Berlin, and only fly into West Germany for their fixtures. FIFA ruled this as being against the tournament's regulations.

East Germany then tried to put in a bid to stay at Ochsenzoll, but that had already been snapped up by the Socceroos. In the end, they stayed at the Quickborn, a fairly spartan sports hotel near Hamburg.

World Cup organisers had also vetoed a plan for East Germany to play a friendly against Hamburger SV, at the Volksparkstadion, before the start of the World Cup. 'We wouldn't like to give this advantage to the East Germans unless we can also make the ground used during the World Cup available to the Australians,' a spokesman said.

The Australian party settled down at Ochsenzoll on 13th June to watch the opening match of the World Cup. It was a game that would especially have interested Rasic as it involved his native Yugoslavia. They managed to hold the defending champions Brazil to a 0–0 draw in a tedious match in Group 2 at the Waldstadion in Frankfurt, before 62,000 fans.

There were more Yugoslavian coaches at the World Cup than any other country. Besides Rasic, there was Miljan Miljanic, who was in charge of Yugoslavia, and Blagoje Vidinic, the coach of Zaire. Rasic may have thought he had to work under difficult circumstances in Australia, but they were nothing compared to those faced by Vidinic.

Vidinic served with Zaire's autocratic President Mobutu Sese Seko scrutinising his every move and decision. Mobutu's hangers-on stole money meant as bonuses for the team, and after the team were beaten 9–0 by Yugoslavia in their second match at the World Cup, Vidinic was forced to tell his players that he was too scared to return to Zaire and never went back to the country again.

Before the opening match had started, the opening ceremony included an appearance from Australian folk group Mulga Bill's Bicycle Band, one of 16 national acts representing countries participating in the World Cup finals and who burst out of a polystyrene soccer ball and played *Waltzing Matilda*.

Australian Soccer Federation president Sir Arthur George was among dignitaries attending the event. 'At the opening ceremony, there was a significant number of Australian supporters,' he said. 'Curiously, most of them who had adopted Australia as their life, as their country. When they played the Australian national anthem, I felt tears go down my face and I looked around and I was relieved to see the same was happening to every Australian there. This was a wonderful moment for me.'

Australia was represented at the World Cup opening ceremony in Frankfurt by Mulga Bill's Bicycle Band

Brazil's victory at Mexico 1970 meant they had won the World Cup three times and were allowed by FIFA to keep the trophy forever, according to guidelines created already in 1930. That meant for West Germany 1974 a new one had been commissioned. Made of 18-karat gold with bands of malachite on its base, it stood 36.8 centimetres high, weighed 6.175 kilograms and had been made by Italian company Stabilimento Artistico Bertoni.

Brazil was missing Pele following his retirement from international football in 1971, after a career which had seen him score 77 goals in 92 appearances for the national team. They started as one of the two top-seeded teams in West Germany and were considered favourites, but were clearly a shadow of the glorious Mexico 1970 side that had entranced so many fans around the globe.

The closest Brazil were to come to triumphing at this World Cup came a few days before it kicked off, when Joao Havelange unseated Sir Stanley Rous as president of FIFA. He had lobbied in 86 different countries for the presidency, including Australia, often accompanied by Pele. It paid off as he beat Sir Stanley by 16 votes in the second round.

It was the start of a 24-year reign as head of the world's most popular sport, during which he was to revolutionise football. In the years to come, the Australian Soccer Federation and Sir Arthur would be among those to benefit greatly from the patronage of Havelange.

Group 1 started on Friday, 14th June, the day after the opening match between Brazil and Yugoslavia. Hosts West Germany and Chile were the first in action, starting at 4pm at the Olympic Stadium in Berlin. Paul Breitner had scored the only goal of the match in the 18th minute to give West Germany a 1-0 victory in front of 82,000 fans.

The Socceroos' match against East Germany was scheduled to start at 7.30pm. They left Ochsenzoll in their special Mercedes bus, decked out in green and gold with 'Australien' on the front and side, and sped through the streets of Hamburg flanked by a phalanx of police cars and motorcycles, arriving at the Volksparkstadion 90 minutes before kick-off.

The English translation for the ground was 'The People's Park Stadium'. It had been opened in 1925 and then renovated in 1953, using building materials from the ruins of Eimsbuttel, a district of Hamburg destroyed under Allied bombing during the Second World War. Like many stadiums in Germany at that time, the pitch was encircled by a running track that increased the distance between the pitch and the stands.

Rasic had officially announced his team before leaving the training base. He had taken Mercer's advice to 'pack the defence' and picked a 4-5-1 formation. Goalkeeper Reilly was playing behind a back four of Utjesenovic, Peter Wilson, Manfred Schaefer and Col Curran. They were supported by a five-man midfield of Johnny Warren, Jimmy Mackay, Jimmy Rooney and Branko Buljevic, with Adrian Alston playing as a lone striker.

The recovery of Curran was a minor miracle, having so severely injured his knee ligaments in the friendly against Indonesia the day after the Socceroos left Australia. He had worked closely with team doctor Brian Corrigan, with plenty of sessions in the

Australia's longest-serving player, Johnny Warren, leads Ray Richards and Jimmy Mackay out in Hamburg for the Socceroos' first World Cup finals match

swimming pool to get back to full fitness and earn his place in the historic line-up.

Alston had been fearful of not starting after being given the squad number '12' behind fellow strikers Garry Manuel and Atti Abonyi, who received numbers '10' and '11', respectively. Alston had also come out in a red rash all over his face a few days before the opening match. He put it down to eating too many strawberries during the training camp in Switzerland, and was relieved when the rash disappeared.

The announcement that Alston had been preferred to Abonyi must have been awkward as the two were sharing a room. 'Atti was absolutely devastated,' Alston admitted in his autobiography, *Noddy*. 'He was a super-

Socceroos captain Peter Wilson takes part in the coin toss with East German counterpart, Bernd Bransch

confident player and a great goalscorer and he proved this throughout his career. He must have been convinced he would play.

'It was tough to take for him and when you're playing in the biggest game of your life and your room-mate is not in the team, what do you say to the guy? It was really hard.'

It was Alston, wearing the traditional gold shirt, green shorts and white socks, who had the honour of kicking off Australia's maiden World Cup campaign when he tapped the ball to Warren to start the match after the referee, Youssou N'Diaye, from Senegal, blew his whistle.

Rasic's instructions to his team before the game were clear and simple. They had to contain the East Germans for as long as possible and try to prevent them getting too close to the Socceroos' goal.

There was a disappointing crowd of 17,000 in a stadium that could hold three times that amount. It is estimated that there were about 2,000 Australian fans in the ground, while only a handful of East Germans had been deemed politically safe enough to make the trip to the West and not defect. The West Germans formed the majority of the spectators and were backing the Socceroos against their communist neighbours. During the match, chants of 'Austral-lien, Austral-lien' could be regularly heard.

The Socceroos' plan of keeping out the East Germans and hoping that frustration set in appeared to be working. Schaefer revealed that at one point early on in the second half, East Germany's top striker, Joachim Streich, had turned to him and said: 'This is unbelievable. We're not creating anything. We can't afford to lose this.'

The Socceroos continued to hold out until 13 minutes into the second half, when Juergen Sparwasser sprinted clear of Utjesenovic as the Australians appealed for offside. The East German midfielder drew Reilly out of his goal and fired a shot towards the far post, which was going in even before Curran helped it into his own net. Rasic was probably

Rale Rasic's plan was to frustrate the East Germans and, thanks to some stout defending from the likes of Col Curran, left, and Johnny Warren, right, it proved to be effective

right in complaining that the goal should not have been allowed to stand because of offside – today, it would almost certainly have been referred to the video assistant referee.

The Australians still battled valiantly, only for East Germany to settle the match with a second goal in the 72nd minute. Streich finally escaped the attentions of Schaefer to meet a cross from Eberhard Vogel and put the game beyond the Socceroos with a shot from a difficult angle into the top of the net.

The match proved to be a tiring affair for Alston, the Socceroos' lone striker. He was forced to spend most of the game chasing long balls from the back over the East German midfield. But his energy and skill in carrying out the role caught the eye of several Bundesliga clubs. Also impressed was England World Cup winner Sir Bobby Charlton. He had retired from playing in 1973 and taken over as manager at Preston North End, the club where Alston had started his career.

There was one particular piece of skill in the first half that had stood out. Alston had chased another long

The Socceroos denied East Germany until the 58th minute, when the unfortunate Col Curran scored an own goal

ball and brought it under control. He was running out towards the left-hand side of East Germany's penalty area, shadowed by defender Konrad Weise. Alston shaped up to pass the ball from just outside the box with his right foot. He instead tucked the ball behind his standing leg and switched direction by 180 degrees.

Joachim Streich scored East Germany's second goal in the 72nd minute

Five days later, in their second Group 3 match, the Netherlands captain, Johan Cruyff, attempted the same trick. The difference was that the defender the Dutch legend performed the trick on, Sweden's Jan Olsson, did not scythe him to the ground, as Weise had done to Alston. The East German did not even get cautioned for the brutal swipe that had sent the Australian crashing to the turf.

The move has since become among the most iconic in soccer, with articles written on the anniversary of the move to celebrate the 'Cruyff turn', which has become the symbol of the Netherlands' 'Total football'. The match programme and ticket for that Dutch match against Sweden are now valuable items when they come up for auction. Cruyff even called his autobiography *My Turn*, in which he claimed the idea of the move suddenly came to him during the match against Sweden.

'The turn wasn't something I'd ever done in training or practised,' Cruyff wrote. 'The idea came to me in a flash, because at that particular moment it was the best solution for the situation I was in. There are impulses that arise because your technical and tactical knowledge has become so great that your legs are able to respond immediately to what your head wants you to do. Even if that's nothing more than a flash in the brain, I've always used feints like that.'

Alston maintains to this day that Cruyff got the idea off him. 'He was in his hotel room apparently, watching our game against East Germany and he said to his room-mate, "I think I can do that,"' Alston said.

'So he did, and then his defender, the wanker, didn't even kick him, whereas the guy I played against flattened me! He was a real defender – he was playing against someone that didn't tackle. Anyway, I should have some recognition, I don't care what it is, I just need some recognition for that …'

There is a film clip available on *YouTube* which unequivocally proves that Alston tried the move before Cruyff. Britain's National Museum in Manchester does give the Socceroos striker credit for doing the move before Cruyff but admitted: 'The Alston turn doesn't have the same ring to it.'

If Weise somehow managed to avoid being shown a yellow card for his foul on Alston, it was testament to the pressure the Socceroos put the East Germans under that three of their team were cautioned, while the Australians left the field with no bookings to their name.

Rasic was delighted with the performance his team had put up, claiming on a different day 'we could have finished with a draw'. The Socceroos had proved they

Adrian Alston impressed everyone against East Germany with his skill and tireless running

'were no pushover', and the predictions they would get beaten six or seven-nil had proved to be horribly inaccurate.

Overall, the Socceroos had won 20 of their 28 tackle attempts throughout their maiden World Cup game – a figure no other country could equal in any other match during the rest of the tournament.

At the final whistle, BBC commentator John Motson praised the Socceroos' performance. 'They proved they are not here just for the ride,' he said.

'Beaten but not disgraced', concluded the *Sydney Morning Herald*, praising the team's fighting spirit and its gallantry in defeat, which had 'won the hearts of the crowd'.

The reports in the world's newspapers the next day were also full of praise for the Socceroos. 'Dwarf grows 10 feet tall', was one. Another said: 'Unbelievable the way these Australians fight'. A leading West German newspaper claimed that 'East Germany narrowly avoids disgrace'.

Buschner, the East Germany coach, was among those to give the most praise to the Socceroos. 'I was impressed with the Australians,' he said. 'They had excellent organisation in defence, they showed above-average flair in midfield, and they had occasional attacks which were dangerous. They are very hard, but fair, and they will not drown in the remaining matches.'

Buschner was joined by his West German counterpart, Helmut Schoen, who had watched the match on television at his team's base in West Berlin. He agreed with Rasic's assessment that they 'deserved' a draw, and that 'only lack of stamina' had let them down.

Johnny Warren picked up an injury during the match that meant this would be his only appearance in the World Cup finals

Schoen added: 'The Australians are every bit as strong as France, Romania, Czechoslovakia or Hungary ... If you weren't so isolated from the hub of world soccer, Australia would already be a world power.'

Warren believed the skill and spirit shown by the Socceroos in the match had earned them immediate respect from the public, media and other teams in the tournament. 'People had been expecting us to be absolutely thumped and we had proved that we weren't imposters,' he wrote in *Sheilas, Wogs and Poofters*.

Australia acknowledge the support after the 2–0 defeat against East Germany

The German media may have started the tournament asking 'why have we got these kangaroos at the World Cup?', but, after only one game, Australia had already got them reconsidering. They were no longer dismissed as 'no-hopers'.

The next match, however, would be the Socceroos' greatest test yet.

CHAPTER FIFTEEN

Cheering for the underdogs

The Socceroos returned to their training base at Ochsenzoll tired but in a positive mood, despite the defeat to East Germany.

Adrian Alston had spent the 90 minutes chasing long balls, often successfully, pulling off that remarkable piece of skill that had caught the eye of a watching Johan Cruyff. He had also been kicked a lot by the uncompromising East German defenders, who probably experienced a much harder evening's work than they had been anticipating.

If any of the players were feeling upset about the result, coach Rale Rasic was on hand to reassure them that they had not let anyone down.

'At first, we were all shattered with the result because we had worked so hard and had played a good match against a world-class team,' said Alston. 'But Rasic told us he was not too disheartened by the result because he had seen a brave effort from us. He picked us up and let us know he was more than happy with the way we played and we did everything that was expected of us.

'He insisted if the first goal had not gone in, anything could have happened because the Germans were beginning to get very nervous about their inability to break us down. Frustration was beginning to creep into their game. So, we just took the defeat on the chin and started thinking about the next game.'

Rasic gave the team the day off after the East Germany match. Some travelled to the coast, others went shopping in Hamburg and the rest stayed at the Socceroos' training base to play table tennis or relax. On the Sunday, the team trained as normal in the morning before they were invited to a barbecue in the afternoon. There is no doubt that all through the weekend, the Socceroos were most focused on what they faced next – the hardest imaginable task with the hosts and World Cup favourites, West Germany, lying in wait.

Besides Brazil, West Germany had been the most successful team in the history of the World Cup since the end of the Second World War, even though the country had been banned from the 1950 tournament as a result of the conflict. When they were allowed to return, even the loss of several top players to East Germany, following the partition of the country, did not seem to weaken them.

At the 1954 World Cup in Switzerland, they had lost 8–3 in the group stage to Hungary. They recovered to reach the final, where they faced the 'Mighty Magyars' again. This time, they won 3–2 – ending Hungary's winning streak of

32 consecutive victories. West Germany's feat in lifting the World Cup was called the *Das Wunder von Bern* – 'The Miracle of Bern'.

After finishing fourth in the 1958 World Cup in Sweden and reaching only the quarter-finals in the 1962 World Cup in Chile, the German Football Association announced a series of major changes.

These included introducing professionalism, and West Germany's best clubs joined a new national league – the Bundesliga. At international level, Helmut Schoen took over as coach, replacing Sepp Herberger, whose 28 years in charge included leading 'The Miracle of Bern' team. Schoen had been Herberger's assistant for six years, so was already well versed in international football.

As a player, Schoen had been a striker representing Dresdner SC, winning the German championship in 1943 and 1944, as well as the cup in 1941 and 1942. He had a remarkable record at international level, scoring 17 goals in just 16 appearances for Germany, although some of the matches are not official due to the start of the Second World War.

Schoen was a member of the army but not directly involved in the War. His entire family was against the Nazi regime and he always refused to join the Party. It was probably only Schoen's status as a well-known footballer that allowed him to continue to resist.

A knee injury suffered shortly towards the end of the War ended Schoen's career, so he turned to coaching. He began his career in football management in his native state of Saxony, then part of East Germany. He was in charge of coaching selections from Saxony and the Soviet occupation zone before political interference in the sport made him flee to West Germany in 1950.

Once there, Schoen accepted a teaching position at the famous Sportschule in Cologne, the administrative and technical football coaching centre of the German Football Association. Later, he took over as chief coach of the autonomous Saarland national team, until the Saar Protectorate was reunified with West Germany in 1957.

Saarland had even faced West Germany during the qualifiers for the 1954 World Cup, with Schoen taking Herberger's team to a decisive qualifier, which went the way of the eventual world champions. In 1958, Herberger invited Schoen to become his assistant, working exclusively with the national team. When Herberger stood down in 1964, Schoen was the obvious person to replace him.

Under Schoen's leadership, West Germany had already finished as World Cup runners-up in 1966, losing 4–2 to hosts England in the final. They also finished third in the 1970 World Cup and were crowned as European champions in 1972, defeating the Soviet Union 3-0 in the final.One of the key tactical changes Schoen had introduced was accepting Franz Beckenbauer's belief that he would be best employed as a sweeper, a position he is widely credited for inventing. The decision by Schoen had helped to give West Germany a new dimension.

The West Germany teams Schoen had built for Mexico 1970 and the 1972 European Championships were among the most exciting around, especially with striker Gerd Muller banging in the goals at a record rate. Key to the success in 1972 was midfielder Gunter Netzer, who Schoen had drafted in to replace the injured Wolfgang Overath.

Netzer had dictated the first leg of West Germany's quarter-final against England at Wembley Stadium, acting as the mesmerising conduit between Muller up front and Beckenbauer at the back. With the resolute Sepp Maier in goal, Schoen had the perfect spine to his team.

But by the time of the World Cup, Schoen had controversially reverted to FC Cologne midfielder Overath as his playmaker of choice. Schoen claimed that Netzer's transfer from Borussia Moenchengladbach to Spanish giants Real Madrid, at a time when it was unusual for players to leave their home country, was behind the decision to restore Overath. Whatever the reason, it was a topic debated endlessly in the German media.

This was not the only subject distracting West Germany's preparations. The West German squad were embroiled in an ugly pre-World Cup row with the German Football Association over their potential bonus for winning the tournament. The players had discovered that the Dutch and Italian teams were both set to earn 100,000 Deutsche Marks if they lifted the trophy, compared to the 30,000 Deutsche Marks they had been promised. There was little support for the players, and German newspaper headlines labelled them 'greedy'.

The German coach was on the side of the media. 'Helmut Schoen said we were greedy, and that people would spit on us in the street if they found out,' said Maier. 'He wanted to have nothing more to do with us.'

At one point, Schoen threatened to drop all the players and replace them with a second-string squad. Paul Breitner, the West German left-back well known for his militant views, even had his bag packed at one stage and was prepared to leave his team's training camp in Malente, a rural area in Schleswig-Holstein. It was a carbon copy of what happened in the Socceroos' camp on the eve of the World Cup qualifying match against South Korea the previous October – except the stakes were much higher.

Beckenbauer personally negotiated with German Football Association president Hermann Neuberger to try to find a solution. Neuberger agreed to double the bonus to 60,000 Deutsche Marks – still a long way short of the 75,000 Deutsche Marks the squad were demanding. When a vote was taken, it was 11 to accept and 11 to decline. It was left to Beckenbauer, in the early hours of the morning following a marathon meeting, to instruct his teammates to accept the 'goodwill gesture' and end their mutiny. Few realised how close the hosts had come to refusing to play in the tournament.

The laboured 1–0 victory over Chile in their opening match must have left the German Football Association confident they would not be needing to write any bonus cheques. It also had the West Germany players doubting whether Schoen had made the right decision about preferring Overath to Netzer. The camp was divided, with senior players like Beckenbauer and Muller offering their opinions to Schoen about who should play. Overath was retained for the match against Australia. When his name was read out before the start of the game, it was booed by the German fans.

Rasic, though, was forced to make a significant change to his team. Johnny Warren had been the victim of a nasty challenge in the game against East Germany when his opponent had been guilty of an over-the-top tackle and then raked his studs across the top of the boot of the Socceroos legend. Warren admitted the 'pain was excruciating', even though he managed to complete the match.

The extent of the injury became clear to Warren when he got back into the dressing room after the final whistle. 'I realised that I might not actually get back on the field for the remaining two matches, and it was one of the worst moments of my entire career,' he wrote in his autobiography, *Sheilas, Wogs and Poofters*. 'After all I had done to get back in the team and to make it to the World Cup, the thought of missing the next two games was just beyond my comprehension.'

Hopes that having ice treatment on the injury would help Warren recover in time for the West Germany match quickly faded, and he had to accept that he would not be fit. It was not only the end of Warren's World Cup, but it was also the end of his career with the Socceroos. Since his debut in 1965, he had represented them in 42 international matches and scored seven goals. His place in the sport's history in Australia was ensured.

It seemed likely that even if Warren had not been injured, Rasic would have dropped him, as he had described his performance against East Germany as 'ineffective' and warned 'now is not the time for sentiment'.

Warren was replaced by Ernie Campbell, a 24-year-old Sydney-born striker who had spent seven months as a youth team player at English First Division club Chelsea before returning home. Campbell admitted it was 'a decision I regret to this day, but the weather compared to Bondi Beach wasn't exactly attractive, and I did miss home.'

Following a four-year spell with APIA Leichhardt, Campbell was signed by Rasic at Marconi-Fairfield in 1971 and later that year given his international debut against Israel. From that point on to the World Cup qualifying campaign, he was a regular in the Socceroos squad and was instrumental in scoring a late goal in the 1–1 draw against New Zealand in March 1973, which helped ensure Australia's progress to the next round against Iran.

In Australian soccer circles, Campbell was nicknamed 'the Fifth Beatle' due to his long hair and moustache which, it was claimed, gave him a distinct resemblance to George Harrison. It was, therefore, appropriate that Campbell should get his opportunity in Hamburg, the German city where in 1960 the legendary group from Liverpool in England had played their first live gig at the Indra Club in the red-light district.

The match had special significance for one member of the team – Manfred Schaefer. The German press remained fascinated by the story of a man born in the East Prussian town of Pillau. His family had fled westward towards Bremen to avoid the advancing Red Army of the Soviet Union in the dying days of the Second World War, before emigrating to start a new life in Australia 10 years later.

Schaefer would be facing Muller, the top scorer at the 1970 World Cup with 10 goals. Muller was the deadliest striker in football. Just the month before the 1974 World Cup started, he had scored two goals as Bayern Munich lifted the European Cup for the first time with a 4–0 victory over Spanish side Atletico Madrid in a replay at the Heysel Stadium in Brussels. That meant Muller had finished as Munich's top scorer for the season with 43 goals.

It was more of a story when Muller did not score than when he did. Schaefer was ready for the challenge, though. 'I have been preparing for weeks for that 90-minute duel,' he told the Australian media before the match. 'I will put everything into it. Should Muller remain goalless in the game against us, it will be the greatest achievement of my soccer career.'

West Germany's World Cup team contained five other members of the Bayern Munich team that, as well as lifting the European Cup, had won the 1973–1974 Bundesliga. There was Maier, considered among the best goalkeepers in the world, centre-back Hans-Georg Schwarzenbeck, Breitner and left-winger Uli Hoeness. Then, of course, there was Beckenbauer – nicknamed *Der Kaiser*.

At 28, Beckenbauer was at the peak of his game. He had already won a World Cup silver medal at England 1966 and bronze at Mexico 1970. At that tournament in 1970, Beckenbauer had dislocated his shoulder after being fouled in the semi-final against Italy, but continued with his arm in a sling as West Germany had already used their two permitted substitutes. It was the enduring image of the match, called the 'Game of the Century' in both Germany and Italy, as his side lost 4–3 after extra time. Beckenbauer was the obvious choice when West Germany needed a new captain, and he had led his country to victory in the 1972 European Championships.

As well as the Bayern Munich players, the West Germany team included stars like Borussia Moenchengladbach defender Berti Vogts and his teammate Jupp Heynckes, a striker. Few would have blamed the Socceroos if their 1pm pre-match lunch, consisting of steak and salad washed down with orange juice and sparkling mineral water, had felt like the last meal of condemned men. After lunch, the Socceroos party boarded their Mercedes coach for another trip to the Volksparkstadion and arrived 90 minutes before the 4pm kick-off.

When the two teams walked out onto the pitch, Australia were led out by quite possibly the oldest mascot in World Cup history. Fifty-eight-year-old Jim Scane was an Englishman who, during World War Two, was wounded and captured in Dunkirk and taken back to Germany as a prisoner of war. When he was released, he married a German woman named Erika and went to live in England before he and his family relocated to Australia in 1960.

A former goalkeeper, he had trials as a youngster with English First Division club Tottenham Hotspur and played for several leading amateur teams in London. Scane was not going to give up his passion for football when he landed in his new country. He got involved in the local scene and began supporting the national team of his adopted country.

Scane invested thousands of dollars to follow the Socceroos to West Germany 1974, leading to his wife divorcing him. When he arrived in the country where he was once a prisoner, he made sure no one would mistake who he was supporting. Scane wore a green hat labelled 'Australia', and a green and gold jacket dotted with badges and inscribed with the names of the Socceroos players and the teams they had beaten to reach the finals.

On his trousers, Scane had painted Aussie slogans, such as 'Hooray, we're here' and 'We fear no bastard' in German, which he had learnt to speak fluently while in the prison camp. Just in case anyone was still wondering who he was cheering on, Scane carried a stuffed kangaroo in one hand and koala bear in the other.

After Schaefer, Scane was the Australian the German media was most interested in.

Australia mascot, 58-year-old Englishman Jim Scane, was the centre of attention before the kick-off of the Socceroos match against West Germany

One article was headlined '*Jim ist der verruckteste Fussball Fan*', which translated to 'Jim is the craziest football fan'.

The Socceroos embraced Scane's eccentricity. 'An incredible man,' Rasic wrote in his autobiography. 'An Englishman who made his home in Australia, adopted the Socceroos and followed us almost everywhere. The boys treated him well – they regarded him as family.'

It all helped reinforce the image in the German media that the Socceroos were figures of fun, not to be taken seriously. The press were still predicting a slaughter, despite their team's poor performance against Chile and Australia's better-than-expected display versus East Germany.

Schoen tried to temper the expectations of the home fans. 'Australia has a few very outstanding players who can make it hard for any team,' he had told the local press. 'We will take our game against the Australians as seriously as any other.'

The Socceroos line up for their second match in Hamburg

The Socceroos must have feared the worst after West Germany, playing in their change kit of green shirts, white shorts and green socks, started the game in such a confident manner before a crowd of 53,000. Overath, in particular, seemed to have something to prove after surviving the campaign for him to be replaced by Netzer. At 31, he was coming to the end of a long international career, the highlight of which was scoring West Germany's goal in their 1-0 victory over Uruguay to clinch third place at Mexico 1970.

Rasic's instructions to the Socceroos had been the same as before the East Germany match: keep them out as long as possible. The West Germans were just too strong in the opening period, however, and it was Overath who put his side ahead in the 13th minute. Australia failed to clear the ball and it fell to Overath 25 metres out. He fired a left-footed shot that eluded Jack Reilly in the Socceroos goal and hit the top of the net.

Wolfgang Overath watches as he scores West Germany's opening goal against the Socceroos

Bernhard Cullmann raises above Australia's defence to head home West Germany's second goal

Muller hit the crossbar with a header before some desperate defending kept West Germany out again until the 34th minute. FC Cologne midfielder Bernhard Cullmann was the first to meet a cross from the right by Vogts, and headed it past Reilly into the net. The West German crowd were confident that, against a group of part-timers, their team of superstars would cash in big time in the second half.

At half-time, Rasic replaced Campbell with Atti Abonyi. The change seemed to give the Socceroos more balance, and they strung a series of passes together. But any thoughts of an unlikely comeback were ended in the 53rd minute, when Hoeness swung in a corner from the left. Muller got a step ahead of Schaefer to flick the ball with the back of his head beyond Reilly for West Germany's third goal.

Gerd Muller finds a gap between Ray Richards, right, and Manfred Schaefer, left, to make it 3-0

For the rest of the match, although West Germany dominated possession, they could not score again. Their best chance was Hoeness heading over in front of an open goal. Muller was kept quiet for the rest of the match by Schaefer, assisted by Peter Wilson. Muller later said of the Socceroos captain: 'Wilson is the roughest man I've played against. He didn't seem to care whether he kicked the ball, a leg or a head.'

Wilson's assessment of Muller was that 'technically, he's not so good, but he can't help but score goals.'

For all of Muller's complaints, the only Australian cautioned was Jimmy Mackay. He became the first Socceroo shown a yellow card at a World Cup, when he was booked by Egyptian referee Mahmoud Mustafa Kamel for kicking the ball away after a disputed free kick for handball was awarded against him.

Muller's comment about Wilson may have been borne out of anger as much as anything because towards the end of the game, the West German crowd began to lose patience with their team. They

Socceroos coach Rale Rasic watches on as his side try to keep West Germany at bay

were expecting to see a lot more goals than just three, and as the Socceroos began to grow in confidence and stifle the West Germans, the Hamburg crowd began to chant for the visitors.

For the second match running, chants of 'Austral-lien, Austral-lien' rang around the Volksparkstadion. Each touch of the ball by a Socceroo player was accompanied by a large cheer. 'This is incredible, the German crowd are cheering for the Socceroos!', John Motson, the shocked commentator on the BBC, covering the match in Britain, proclaimed.

The local television director regularly cut to shots of Netzer sitting on West Germany's substitutes bench as he slumped back into his chair shaking his head.

Beckenbauer was particularly riled by losing the support of the home crowd, which he blamed on the fierce rivalry between Hamburg and Munich. The man who did not think Australia deserved a place at the World Cup at the expense of England was booed after being muscled off the ball by Mackay, a Scotsman, remember, to concede a corner.

Beckenbauer's reaction was to spit in the direction of the supporters giving him the bird. 'I was called a "Bayern pig" and just went ballistic,' Beckenbauer said after the match. 'I regret this. However, my reaction was only directed at those 10 or 15 people. I am sorry that the spectators felt offended.'

The row over bonuses and Beckenbauer's behaviour had badly hit the popularity of the West German team. Criticism

Jimmy Mackay is shown the yellow card after kicking the ball away

in the German media was mounting. The West German captain was forced to call a special press conference after the Australia match, and apologise for his personal conduct. 'I'm really sorry that I have allowed myself to be provoked into this gaffe,' he said. 'I can only hope people won't stop supporting us now.'

Gerd Muller was restricted to just one goal versus Australia

Australia may even have scored a consolation goal when Abonyi found a bit of space, following a pass by Mackay, and crashed a shot against the inside of West Germany's post. There was also another moment of fantastic skill from Alston. He chased another long ball and, with no one alongside to help him, he decided to firstly take on Beckenbauer and then Schwarzenbeck, the defender who had stuck close to him all match. Alston fired in a shot which Maier saved.

The striker later claimed he should have done better. Maybe, but his performance had again caught the eye of a number of Bundesliga clubs, who were growing increasingly interested in making his stay in Germany permanent.

Alston believed that the home crowd were unrealistic in expecting their team to score a hatful of goals. 'We respected them, but we were never going to let them humiliate us,' he said in his autobiography, *Noddy*. 'That's just not us. The crowd was getting agitated towards the end because the spectators were probably expecting more goals, but we did not let them do that.

'Beckenbauer said after the game that the team was surprised with our determination. I would like to think that our overall performance had changed a few people's minds about our football, especially those who questioned our right to be in the competition in the first place.'

At the final whistle, as boos rained down on the West German team, Wilson approached Beckenbauer to swap shirts. Wilson can be seen pulling at Beckenbauer's sleeve as he walked off, with the West German captain pushing him away. 'If Mr Beckenbauer wants to keep this shirt, then he can do so,' Wilson said in the post-match press conference.

What Wilson did not know was that his teammate Alston had already arranged the swap with Beckenbauer before the game even kicked off. 'We arrived at the ground one and a half hours from kick-off and to our surprise, we found out that the Germans were already warming up,' Alston revealed in his autobiography. 'We said to ourselves

Socceroos substitute Peter Ollerton challenges West Germany goalkeeper Sepp Maier for a high ball

that by the time the match started, they would be knackered.

'The group went into our dressing room to prepare, but I did not follow the lads to the sheds and instead I went over to where Beckenbauer was warming up, and when he was done, I got in early and asked him if we could exchange jerseys after the match. He asked me what number I would be wearing and when I said my jersey number was 12, he said, "Okay, I'll look out for you." I said to him, "Don't worry about that, mate. I'll be looking out for you wherever you are."'

The West German captain was not the only one reluctant to do a swap on the pitch. At the end, Reilly approached his counterpart in the German goal and tried to get Maier's top. 'He said to me, "Dressing room, dressing room, dressing room," but when I caught up with him later, I could see to my embarrassment that he had so many layers of clothing on him that I had nearly castrated the poor man in trying to rip his jersey off on the pitch,' Reilly revealed.

There was a happy ending, however, as the swap occurred in the changing room and Reilly later auctioned it for charity.

Wilson's failure to snare Beckenbauer's shirt did not damage his opinion of the West German legend. 'You'd heard so much about them, then you played against them and found out that they were even better than you had expected,' he said. 'Beckenbauer is the greatest, most incredible player I have ever seen.'

There was an unfortunate incident in the first half involving Socceroos' right-back Doug Utjesenovic and Heynckes, who was playing on the left. 'He tried to pass me from the outside and when he got to the by-line to put in a cross, I lunged at the ball in a sliding tackle and he did his ankle upon impact, probably because the momentum was all with me,' Utjesenovic later recalled.

Peter Wilson, left, tries to swap shirts with West German captain Franz Beckenbauer, but Adrian Alston, right, had already pre-arranged to get Der Kaiser's prized jersey

'He never came back in the second half and his World Cup would be over. It was just unfortunate, and I'll never forget that.'

The accident did not detract from another great Socceroos performance that once again earned praise from both the German and international media. Rasic claimed that this was the match where 'Australian soccer arrived on the world stage'.

To put the Australians' performance into perspective, the other two newcomers to the World Cup were not faring so well. On the same day the Socceroos had restricted West Germany to just three goals, Zaire were beaten 9–0 by Yugoslavia at the Parkstadion in Gelsenkirchen. The next day, Haiti were thrashed 7–0 by Poland at the Olympic Stadium in Munich. Zaire and Haiti would both finish the tournament having conceded 14 goals.

It made it all the more ridiculous that some of the uneducated media in Australia had criticised Rasic for adopting an overly defensive approach. Those close to the Socceroos were fully on board with his tactics. 'Realistically, trying to establish a defensive platform was the only sensible option we had,' said Warren. 'It would have been disastrous for the game in Australia if we had come out, all guns blazing, and been beaten by a huge margin.'

Those who understood the game had taken note of how well organised and professionally set up the Socceroos were. After the West Germany match, Rasic revealed that he had received offers from teams in Austria, France and Switzerland to coach them. At the same time, he announced that he wanted to renew his contract with the Australian Soccer Federation to have a crack at qualifying for the 1978 World Cup in Argentina.

With the Socceroos riding so high and being praised all around the world, it seemed a straightforward decision for Federation president Sir Arthur George to make.

Surely?

CHAPTER SIXTEEN

Playing for more than just pride

When the Socceroos returned to Ochsenzoll for their last night after their defeat against West Germany, Rale Rasic allowed the players the opportunity of an evening off and to go into Hamburg to grab a few drinks.

He imposed a curfew but admitted he did not think anyone would observe it and was expecting to see a group of bleary-eyed players at breakfast the next morning. He was, therefore, delighted when every single player returned to the training base well before his deadline. It demonstrated to him that they remained focused with one last match in Group 1 coming up, even though two defeats meant they could not go any further in the competition.

Adrian Alston claimed that the players never considered the match against Chile a 'dead rubber' because 'that is not the way we were'.

After breakfast on 19th June, the Socceroos packed their bags to end their nine-day stay at Ochsenzoll. The staff there were sad to see them go and praised them for being such great ambassadors for their country. Ernst Kreuz, chief chef at the centre, was pleased they had enjoyed his cooking and was shocked that the players had even washed their own dishes.

Rasic was proud that his team had made such a favourable impression but wanted more than just that in the final game. 'We must stop winning friends and start winning points,' he told the squad before they boarded the plane for the two-and-a-half-hour flight to West Berlin. As well as achieving that first point, Rasic also wanted his team to score their first World Cup goal and lift the Fair Play Trophy.

There was a treat for the party when they arrived in Germany's divided former capital. Rasic had arranged for them to stay in the five-star Gersthus Hotel, instead of another training camp. 'I did not want the players to be caught up in the regimented atmosphere we had to endure in Hamburg,' Rasic explained in his autobiography. 'They needed some space and some extra care. It was a reward for the players who had given so much, not only in the first two matches but over the last four years. They deserved it.'

When the Socceroos party landed in Berlin, Australian Soccer Federation president Sir Arthur George was immediately taken to an engagement at the local zoo. There, he presented the Berlin Zoological Garden, Germany's oldest surviving and best-known zoo, with two souvenir toy kangaroos. Sir Arthur promised that he would arrange for two live kangaroos to be sent to the zoo if the German fans continued to support Australia in their last match. Whether Sir Arthur really did sort it out or whether it was just a coincidence is not known, but two kangaroos were sent from Australia to start residence at Berlin Zoo in 1975, and survived there for 14 years.

The delegation from Chile had more urgent matters on their minds. Following their narrow 1–0 defeat to hosts West Germany in the opening match, they had drawn 1–1 with East Germany in the second, thanks to a 69th-minute equaliser from Sergio Ahumada. Unlike the Socceroos, it meant they still had the chance to qualify for the next stage of the tournament.

Overshadowing everything, however, was what was happening back home in South America. Chile was still in a state of extreme crisis after the American-backed *coup d'état* in 1973, in which the democratically elected government of Salvador Allende had been overthrown by the military, led by General Augusto Pinochet. Pinochet had ended civilian rule and installed himself as the head of state. It started a 17-year military dictatorship in which thousands of political opponents were tortured, beheaded, burned alive and disappeared.

Several members of Chile's team – nicknamed 'La Roja' – had openly supported Allende and his progressive socialist policies before he was deposed, and feared for their safety under the new regime. Indeed, many of the players had been happy when Allende had paraded them as symbols of pride and unity for the new socialist Chile.

Chile had qualified for West Germany 1974 in controversial and farcical circumstances, when the Soviet Union had refused to take part in the return leg of the play-off because of claims that Pinochet had used the Estadio Nacional in Santiago to intern political prisoners. FIFA, who had conducted the briefest of inspections while the prisoners were held in the bowels of the stadium with guns pointed at their heads, had ordered the match to start. Chile walked the ball into an empty net to qualify for the World Cup finals.

Among the most strident opponents of Pinochet was Carlos Caszely, who had only agreed to play in the 'ghost match' that day because he feared for the safety of his family. 'That team did the most ridiculous thing in history,' he said. 'It was a worldwide embarrassment.'

Just as Allende wanted to associate himself with La Roja for political reasons, so did Pinochet. That is why he was keen to be seen wishing the team farewell before they departed for West Germany. Caszely recalled how he and his teammates were approached by a man wearing a cape, dark glasses and a hat. 'A cold shiver went down my back from seeing this Hitler-like-looking thing, with five guys behind him,' he said. 'When he started coming closer, I put my hand behind me and didn't give it to him.'

It was the first public act of dissent towards Pinochet, and Caszely's family paid a high price. 'I said no to dictatorship on every level: no to dictatorship, no to torture,' he recalled sadly. 'So, they made me pay for that with what they did to my mother.'

Caszely's mother, Olga, was arrested and tortured for her son's political views.

Chile went to the World Cup underprepared as they struggled to find anyone that would play warm-up matches against them due to the country's pariah status following Pinochet's coup. In West Germany, the squad were surrounded by Pinochet's military men and not allowed to speak to any outsiders in case they criticised the junta.

In this pressure cooker of an atmosphere, it was no surprise that Caszely lost his temper in Chile's opening match against West Germany. He retaliated after being fouled by Berti Vogts and became the first player in World Cup history to be shown a red card when he was sent off by Turkish referee Dogan Babacan. Red and yellow cards had been introduced for the first time at a World Cup at Mexico 1970, but no one had been sent off.

Caszely was banned for Chile's match against East Germany, but was back in time to face the Socceroos. The 23-year-old, who had moved in 1973 to play his club football in Spain for Levante, had, by his actions in refusing to shake Pinochet's hand, unwittingly become a figurehead for the millions of Chileans opposed to the military dictatorship.

Soon after Chile's qualification for West Germany, a number of Chile solidarity groups, founded across Europe, saw the World Cup as the ideal platform to express their dissent towards Pinochet. As fate would have it, Chile were due to play all their matches in West Berlin at the stadium built for the 1936 Olympic Games, the most politically charged in history.

The Nazi Party had risen to power in Germany in 1933, two years after Berlin was awarded the Olympics, and its racist policies led to international debate about a boycott of the Games. Fearing a mass boycott, the International Olympic Committee pressured the German government and received assurances that qualified Jewish athletes would be part of the German team, and that the Games would not be used to promote Nazi ideology. Adolf Hitler's government, however, routinely failed to deliver on such promises.

Pamphlets and speeches about the natural superiority of the Aryan race were commonplace, and the Reich Sports Field, a newly constructed sports complex that covered 325 acres and included four stadiums, was draped in Nazi banners and symbols. The main focal point of the entire complex's composition was the Olympic Stadium, which was located at the middle of the Reich Sports Field.

Work on the Olympic Stadium began in 1934 and was completed in time for the Games in the summer of 1936. Taking the symmetrical form of a large oval, it was built in the monumental Neoclassical style favoured by the Nazis and was capable of holding 110,000 spectators. The structure was partially dug into the ground, so that the field itself was some 12 metres below ground level. Its sheer scale was intended to impress the world and inspire awe, and in this it succeeded.

Although Germany topped the medal table, the 1936 Olympics were most memorable for the performances of American athlete Jesse Owens, who won four gold medals in the track and field events and, because he was black, completely undermined the myth of Aryan superiority.

After the Second World War, the stadium was taken over by the British and became part of their military occupation headquarters, where it was used for general sporting activities as well as acting as the home for the local Bundesliga football team, Hertha BSC Berlin.

A group representing the Chile Solidarity Committee and the Socialist Work Collective, founded at the Department of Jurisprudence of the Berlin Free University, were put in charge of planning activities to highlight their cause during the World Cup under the slogan 'Chile Si, Junta No!'.

They started planning to organise a pitch invasion during their country's opening match against West Germany. The event was broadcast worldwide, including in Chile, and promised maximum exposure.

The group soon realised how difficult a task this would be. The pitch was separated from the spectators by Plexiglass barriers along with a deep trench designed to keep out potential pitch invaders. Plus, like many of the stadiums being used during the World Cup, there was a running track around the arena. That was before the incredibly tight security employed by the West German authorities desperate to avoid any more security problems after the massacre of the Israeli athletes at the 1972 Olympic Games in Munich was factored in.

About 1,500 demonstrators managed to obtain tickets in block 41 for the match against West Germany, and when the local army band began playing the Chilean national anthem, they started chanting 'Chile Si, Junta No!' A large flag measuring six by four metres was also unfurled, covering the heads of most of the block. Boos from West German fans among the attendance of 82,000, angry at the disruption, greeted the protest.

West German police were already moving in to quell the protest, but their urgency intensified when a group unveiled a banner in which the 'CH' in 'PINOCHET' had been replaced by a swastika that was clearly visible from a distance. Displaying the swastika had been a criminal offence in Germany since the end of the War.

Although they had failed to get onto the pitch as they had hoped, the Chilean demonstrators considered their protest to be a success. The day after the match, they organised a march, attended by 7,000 supporters, to FIFA's World Cup headquarters at the Hotel Schweizerhof in West Berlin. There, they presented a petition against the suppression of anti-Pinochet protests.

At their next match against East Germany on 18th June, however, the German authorities were much more alert to the dangers of another protest by the Chilean groups. Even though the attendance of 28,000 meant the Olympic Stadium was not even half full, nearly 2,000 policemen were deployed. They conducted thorough bodychecks designed to ensure no banners were smuggled into the stands.

The Chile Solidarity Committee had hoped for some support from the 3,000 East German fans brought to the match in special trains, but they had been warned to stay clear of any sort of political activity that could be seen as overshadowing their country's first appearance in the World Cup.

The Chilean dissident groups knew that the match against Australia on 22nd June could be their last opportunity to mount a protest that would be seen around the world. It is fair to say that they were not optimistic and feared they had missed their chance to send a powerful message that would embarrass Pinochet and the military junta.

Following the takeover by Pinochet, about 10,000 Chilean supporters of Allende sought asylum in Australia. The Chile Solidarity Committee flourished in Australia. In February 1974, unionised airport workers in Sydney grounded a plane of LAN Airlines, the national carrier of Chile, after discovering its passengers included a military general from the junta.

Socceroos goalkeeper Jack Reilly admitted that they were oblivious to the Chileans' ordeal. 'We were a group of guys who'd given up our jobs for six to eight weeks who weren't very politically minded,' he said. 'Our only thought really was that we'd lost the first two games, and we didn't want to lose all three.'

Rasic also concentrated on the strength of Chile's players, ignoring the turmoil that was happening in their camp.

Chile is a long, narrow country stretching along South America's western edge, with more than 6,000 kilometres of Pacific Ocean coastline. At the time, it had a relatively small population of about 15 million. The Football Federation of Chile was the second oldest in South America. It had been founded in 1895 by David Scott, a Scottish journalist who had emigrated to the country.

West Germany 1974 was Chile's fifth appearance in the World Cup finals, including the first two at Uruguay 1930 and Italy 1934. Chile had hosted the World Cup in 1962, when they had finished third after being knocked out in the semi-finals by eventual champions Brazil. Brazil had won the tournament, beating Czechoslovakia 3–1 in the same Estadio Nacional that was now being used as a prison and torture chamber by Pinochet for his political opponents.

The team in West Germany was coached by Luis Alamos. He had returned to the role having also been Chile's coach when they were knocked out in the group stages of the 1966 World Cup in England. He had replaced German Rudi Gutendorf, originally tasked with the job of guiding Chile to the 1974 World Cup.

After leaving Peru to accept the role in Chile in 1972, Gutendorf had grown close to President Allende. 'I spent a lot of time with the president on his estate outside of Santiago,' he said. 'We often drank whisky at his place, and afterwards, we'd return to Santiago by helicopter.'

Gutendorf's role in Chile extended far beyond football, however, and he was invited by Allende to perform several actions as an honorary government official. This included opening public buildings, such as schools, and crowning the winner of Miss Chile.

The then 46-year-old Gutendorf had also started an affair with a woman 20 years his junior who was rumoured to be secretly working for the CIA, the United States spy agency. One night, when Gutendorf and his lover were lying in bed, a man entered the room and shot the woman in the head, killing her instantly. Gutendorf suffered a shattered jawbone and bore the scar to remind him of the incident until his death at the age of 93 in 2019.

When Pinochet seized power and ousted Allende, who committed suicide following a farewell address on the radio to his supporters, Gutendorf was advised by the German Ambassador in Santiago to flee the country. He did so reluctantly, torn between wanting to complete the job he had started and support his players or facing the real prospect of being imprisoned and murdered by the new junta.

One unintended legacy that Gutendorf unwittingly left behind when he fled the country was a practice wall at the Estadio Nacional, where Chile's team warmed up for matches by kicking balls at it to increase accuracy. Pinochet decided to use Gutendorf's practice wall as the place against which hundreds of dissidents were shot.

After leaving Chile, Gutendorf had brief spells in Bolivia and Venezuela before taking over the national teams of Botswana and Grenada. He eventually ended up coaching the Socceroos in 1979 as Australian Soccer Federation president Sir Arthur tried to halt a decline in fortunes he had set in motion with the dismissal of Rasic. By the time he eventually retired in 2003, Gutendorf had set a Guinness World Record for coaching 55 teams in 32 countries, located in six continents.

Rasic had sent the Australian Soccer Federation's director of coaching, Eric Worthington, to scout Chile during their match against East Germany. Rasic had already done a lot of analysis on their opponents but was hoping for some fresh insight. He was not impressed when Worthington failed to produce a written report, and his only observation was 'Chile is nothing much except they have two big lads at the back.'

Australia line up for their last match of the 1974 World Cup finals against Chile

Rasic's only change from the match against West Germany was replacing Ernie Campbell up front with Atti Abonyi, who had come so close to scoring the Socceroos' first goal in World Cup history when he hit the post after coming on as a substitute in Hamburg. It was the most adventurous line-up that

The Olympic Stadium in Berlin was not even a quarter full for Australia's match against Chile

Rasic had selected in West Germany, with the trio of Abonyi, Alston and Branko Buljevic nicknamed 'the three gangsters'.

Another important change was that for the first time in the tournament, the Socceroos lined up wearing green socks with gold piping to avoid clashing with their opponents dressed in red shirts and white shorts and socks.

Before the match, Rasic compared the Socceroos' situation to defending world champions Brazil. They had drawn their opening two matches, against Yugoslavia and Scotland, with 0–0 draws. 'Boys,' he told his team in the changing room, 'we are without a victory in the tournament, just like Brazil, but that will change today.'

In those days, the final group matches at the World Cup did not start simultaneously, so Chile knew they had to beat Australia in a game that kicked off at 4pm and hope West Germany beat their neighbours East Germany in the fixture that started three and a half hours later.

As an added incentive, the Football Federation of Chile, now under the control of Pinochet, offered the players a bonus of $8,000 if they beat the Socceroos and qualified for the next stage of the tournament. What would happen if they lost, no one knew, but there were real fears among the Chile players their families would be in danger.

It was no surprise, with so much on the line, that Chile started the more aggressively of the two countries. The Socceroos were well drilled, however, and with Peter Wilson and Manfred Schaefer superb in the middle at the back,

Jimmy Mackay tackles Chile's Elias Figueroa as a torrential downpour just before half-time left the pitch covered in water

brilliantly supported by full-backs Doug Utjesenovic and Col Curran, La Roja did not look like scoring.

Rasic was delighted with his team's performance; the only moment of annoyance was when Ray Richards received a yellow card from Iranian referee Jafar Namdar for arguing with him in the 37th minute. Namdar was making history as only the second Asian to referee a World Cup finals match, having been beaten to first by only three days by Singapore official George Suppiah, who had taken charge of Poland's match against Haiti.

Shortly before half-time, the dark clouds that had hovered over the Olympic Stadium since the game started opened up and there was a torrential downpour. The rain was so bad that the interval was extended to 22 minutes. Rasic claimed he 'had to literally drag' Namdar out to start the second half.

The rain provided an unexpected opportunity for members of the Chilean protest groups among the attendance of 17,400. There were reportedly 1,600 police on duty for the match, along with hundreds of undercover security officers dressed in tracksuits. To avoid getting soaked, they had sought cover under the grandstands, where they remained when the second half finally got underway.

The rain was so bad that the half-time interval was extended to 22 minutes

A group of 11 students from Chile seized their moment, climbing over the Plexiglass barriers, scrambling over the trench and running onto the pitch. They reached as far as the centre circle where they unfolded a Chilean flag bearing the words 'CHILE SOCIALISTA' and tried to lay it on the ground.

It seemed to take a few moments for the West German security forces to realise what had happened, and they rushed onto the pitch to halt the protest, which had been accompanied by loud boos and whistles from the mostly West German crowd. The demonstrators did not resist and gave up immediately when the police reached them.

Like Berlin's security forces, television producers in Chile were also caught off guard by the protest. They allowed it to be broadcast live to the country for several minutes before interrupting the match with a notice blaming 'technical problems'. The fate of the television executives that did not react quickly enough is unknown, but it was probably not pleasant.

The Socceroos' West German-appointed security man later told members of the Australian party that, after their arrest, he had witnessed the Chilean students being taken round the back of the Olympic Stadium and beaten by the police. They were later taken to a detention centre set up by the Charlottenburg police station on the Kaiserdamm, where they probably suffered more 'punishment'. They were charged with trespassing but were released soon after their personal data was recorded.

The West German media were heavy in their criticism of the police's performance. 'Only three goals were scored in three World Cup games played in the Olympic Stadium,' *Die Welt* said in an editorial. 'The police contributed two "own goals" to the tournament: first, with insufficient protection for the Chilean consulate, which was attacked on 12 June; then on Saturday, when demonstrators managed to exploit the Berlin World Cup final for political purposes.'

Chileans protesting against Pinochet took advantage of the rain storm to breach security before police could stop them

The next day in Santiago, after the match against the Socceroos, Pinochet was publicly declared 'Supreme Chief of the Nation', effectively appointing him president. His reign of terror continued until he stepped down in 1990. Pinochet continued to serve as Commander-in-Chief of the Chilean Army until 1998, when he retired. Later that year, Pinochet was arrested during a visit to London, under an international arrest warrant, in connection with numerous human rights violations. By the time of his death in December 2006, there were 300 criminal charges still pending against him in Chile for numerous human rights violations during his 17-year rule, as well as tax evasion and embezzlement during and after his rule. Pinochet was also accused of having corruptly amassed a personal fortune of at least $28 million.

Whether it was the heavy rain or the protest, Chile were not the same side in the second half, and the Socceroos gradually got on top on a pitch that resembled a shallow lake. Jimmy Mackay wasted a chance when he blasted the ball over the crossbar from close range after running up the field to try to complete a move he had started, and then had a clear penalty appeal turned down.

Abonyi and Alston also had opportunities to score Australia's first World Cup goal. The performance of the Socceroos once again caught the imagination of the West German fans. For the third consecutive match, chants of 'Austral-lien, Austral-lien' could be heard echoing around the stadium.

In the 79th minute, Curran was fouled by Chile's Rolando Garcia before crumpling to the turf in agony and having to be carried off on a stretcher. The medial ligament of his knee had been snapped in the tackle. It was dreadful bad luck for a player who had nearly missed the World Cup because of an injury sustained at the start of the Socceroos' preparation, but who had worked so hard to recover from that setback.

It meant that Harry Williams, the first Indigenous player to represent Australia, was sent on for the final few moments of Socceroos' World Cup adventure.

Rasic had signalled to Richards to delay taking the free kick so he could get Williams ready to come on. The ploy backfired because referee Namdar issued Richards with another yellow card. That should have meant he was shown a red, yet the official inexplicably allowed him to continue.

Another four minutes passed before the reserve referee, Wales's Clive Thomas, managed to make his way down from the stands and informed the linesman what had happened. That linesman was Belgian official Vital Loraux, who the previous October had refereed the Socceroos' World Cup qualifying match against South Korea in Sydney. He called over Namdar to explain the situation. The Iranian then consulted the FIFA match supervisor about what he should do next.

'After getting the second card I played on, but after about five minutes the linesman was alerted to the fact that the number six had received two yellow cards and should not be on the field,' Richards said. 'So, the referee came up to me and said I had two yellows to which I replied, "Nah, it's only one." I pointed to Doug [Utjesenovic] and told the ref that he had got the card, not me. By this time, the Chileans came up to the referee and, gesturing at me, told him, "It was him, it was him."'

Schaefer also tried to take the blame with Mackay pointing at the German trying to convince the referee that is who he had cautioned, not Richards.

'To cut a long story short, the referee was completely confused and he gave me a third yellow card before sending me off with seven minutes to go,' said Richards. 'So, I must be one of only a few players to get three yellows and a red in one game. I laugh about it now, but I was upset at the time because I thought I had let the team down.'

This incident has only ever happened once since in the World Cup and, remarkably, Australia were again involved. This time, the guilty man was Croatian defender Josip Simunic, shown three yellow cards during his side's match against the Socceroos in Stuttgart at Germany 2006. The centre-back received his first yellow card from English referee Graham Poll in the 61st minute, for sticking a hand out to stop Harry Kewell. His second came after 90 minutes, when he was guilty of a poor challenge in the middle of the pitch.

Simunic saw the yellow card and walked away slyly without being shown the red card that should have come with it. At the end of the match, Simunic then berated Poll to get his third yellow card of the game and the elusive red card he should have been handed minutes earlier.

After the match, Poll claimed he had got confused by the broad Australian accent of Simunic, who had been born in Canberra to Bosnian Croat parents and started his career at Melbourne Knights before moving to Europe. Poll

Socceroos goalkeeper Jack Reilly feared he had presented Chile with a late opportunity to score the winner

never refereed another international match again. Namdar fared better and was rewarded by FIFA by being appointed as a linesman for the third-place play-off at West Germany 1974, between Brazil and Poland. He also officiated at the 1976 Olympic Games in Montreal.

Even after being forced to play the last few minutes with 10 men, the Socceroos defended staunchly as Chile poured forward, trying to score the goal they needed. The one time that Chile looked likely to score came in the final seconds, when Reilly, in the Socceroos goal, collected a ball, only for his feet to slip on the wet turf. 'My elbows hit the ground and the ball popped up in the air,' he recalled. 'Luckily, Peter Wilson was there to save the day. I almost lost us the match.'

A few moments later, the final whistle went to signal a 0–0 draw, with Wilson throwing his hands in the air to celebrate Australia's first World Cup point.

The Socceroos had failed to fulfil Rasic's target of scoring their first goal, and their chances of lifting the Fair Play Trophy were gone after Richards's red card. But Australia's point meant they finished on the same total as Uruguay, one of the four seeded teams, and better than the other two newcomers, Zaire and Haiti.

'It was a huge result for Australian soccer,' Rasic said.

CHAPTER SEVENTEEN

You're fired!

After the historic draw against Chile, the Socceroos showered and boarded their specially branded Mercedes bus to head back to their luxury hotel for one final meal together.

Before dinner, coach Rale Rasic gathered the party together and delivered an emotional six-minute speech. 'I thanked them for everything they had done for their country, themselves and family, and for me,' he recounted in his autobiography. 'I thanked them for their sacrifices, both family and workwise. They had bled for their country and their mates, and they had done themselves proud.'

It was not just Rasic who thought his Socceroos had surpassed expectations. The next morning, *Bild-Zeitung*, the German tabloid newspaper that had asked 'Why have we got these kangaroos at the World Cup?', carried an editorial apologising for its earlier comments.

'When Australia was drawn on January 5 to play in the same group as our national team, everyone laughed,' *Bild-Zeitung* wrote. 'What could these greenhorns be dreaming of playing East and West Germany. They will get thrashed … We would like to apologise for the statements we made. We were wrong … The Australians have been a wonderful squad. Thank you very much, and goodbye and good luck Aussies.'

Other international media also admitted their shock at how well the Socceroos had acquitted themselves. Influential French sports newspaper *L'Equipe* wrote that they had delivered a 'surprisingly mature brand of football'. They added: 'Their football was precise, intelligent and thoroughly modern. It was impossible to tell that their players came from the far end of the world, where they are isolated from the mainstream of soccer.'

L'Equipe were especially impressed by Adrian Alston, claiming his 'technique was remarkable, a revelation'. Captain Peter Wilson was another to catch the eye of the French. They called him one of 'the tournament's most competent liberos'.

There was no major celebration after the last dinner. Some of the players went out for a drink, a few visited clubs, others met up with their families, a couple stayed in the hotel to soak up the atmosphere for the last few hours. The team had been together for nearly two years now, travelling the world chasing a dream, which they had now fulfilled. Everyone was wondering what was to come next.

Rasic already knew his fate.

At the end of the Chile game, Australian Soccer Federation president Sir Arthur George had paid a fulsome tribute to the Socceroos. 'You have put Australia on the map for 700 million TV viewers much more effectively than all the diplomatic people, who go overseas and spend hundreds and thousands of dollars.

'When the players of Haiti lined up before their first match and their national anthem was played, they wept openly, so proud were they to represent their country. In Australia's case, it is the country which was proud to have such a team wearing the green and gold.'

Shortly after these words, Sir Arthur called Rasic and told him that they would not be renewing his contract. A coach who had overseen a team winning 27 matches out 58, drawing 17 and losing just 14, and scoring 96 goals and conceding 58 in the process, had been fired.

A coach who had taken Australia to the World Cup finals for the first time, earning praise from all around the world, had been sacked. It probably ranks as one of the worst decisions ever taken in Australian sport.

Rasic had wanted to continue but feared what was coming. There had been too many rows in the past four years. Throwing Sir Arthur out of the dressing

Tributes were still being paid to the Socceroos' performance when Sir Arthur George informed Rale Rasic he would not be retained as coach

room at the end of the Uruguay friendly in Melbourne in April had been a silly thing to do, and probably sealed his future.

Rasic had also, unfairly, been portrayed as the ringleader of the players' pay dispute on the eve of the World Cup qualifying match against South Korea in Sydney, when the Australian Soccer Federation had been forced to back down.

During one row with Sir Arthur, it was reported that Rasic yelled at him: 'Either you go, or I go!' There was room for only one giant-sized ego in Australian soccer – and it was not Rasic's.

Rasic was still furious when it became public that he had been fired. 'The treatment I received as national coach, I would not wish on any person,' he said. 'I fought battles with everyone for four years.'

Team doctor Brian Corrigan had witnessed Rasic in action from close quarters during his four-year spell as coach. 'Throughout the World Cup campaign, Rasic had his critics,' he wrote in his autobiography, *The Life of Brian*. 'Some reckoned he was too abrasive. Rale's reply: "I was a coach, not a diplomat. If I were a diplomat, we would never have qualified." Many believed he played too defensively, especially when we were lucky to escape with those two draws against New Zealand in the preliminary matches.

'Rale was always supremely confident in his own ability. At the World Cup finals, when any coach there for the first time, and especially one so young as he was, would be entitled to be overawed, he took to it as though he had been coaching World Cup teams all his life.

'He had some monumental quarrels and arguments with ASF president Sir Arthur George over a whole range of matters – they were very different personalities. Rale had never been afraid to speak his mind and criticise the powers that be about the many things that he – and many other people for that matter – thought was wrong about Australian soccer.'

The Socceroos left Berlin to return home to Sydney unaware that the coach that had guided them to the greatest moment of their careers had been fired. Rasic stayed behind in West Germany after being employed as a columnist for the rest of the tournament by *Bild-Zeitung*, the same newspaper who had originally mocked the Socceroos. He watched as hosts West Germany put all the early criticism behind them by lifting the World Cup trophy with a 2–1 victory over the Netherlands in the final at the Olympic Stadium in Munich.

Peter Bizer, the German journalist who had travelled to Australia earlier in the year to produce a television programme on the Socceroos, remembered how much Rasic enjoyed being at the centre of the World Cup.

'Rale wanted to soak up every hour, every day, every game of the World Cup like a thirsty sponge,' he said. 'In the evenings, many of the football celebrities met in the "Zum Grauen Bock", a traditional Frankfurt restaurant, where the popular apple wine was a special challenge for every foreign guest.

'Always there and often enough in the centre was Rale. Here he felt like a fish in the water among all the experts and enthusiasts, the coaches, former world stars like the unforgettable Alfredo Di Stefano and international sports journalists. He inspired his table mates with his knowledge, his noticeable love for football, his humour and art of communicating with everyone.'

The first the players knew of what had happened to Rasic was when they landed back home. 'We were coming down the steps from the plane at Sydney airport and Arthur George greeted us by telling us that Rasic had been dismissed,' said goalkeeper Jack Reilly. 'His contract was up, and it was not renewed. We were all shocked and in complete disbelief. I think that moment sent our football so far back that it was going to take the game many years to recover.'

Alston summed up the shock the squad felt when they found out. 'We could not believe what we were hearing about Rasic,' he wrote in his autobiography, *Noddy*. 'It was like snapping the head off our game. The drama with Rasic should never have happened. He would have added to that squad and made it better.

'Clearly Rale was sacked because he was never prepared to be a "yes" man. It was always an issue with him ... he always put his players first and it had to be his way, and some people from the Federation did not like that.'

The mainstream Australian media were still praising the Socceroos' better-than-expected performance in West Germany, not knowing that the architect of it had been dismissed. 'For a team of part-time players, they did remarkably well in their first appearance at the World Cup finals,' an editorial published in *The Australian*, to coincide with the squad's arrival home, said.

'They surprised everyone who saw them play with their determination and ability, and while they lost two of their three matches, they won Australian soccer a new and more respected position in the sporting world.'

Soccer World concentrated on the potential impact that the Socceroos' performance could have on the sport in the future in Australia. 'They aroused tremendous interest back home; people who have never been to a soccer game in their lives sat up to watch the games televised early in the morning,' they wrote. 'Soccer's image in Australia has steadily changed from migrant sport to a populist game, and the World Cup challenges both in Munich (sic) and earlier games in Korea and Iran, highlighted and hastened this trend.

'The growth of the game raises some interesting possibilities ... It is quite possible that soccer could be Australia's national winter game in the next 20 years or so.'

Outside of the Australian Soccer Federation, Rasic's reputation was at its peak. The Department of Tourism and Recreation appointed him to join a panel of six experts, including Andrew Dettre, which travelled around the world in

September 1974 to research the success of national training centres and produce a feasibility study about creating an Australian institute of sport.

In the end, the recommendations of the study group were largely ignored until Australia's disastrous performance at the 1976 Olympic Games in Montreal, when the team failed to win a gold medal. It led to the establishment in 1980 of the Australian Institute of Sport, laying the groundwork for the country to become a leading power in the Olympics. It culminated in Australia finishing fourth overall when Sydney hosted the Games in 2000, with a total of 58 medals, including 16 gold.

Soccer World's Lou Gautier, summing up the Socceroos' performance at West Germany 1974, laid the credit squarely at the door of Rasic. He wrote that his 'stature has grown even more during the World Cup'.

Gautier warned the Australian Soccer Federation 'would be criminally stupid not to give Rale Rasic everything he wants to stay at the helm for the next four years'.

Quite how stupid, Gautier could not have imagined. Sir Arthur had allowed his personal antagonism towards Rasic to cloud his judgement. He had no plan as to who was going to replace the successful coach he had just fired. There were no friendly matches arranged for the Australian Soccer Federation to capitalise on the new interest in the Socceroos. The celebrations for Australian soccer's finest moment had not even finished, and the sport was facing a wasteland.

Soccer World tried to engineer a reconciliation between Sir Arthur and Rasic with an eye on the next World Cup, set to take place in Argentina in 1978. 'It would be a tragedy for Australian soccer if petty jealousies and clashes of personalities robbed the national team of the coach who made our creditable showing in West Germany possible,' Gautier wrote after the news about Rasic's firing had become public knowledge.

'Sir Arthur George has to call Rasic in for a heart-to-heart talk to dispel any misunderstandings. Both should lay their cards on the table. I am sure that an arrangement can be reached that will ensure that Rasic remains in charge of Australia's bid to reach Argentina in 1978. It will be tough enough finding what virtually amounts to a new team without the added hardship of breaking in a new coach.

'It is ridiculous to suggest we should advertise nationwide and worldwide for a coach when we have the best man for the job right here. His build-up of the team over four hard years puts him in good stead to achieve similar, if not better, results with the new Socceroos who will be carrying our hopes over the next four years.'

Soccer World's pleas were ignored. Sir Arthur refused to entertain the idea of going back on his decision and renewing Rasic's contract. Instead, the Australian Soccer Federation's director of coaching, Eric Worthington, the

Englishman of whom Rasic had such a low opinion, was put in charge of finding a replacement.

Perhaps Sir Arthur believed he was really the power behind the Socceroos' success. Shortly after returning home from West Germany, the now former FIFA president Sir Stanley Rous had travelled to Sydney to meet him. He told Sir Arthur over lunch at Tattersalls Club, where in 1972 the Socceroos' brand had been launched, that 'Australia has the basic structure and the ability to develop to European or South American standards'.

Sir Stanley told Sir Arthur that 'much of the push had come from' him and that he was a 'forceful spokesman for Australia over the years in both Oceania and FIFA'. Sir Arthur no doubt loved it when the former leader of FIFA told him that he was an 'influential man whose energetic support of soccer has been a boon to the game'.

Whatever Sir Arthur really thought, more than a year after the World Cup had finished and Rasic fired, the Australian Soccer Federation was still looking for a new coach. Rasic had applied for his old job but was never going to be considered.

'The ASF is not happy with the quality of applicants, who include former coach Rale Rasic,' the *Sydney Morning Herald* reported in July 1975. 'It plans to intensify its search for a top man.'

In the meantime, a row between Rasic and the Australian Soccer Federation, over bonuses he claimed he was due for steering the Socceroos to the World Cup finals, had become public. Rasic claimed that there had been a verbal agreement, but secretary Brian Le Fevre contradicted him. 'He is completely wrong,' Le Fevre told *Soccer World*. 'His claims are incorrect. Up to date, the ASF has paid every cent they owe to him.'

In March 1975, Le Fevre mailed Rasic. 'Please find attached hereto your cheque for the sum of $2,400, which represents the West Germany qualification bonus of $3,000 minus a tax deduction of $600,' he wrote. 'You will recall that this was the amount that was agreed to be recommended to the Executive for payment to you, and subsequently the Executive approved such payment.'

The Australian Soccer Federation annual accounts later revealed that they had made a $252,000 profit from the Socceroos' appearance at the World Cup. Of that figure, a total of $115,309.46 was paid out in bonuses to the players, which worked out at about $5,000 for each member of the 22-man squad.

While he searched for the 'top man' to take over the Socceroos, Worthington himself took charge of several matches on a caretaker basis, including to Indonesia to take part in the Djakarta Anniversary Cup Tournament. The squad was selected to ensure that every Australian state was represented, rather than on player merit, and did not include any members of the Socceroos team from the World Cup. Australia failed to win either of their two matches and were beaten 2–1 by Burma.

Worthington shared the caretaker role with Italian Tony Boggi, the coach of Victorian State League club Juventus. Boggi led the Socceroos in friendlies against Scotland's Glasgow Rangers, England's Manchester United, China's national team and Portugal's Benfica. He had quite a good record, winning against Rangers and China, drawing with Benfica and losing against a full-strength Manchester United. Boggi, however, failed to fit the criteria that the Australian Soccer Federation was looking for, and he was never in with a chance of getting the job of coach on a full-time basis.

Australian Soccer Federation director of coaching, Englishman Eric Worthington, led a squad to the Djakarta Anniversary Cup Tournament

Finally, in September 1975, the identity of the 'top man' the Australian Soccer Federation had been seeking as its new coach for more than a year was revealed. His name was Brian Green, plucked from the Fourth Division of English football. The 40-year-old had played for a series of lower league clubs in England, including Rochdale, Southport and Exeter City in the Football League, before finishing his playing career with a short spell at Sydney Prague.

He was a coach under manager Ken Roberts at Chester City, who had just enjoyed the best season of their 89-year history by getting promoted from the Fourth Division and reaching the semi-finals of the League Cup, where they had been narrowly beaten 5–4 over two legs by First Division side Aston Villa. Chester's star striker that season was Terry Owen, whose son Michael went on to play for Liverpool, Real Madrid and England.

The club's success saw Green voted Coach of the Year by the Football League Coaches' Association. Sir Arthur flew to London to interview Green after former Manchester United manager Sir Matt Busby had given him a glowing reference. Green told Sir Arthur that he was the 'best man in England for the job'.

The decision to give Green the job immediately upset the New South Wales Soccer Federation as the successful applicant would also be appointed as their director of coaching, with them contributing $3,500 towards his annual salary. They had not been consulted, but Sir Arthur brushed off their complaints by claiming he had a mandate from all the states to appoint who he thought was the best man for the job.

News of the appointment was met with overwhelming disappointment. The *Sydney Morning Herald*'s soccer writer, Brian Mossop, wrote that Green deserved a 'measure of respect', but noted that his qualifications did not meet the 'original advertisements for a national coach with first division and/or national team experience'. Mossop concluded that the Australian Soccer Federation 'seems to have lowered its standards'.

The decision to hand the reins to Green was another slap in the face to the former coach, Mossop claimed. 'Rale Rasic was the only man who qualified on both counts,' he wrote. 'He knows the game in this country, is a professional man and took Australia to the World Cup finals. That sort of success deserved a better recognition than he received.'

Dettre, at *Soccer World*, was another who could not understand why the Australian Soccer Federation had placed its faith in a coach from such a low level of English football. The front page of the newspaper read 'ANGLOMANIA PREVAILS – RASIC DUMPED', with Dettre furious at Green's appointment. 'What I find more depressing is that the ASF seems hell-bent on prodding Australia even further towards becoming a pale imitation of English soccer,' he wrote.

The appointment of the Englishman came at a time of great soul-searching within Australian society. In November 1975, Rasic's great friend Gough Whitlam was forced out of office after a controversial deal between Sir John Kerr, Australia's governor-general appointed by the Queen in London, and the opposition saw the Liberal Party's Malcolm Fraser put in charge as caretaker prime minister. A snap general election was called, which Whitlam's Labor lost by a landslide.

Rasic dismissed Green as one of Worthington's English 'boys' he seemed so keen to promote. *Soccer World* looked back in its archives and discovered that Green had played only two matches in 1964 for Sydney Prague, earning a mark of just two from its reporters in both games. He was then dropped and flew back to England, running out on a three-year contract. That left Prague badly out of pocket as they had lodged a £140 bond with the Australian Immigration Department when Green landed in the country as an assisted migrant.

Geoff Sleight, an English teammate of Green's during his brief time at Prague, elaborated in more detail in his autobiography, *Sporting Memories of a Yorkshire Aussie*, about the controversial departure. He claimed that Green had told him that he did not like it in Australia and was going to tell the club his father had died and needed to return home.

'A week later, I went to training and asked where Greeny was,' Sleight wrote. '"He had to go home," they told me. "His dad's died."

'Bizarrely, that turned out to be the truth! His dad had actually died that week. The next time I saw him, I said: "I bet your dad didn't realise that you'd put his name down as a payment for you leaving Australia."'

That was all forgotten when Green landed in Australia to start his new role. 'I'm a winner,' he told the press upon his arrival. 'I have not come 12,000 miles to fail. I'm a man who doesn't fail. I'm a positive thinker. My track record is good after nine years as a coach and 15 years as a player, in all four divisions and in nine positions on the field. I've had a long apprenticeship. I'm supremely confident.'

Brian Green was not the big-name coach Socceroos fans had been promised

Green's appointment as the new national team coach was a complete disaster, and not just on the pitch. He arrived in Australia in time to take charge of the Socceroos in a six-match series in November and December against the Soviet Union, who, to the disappointment of the Australian Soccer Federation, had sent a B-team.

The first match, at the Perry Lakes Stadium in Perth, ended in a goalless draw, with the Socceroos featuring only four players who had represented them in the previous year's World Cup. The Soviet Union won three of the remaining five matches, with the other two finishing in draws.

The Soviets had won the third game of the series, at Olympic Park in Melbourne, 2–1 after Ernie Campbell had put the Socceroos ahead. In the fifth match, at Sydney Sports Ground, Australia were leading 2–0, with goals from Peter Ollerton and newcomer Murray Barnes, before throwing it away and losing 3–2.

Rasic was a spectator at the match in Sydney and mocked Green, who had promised to introduce a more attacking style of play. 'Don't be stupid,' he told *Soccer World*. 'In the second-half, the Australians had nine men in their own penalty area as the Russians bombarded them.'

The Socceroos started 1976 with a 2–2 draw against Velez Mostar, the Yugoslavian club from the city where Rasic had been born, at the Sydney Sports Ground on 8th February.

Then, four days later, there appeared a small item on page 21 of *The Age* newspaper under the headline 'Australia's soccer coach put on bond'. The story reported: 'Brian Green, Australia's new soccer coach, was placed on a $200, two-year bond for shoplifting in Central Court yesterday.

'Green, of East Esplanade, Manly, pleaded guilty to stealing two long-playing records, valued at $12.74, from Nicholsons Pty. Ltd.

'Mr. K. Anderson, SM, found the charge proven, but dismissed it without penalty under the first offenders' section of the Crimes Act.

'Green said last night that the president of the Australian Soccer Federation, Sir Arthur George, "accepted my word and the whole thing is forgotten. It is in the past – I am here to stay and coach Australia."'

The New South Wales Soccer Federation withdrew their portion of funding for Green's salary, claiming that it was unclear what his role was actually supposed to be. But the coach survived for a two-match series against New Zealand, with the Socceroos winning 1–0 at Newmarket Park in Auckland on 29th February and 3–1 at Olympic Park in Melbourne three days later.

Green claimed to retain the support of Sir Arthur and the players but shortly after the second game against the Kiwis, he fled home to England without telling anyone. 'He came, he didn't conquer, and he left,' was Rasic's curt summary of Green's bizarre spell as Socceroos coach.

The Australian Soccer Federation later issued a statement in which they claimed that while Sir Arthur had been prepared to 'overlook the matter' of the shoplifting offence, 'continuing pressures from many different sources have affected Mr Green's health'.

The statement added, 'In his letter of resignation to the Federation, Mr Green stated that these pressures had left him mentally drained and that if he had continued in the position of national coach, his health would have suffered further.'

Upon his arrival home in the north of England, Green appeared on Granada Television to let people know he was back and available for work. In the days before social media, the real reason as to why he had quit as the Socceroos coach had yet to reach England. Green instead blamed the Australian press and the fact that they never wanted him to replace Rasic.

'There had been a campaign for the reappointment of the previous coach, and this was a burden from the start,' Green told the local television channel without mentioning Rasic's name. 'My predecessor had taken the Australian team to the World Cup finals in Munich (sic) and there was antagonism to my appointment.'

Green also blamed the Australian Soccer Federation and complained: 'I thought they might have told me of the situation before I went.'

Then Green cryptically added that he 'had decided to quit about a month ago when pressures were becoming greater, and the job was drifting away' and stopping him doing what he 'had principally set out to do – coach soccer'.

He did not mention the shoplifting offence.

Green managed to land a new job for the 1976–1977 season as manager of Rochdale, one of the former clubs he had played for, but left at the end of it after they finished 18th in the English Fourth Division. The Englishman then ended up coaching a number of clubs in Norway, until he returned home in 1991. Green finished his working life delivering medicines from his local chemist. He died in Rochdale in 2012, at the age of 77.

Rasic had little sympathy for his successor. 'In Australia, if you are caught shoplifting and are a national coach, Aussies will take the piss out of you for the rest of your life,' he said.

The national coach's job was re-advertised and the Australian Soccer Federation received 23 applications, including from Rasic and former skipper Johnny Warren. Both made it to the four-man shortlist drawn up by Worthington, along with two English-born former players.

One was Alan Vest, who had emigrated to New Zealand and played in 17 matches for the All Whites, including in the 1974 World Cup qualifying campaign when he had scored one of the goals in the 3–3 draw against Australia in Sydney.

The other was Jim Shoulder, who had spent his career in England as a defender with Sunderland, Scarborough and Hartlepool United. He had combined his football career with higher education, and graduated with a degree in sociology from Durham University in 1973. At 29 years old, Shoulder had no coaching experience, however.

Rasic and Warren had a pact that if one of them was appointed as Socceroos coach, they would take on the other as an assistant. Their inclusion on the shortlist, though, was mainly for public show. Rasic was never going to be given a second chance by Sir Arthur, and Warren was tainted by having led the players' revolt over money before the final phase of World Cup qualifying against South Korea in 1973. Rasic and Warren were both eliminated after the first round of interviews at the Macleay Travelodge in King's Cross in Sydney.

Rasic's interview lasted only three minutes after he took exception to the opening question from Ian Brusasco, the official with whom he had fallen out during Australia's world tour in 1970. Brusasco asked Rasic whether he would 'give away playing defensive football'. Rasic took a pen and threw it at the official, and asked him to explain the difference between attacking and defensive football before walking out.

Warren's interview lasted an even shorter time. He left after one of the panel asked him: 'Tell us about yourself.' This to a man who was probably Australia's best-known soccer player, having appeared in 42 internationals for the Socceroos, including 24 as captain.

Of the remaining two, Vest was clearly the only choice. At the age of 36, he had played in Australia for Perth Azzurri and worked as director of coaching in Western Australia. Most importantly, he was also the choice of Sir Arthur and Worthington.

But when the Australian Soccer Federation Board of Directors voted, Sir Arthur had the tables turned on him. New South Wales, still angry after not being consulted about the appointment of Green, had decided beforehand that they were going to vote for Rasic and Warren to do the job together. After they were both eliminated, they decided to teach Sir Arthur a lesson. 'If he wants to turn this into a joke, let it be a joke,' New South Wales delegate Tony Palumbo said.

The votes from New South Wales ensured that Shoulder was elected as the new Socceroos coach, by 17 to seven. If they had voted for Vest, he would have won 13–11. One delegate reportedly told Sir Arthur: 'You have got the coach you deserve.'

St George Budapest president Alex Pongrass claimed: 'It's a disgraceful decision, and one that must be revoked as soon as possible.'

Shoulder, whose salary was $16,500 a year plus car and expenses, actually started quite well but the wheels fell off during the Socceroos' qualifying campaign for the 1978 World Cup. They topped their first group, finishing above New Zealand and Taiwan. In the second round, they finished fourth out of five teams, including losing both home and away against Iran and Kuwait.

The retirement of so many of the West Germany World Cup team had obviously weakened the Socceroos, but Alston believed firing Rasic was the main reason the team had done so poorly. 'Everything had changed from 1974,' he wrote in his autobiography, *Noddy*. 'It just seemed a very different set-up from the one I was used to. Too different. It was like going from day into night.

Jim Shoulder was the shock choice as Socceroos coach after Rale Rasic and Johnny Warren walked out of their interviews

'If Rasic had carried on, he would have built on the 1974 success and not sacrificed most of the team at the same time. He would have brought in new faces, for sure, but only gradually. I tell you, some of the players who quit after the 1974 World Cup would have stayed on if the Federation had done the logical thing and retained Rasic. I have no doubt about this.'

Chapter Eighteen

I told you so

The performances of several members of the Socceroos at the World Cup finals caught the eye of European clubs. These included goalkeeper Jack Reilly and centre-back and captain Peter Wilson, who it was reported had received offers to return to Scotland and England, respectively. Branko Buljevic was another name linked with clubs in Germany.

In the end, the only member of Australia's 1974 West Germany team who left Australia to play overseas was Adrian Alston. His performances, playing up front on his own for the majority of the tournament, had earned praise from some of the most prominent names in football, including West Germany manager Helmut Schoen and England and Manchester United legend Sir Bobby Charlton.

The end-of-tournament statistics told their own story. Alston had taken six of the Socceroos' 20 shots, ahead of Jimmy Mackay with four, Ray Richards three, Atti Abonyi and Col Curran two each and Johnny Warren, Peter Ollerton and Buljevic one each.

As the World Cup progressed, several clubs from the Bundesliga contacted Alston by calling him on the telephone at the Socceroos' training camp. Hertha Berlin were the keenest of the German teams, who also included Hamburger SV and Eintracht Frankfurt, to sign Alston, so adopted a novel approach to attract his interest and steal a march on their rivals.

The tired striker had been substituted in the 65th minute of Australia's final group match against Chile at the Olympic Stadium in West Berlin, and replaced by Peter Ollerton. After coming off, Alston quickly changed into some dry clothes and joined the rest of the Socceroos party on the bench to watch the closing minutes of the World Cup adventure.

As Alston sat down, a Hertha Berlin representative attracted his attention and passed him, over his shoulder, a three-year contract with a $40,000 signing-on fee and an apartment in the city while he found somewhere to live.

'I could not believe what I was seeing,' Alston admitted in his autobiography, *Noddy*. 'He wanted me to sign there and then, but how could I do that – apart from the fact that it was in German? I just had to say to him, "Mate, let's first finish this match first, eh – then we can talk." I felt embarrassed because the players on the bench saw what was going on and were jumping on me and urging me to sign up.'

It helped make up Alston's mind, however, and soon after the match, he agreed to join Hertha Berlin. A transfer fee of $100,000 was agreed between the Germans and Safeway United, Alston's club in Australia. He returned home and he and his family prepared to start a new life in Germany. Then there was a twist.

Luton Town, just promoted to the English First Division, had been tracking Alston since he had scored against them in a friendly at Kenilworth Road, during Australia's world tour in 1970, and were impressed with his performances at West Germany 1974.

They agreed to match Hertha Berlin's offer and it proved irresistible to Alston. 'The prospect of returning to England and playing in the First Division, like my brother Alec did, was too strong to knock back, especially since it also meant a lot to my family,' he wrote in his autobiography.

Adrian Alston joined English First Division club Luton Town after a late offer

Alston spent a season at Luton Town, finishing joint top scorer with eight goals in 29 appearances, before the club began suffering financial problems which resulted in him not being paid. In 1975, Alston joined Third Division club Cardiff City for a transfer fee of £20,000. He scored twice on his debut, in a 4–3 win over Chesterfield, and later went on to become the first post-war Cardiff player to score a hat-trick in the FA Cup in a 6–2 win over Exeter City.

In Alston's first year, the club won the Welsh Cup, qualifying for the European Cup Winners' Cup the following season. In the first round of the competition in September 1976, Alston became the first Australian player to score in a European competition when he hit the only goal in a 1–0 victory over Soviet Union side Dinamo Tbilisi.

After helping the club win promotion to the Second Division, scoring the goal that confirmed the achievement in a 1–0 victory over Bury, he struggled to reproduce his form the following year and in 1977 left Cardiff to play in the North American Soccer League for Tampa Bay Rowdies for $250,000. There, he got the opportunity to play again against Pele and Franz Beckenbauer, who had both joined the New York Cosmos.

Beckenbauer told Alston he had been 'very surprised' he had turned down the Bundesliga to go to a country that had not even reached the 1974 World Cup finals. With hindsight, Alston agreed with Der Kaiser. 'It was the biggest mistake I ever made,' he admitted in his autobiography. 'It was the only time I put family first and football second.'

Playing overseas, it was difficult for Alston to continue representing the Socceroos. His first game after the World Cup finals was when he answered a call from new coach Jim Shoulder for the match against Kuwait at the Sydney Sports Ground in October 1977, in the qualifying campaign for Argentina 1978. He played in midfield in a 2–1 defeat, which effectively ended Australia's hopes of returning to the World Cup finals.

Alston played another three times for the Socceroos. His final appearance came in November 1977 at the Aryamehr Stadium in Tehran, where four years earlier he had been sacrificed at half-time to help Australia hang on for a 3–2 aggregate victory. This time, Alston played the whole game as Iran won 1–0 in front of 100,000 fans to qualify for the World Cup finals for the first time.

A number of the Australian players had retired from international football after the 1974 World Cup. They were led by 'Mr Socceroo', as the press had nicknamed Johnny Warren. His final appearance in a green and gold shirt was at the opening game of the World Cup finals against East Germany, when he had got injured.

It was a fitting stage to bow out on for a man who had shown such faith and belief that one day soccer could be a major sport in Australia. 'The World Cup is bigger than the Olympics and our era were the pioneers,' he said. 'That achievement in qualifying, in relative terms, has never been matched. We were part-time players who had never before seen Brazil play, who had never seen Holland play, who had never seen the Italian first division.'

After he returned from the World Cup, Warren had been appointed as player-coach of St George Budapest, the club he had played for since 1963 apart from a brief spell in England with Stockport County the following year.

He steered the team to the 1974 grand final of the New South Wales League, where they beat Sydney Hakoah 4–2 after extra time. Warren had scored the third goal with a curling shot that *Soccer World* compared to 'something a Rivelino or Tostao can imitate at their best'.

It was Warren's last touch as a footballer after he immediately substituted himself and, following the match, announced he was retiring, although at 31 he was still relatively young.

Even the mainstream Australian media marked Warren's decision to hang up his boots with tributes. 'It is one of the great sporting success stories of our time that Warren came back from the operating table to play in the World Cup finals and lead St George Budapest to the 1974 soccer championship,' columnist Rod Humphries wrote in the *Sydney Morning Herald*. 'John Warren, the all-Australian boy ... the son every mother hopes for ... the man every sportsman should live up to.'

Johnny Warren is carried off the pitch after scoring in his last match for St George Budapest

Warren led St George to victory in the grand final again in 1975, when his coaching staff included former Socceroos teammate Manfred Schaefer. Schaefer, who had been at St George Budapest as long as Warren, had announced his own retirement a few weeks after his former captain. Shortly after winning a second consecutive grand final, Warren fell out with the club and left. He was replaced as coach by Schaefer.

There was a major change to the structure of Australian soccer when, in 1977, the National Soccer League was launched. It was Australia's first domestic national league competition in any sport. The competition was very much the dream of Alex Pongrass of St George Budapest and Frank Lowy of Sydney Hakoah. Just as they had been when the new Australian Soccer Federation had been formed in 1963, initially, the Victorian Soccer Federation was reluctant to allow its clubs to join.

They finally relented and the new competition was introduced as the Philips Soccer League, with 14 clubs from New South Wales, Queensland, Victoria, South Australia and the nation's capital, Canberra.

Warren was recruited to coach Canberra City, but the club did not have the depth of talent of St George Budapest, and they finished second from bottom in the inaugural season.

The first champions were Eastern Suburbs, the club known as Sydney Hakoah before changing their name for the new league. Unlike the state leagues, the champions were initially determined by first past the post. But, after seven seasons, the league introduced a grand final to crown the champions.

Eastern Suburbs clinched the title ahead of Marconi-Fairfield, coached by Rale Rasic, on goal difference. Rasic was still voted Coach of the Year – another sign of the high esteem he continued to be held in by those who really knew the sport – and Jimmy Rooney Player of the Year.

Besides Rooney, Rasic's Marconi-Fairfield side included a number of players from his World Cup finals. There was also Ray Richards, Ernie Campbell and Allan Maher, the third-choice goalkeeper at West Germany 1974.

In addition, the team included Roberto Vieri, whose sons Christian and Max also went on to become professional footballers, appearing at international level for Italy and Australia, respectively. Vieri had played for several leading Italian clubs, including Sampdoria, Juventus and AS Roma, and had become one of the first players from his country to play abroad when he accepted an offer from Marconi in 1977.

Even Vieri's exalted status did not prevent him from having to follow Rasic's strict standards. 'Roberto hated training and I used to trick him and play small games to get him moving,' Rasic revealed. 'His wife would call up late at night and say: "Mr Rasic, Roberto said, '*Te grande bastarde!*' You're a big bastard. He has big cramps." We did an hour and a half of training. I didn't make him sprint, but I got him to train.'

Rooney continued playing international football until 1980, when his final appearance in the green and gold came at the Hindmarsh Stadium in Adelaide.

Northern Ireland were the opposition in a match to celebrate the centenary of football in Australia. It was Rooney's 57th cap of a career that also included 20 goals for the Socceroos.

Richards did not play another international match after his red card against Chile but did appear for the Socceroos in 1975 in a series of matches against touring club sides. His last game was against Manchester United on 18th June – the first anniversary of the Socceroos' game against West Germany in Hamburg. Australia were beaten 4–0 in Sydney by a strong English side coached by Tommy Docherty, and which included Alex Stepney, Sammy McIlroy, Lou Macari, Steve Coppell and Stuart Pearson.

Richards had combined his later career at Marconi-Fairfield as player-coach, but was replaced by Rasic in 1975. The relationship between the two business partners deteriorated after the World Cup, with Richards regularly criticising his former coach in the media.

West Adelaide were crowned the Philips Soccer League champions the second season in 1978, but Marconi-Fairfield, under Rasic, did lift the title in 1979. Warren's Canberra City continued to struggle, however, and after they had finished second bottom again in 1978, he decided to leave and return to Sydney.

Warren started a successful media career, commentating on football for the Australian Broadcasting Corporation and Special Broadcasting Service television networks. On SBS, Warren formed a legendary partnership with Les Murray. Murray, a Hungarian refugee who came to Australia with his family in 1957, and Warren became the indomitable face of a sport still trying to rise above ethnic divisions. The Australian media dubbed them 'Mr and Mrs Soccer', although it was never really distinguished which was which.

In 2002, Warren published a best-selling book, *Sheilas, Wogs and Poofters, An Incomplete Biography of Johnny Warren and Soccer in Australia*, which brilliantly captured the history of soccer in the country from the darkness of the 1950s through to the solemn days of administrative greed, redundant power struggles and political self-destruction.

The year after the book was published, Warren, a heavy smoker for most of his life, announced that he had been diagnosed with lung cancer. A few months later, FIFA president Sepp Blatter presented a frail Warren with the FIFA Centennial Order of Merit for his services to the game in Australia.

At the ceremony, Warren delivered an emotional speech in which he said: 'I want Australia to embrace this fabulous game. It's not "wogball". This is the game of the world. We are on the verge of doing big things. I'm sure it will happen.'

Warren died at the Royal Prince Alfred Hospital in Sydney on 6th November 2004, at the age of 61. He was awarded a full state funeral, the first to be held for a sportsman in Australia.

Johnny Warren received a state funeral following his death in November 2004

The first member of the Socceroos' 1974 team to die was Jimmy Mackay, the scorer of that famous play-off goal against South Korea. He died in December 1998, at the age of 54, after a heart attack following an accident he had suffered at work as a roof plumber.

The goal in Hong Kong did not change Mackay's life. 'People soon forget you when you are no longer hanging around the soccer grounds but I've no regrets,' he said shortly before his death. 'Occasionally, I meet a person who remembers that I played in the 1974 World Cup and scored the goal that got us to the finals, but, to be honest, I can walk down any street in Melbourne and go unnoticed.'

Rasic was affected deeply by Mackay's death. They had huge mutual admiration for each other, even if Rasic sometimes used to get upset with the lack of effort he believed Mackay was putting in during practice. 'Rasic used to say that I was always injured, but that was only when we were training!' Mackay admitted. "One of the advantages we had in the 1970s was

Rale Rasic wore Jimmy Mackay's Socceroos cap on the 47th anniversary of his famous goal against South Korea as a tribute

that seven of the players that starred in the 1974 World Cup finals had been together for three or four years.'

On the 47th anniversary of Mackay's goal in 2020, Rasic donned Mackay's Socceroos cap as a tribute during a special television programme titled *Rale Rasic: A Celebration.*

Mackay had decided before Australia's match against Chile at the World Cup that he would retire from international football. At the end of the game, he threw both his boots into the crowd.

The statistics Mackay chalked up during West Germany 1974 were the most impressive of all the Socceroos. As well as having the second most shots behind Alston, Mackay was one of the best tacklers in the tournament. He made eight tackle attempts throughout the World Cup without missing a single attempt. Only the Netherlands' right-back Wim Suurbier, with 13 from 13, made more tackles and maintained a 100 per cent success rate.

Indeed, the Socceroos finished the World Cup campaign with a tackle success rate of 78 per cent, winning 73 out of 93 attempts. It was the second highest of any team at the tournament behind Scotland's 84 per cent.

Mackay continued, though, for a short while after the World Cup and, in February 1975, appeared in the Socceroos' two matches against Polish club side Legia Warsaw in Sydney and Brisbane, respectively.

Mackay finished his club career by returning to the city he had settled in after arriving for his two-year working holiday in 1965. He signed for South Melbourne Hellas, the club he had agreed to join originally before being

Jimmy Mackay, second right in back row, did finally sign for South Melbourne Hellas and led them to the Victorian State League title in 1976

kidnapped on arrival at the airport by former Celtic captain Duncan MacKay and persuaded to join Melbourne Croatia instead. In Mackay's final full season in 1976, Hellas lifted the Victorian State League.

There was one youngster at South Melbourne Hellas who remembers being inspired by Mackay. Born in Athens, Ange Postecoglou's family joined the burgeoning Greek diaspora in Melbourne in 1970 when he was five. For a while, Postecoglou decided the best way to fit in with his new environment was to shun soccer and instead played Australian rules. But his father took him down to South Melbourne Hellas when he was eight and he joined the club when he was nine.

'Those are the strongest memories of my youth,' Postecoglou said. 'It was a big part of my childhood. For us, Middle Park became almost the social hub for Greek-Australian migrants. It almost became our church and it is significant that it was a Sunday because it was a place where we found community.

'It was a unique atmosphere, a sense of community, a passionate vocal crowd, and it made a strong impression on me as a young kid.'

Postecoglou recalls the impact that watching the Socceroos at the World Cup finals had on him and the fact that the team contained so many immigrants, like him. 'The men representing us were a microcosm of our country at that time,' Postecoglou said. 'Some names rolled off the tongue, others not so much. Wilson, Warren, Alston and Mackay alongside Buljevic, Utjesenovic and Abonyi and Harry Williams, one of our greatest-ever Indigenous players. Some born here, some abroad. But all proud Australians.

'We played against the best in the world and surprised everyone with our competitive spirit and our fearless attitude. The concern was that these amateurs would be outclassed and maybe as a nation we would be embarrassed. We nicknamed them the Socceroos and in part it suited us, because we could disassociate ourselves from them if the results were disastrous. What country is Socceroos?

'In the end these players, from varying backgrounds, showed the best of us. A young country, in many ways underestimated like these men, had always punched above its weight and believed it could conquer the world.

'I was nine years old sitting with my father in the early hours of the morning, watching a grainy black-and-white TV, and for me it was the equivalent of the moon landing. Anything was possible.'

Postecoglou went on to play more than 200 games for South Melbourne Hellas and was capped four times for the Socceroos. He later managed South Melbourne Hellas and was Australia's coach at the 2014 World Cup finals in Brazil. It laid the groundwork for a coaching career that has taken him all over the world, including to Celtic in Scotland and Tottenham Hotspur in the English Premier League.

In 2013, Postecoglou was a guest at an event to celebrate the 40th anniversary of the Socceroos reaching the World Cup finals for the first time. He was noticeably emotional at meeting these pathfinders.

'I don't think we have done our history well as a code,' Postecoglou said. 'There were times when we seemed to have tried to bury our history as a dirty little secret. Ultimately we are all here because of pioneers of the past. I remember watching the likes of Jimmy Mackay and Jimmy Armstrong playing for South Melbourne in the early 70s and it had a significant impact on me as a person.'

In 1997, the year before he died, Mackay joined his former Socceroos teammates when they were rewarded with a lap around the Melbourne Cricket Ground in open-roof luxury cars, prior to the World Cup qualifying match between Australia and Iran. In front of 85,000 people, a grateful public were finally able to pay their respects to a side that had put Australia on the soccer map.

Mackay and Warren were both among the former players who publicly cried that night, when the Socceroos blew another opportunity to finally return to the World Cup finals.

Since West Germany 1974, Australia had endured a series of disasters and near misses. Under Shoulder, the team had been out of its depth trying to qualify for Argentina 1978.

Shoulder was replaced by Rudi Gutendorf, the former coach of Chile who had been forced to flee the country after the military *coup d'état*. He claimed he had been inspired to take the job by the Socceroos' performance at West Germany 1974.

Before Gutendorf got the job, it had been reported that Rasic and Australian Soccer Federation president Sir Arthur George had met to sort out their problems. It was even claimed that Sir Arthur would not oppose the reappointment of Rasic. The fact that he still did not get the job probably finally proved to Rasic that he was never going to be given another opportunity.

Gutendorf promised to give local youth its chance, but his reign started and ended with defeats to New Zealand. The first, in 1979, was the Socceroos' first loss to the Kiwis since 1954. The second, a 2–0 defeat at the Sydney Cricket Ground in May 1981, ended Australia's hopes of qualifying for Spain 1982 and led to Gutendorf resigning.

He was replaced by Frank Arok, Rasic's fellow Yugoslavian and one of the most successful coaches in Australian history following spells with St George Budapest, South Melbourne, Port Melbourne, Gippsland Falcons and Sydney Olympic.

Arok was in charge of two Socceroos World Cup qualifying campaigns. For Mexico 1986, Australia were beaten 2–0 on aggregate in a play-off against

Scotland, who were managed by Alex Ferguson. As it had for Mexico 1970, the failure to beat Israel in Sydney cost the Socceroos dearly and meant they missed a play-off for Italy 1990.

Scotsman Eddie Thomson, who had played nearly 300 matches for Heart of Midlothian and Aberdeen in the Scottish league before emigrating to Australia, was put in charge of the Socceroos' efforts to qualify for the 1994 World Cup finals in the United States.

Australia again had to travel the world and earned a final play-off against the 1978 and 1986 World Cup winners Argentina. Diego Maradona was persuaded to come out of retirement and was part of the team that drew 1–1 in Sydney, before the Socceroos lost the second leg 1–0 following an own goal from Alex Tobin.

In a bid to qualify for France 1998, the Socceroos broke the bank by hiring Terry Venables. Venables had had a distinguished playing career, representing England and having turned out for Chelsea, Tottenham Hotspur, Queens Park Rangers and Crystal Palace. It was as a coach he had really made his name. Venables had become a legend at Barcelona by winning La Liga in 1985 and the following season taking them to the final of the European Cup. As England manager, he had led his country to the semi-finals of the 1996 European Championships with a bold, innovative style of football that reinvigorated supporters.

Beset by legal problems in Britain, Venables had taken the Socceroos job in November 1996 after the resignation of Thomson. Australia reached the final of the 1997 FIFA Confederations Cup in Riyadh, beating Mexico 3–1 in the group stages and Uruguay 1–0 in the semi-finals. They lost the final 6–0 to Brazil, for whom Ronaldo and Romario both scored hat-tricks, but expectations were high for the World Cup campaign.

The Socceroos steamrolled through their group in Oceania featuring the Solomon Islands and Tahiti, averaging over six goals a match. They then beat New Zealand 5–0 on aggregate in a play-off to qualify to meet Iran in a final decider. A Socceroos team including well-known names like Mark Bosnich, Mark Viduka and Harry Kewell drew the first leg 1–1 in Tehran in front of 128,000 fans.

The parading of the 1974 Socceroos before the kick-off of the second leg, at the Melbourne Cricket Ground, raised expectations even higher than they were already. When Australia took a 2–0 lead thanks to goals from Kewell and Aurelio Vidmar, the arena was a cauldron of massive celebration. Then, goals in the 75th and 79th minutes pulled Iran level. At the final whistle, it was 3–3 on aggregate, and Iran qualified on the away goals rule. Australia had been eliminated from the World Cup without losing a match.

Before the match, a narrative had begun to form that the team of 1974 were happy to see their successors fail so as to keep their unique place in Australian soccer history. But what happened that night against Iran dispelled that ridiculous theory.

'I have never been involved in a more shattering night for our game,' Rasic wrote in his autobiography. 'There was a huge sense of excitement and expectation as the game drew near. But I can tell you, it was a whole lot different when the final whistle went. Many of the 1974 Socceroos cried.

Former England manager Terry Venables was among the coaches who failed to guide the Socceroos to the World Cup finals

'Poor Jimmy Mackay was totally devastated. He took the result very hard. Jimmy was sitting next to me when Iran scored their first goal. He could always read a game and how it was shaping. He turned to me and, with tears, he said quietly, "We are gone." When Iran scored the second, the tears really flowed. He was stunned. He could not say a word.'

Mackay and Warren both died without seeing the Socceroos qualify for another World Cup, but each were very much in everyone's thoughts when they did finally make it. Venables resigned shortly after the disaster against Iran. He was replaced by Frank Farina, a former Socceroo himself and the first Indigenous Australian to manage the national team.

Under Farina, the Socceroos started the campaign to qualify for the 2002 World Cup in Japan and South Korea in record-breaking fashion. They beat Tonga 22–0, then American Samoa 31–0 in a match where Australian striker Archie Thompson scored 13 goals, then Fiji 2–0, and, finally, Samoa 11–0. In four group matches, the Socceroos scored 66 goals and conceded none.

The Socceroos then beat New Zealand 6–1 over two legs in the Oceania play-off, and hopes were high they would beat Uruguay in the final preliminary match to qualify. Before the first leg at the Melbourne Cricket Ground, much of the media attention focused on what had happened during the friendly between the two sides in 1974, when Ray Baartz had been karate chopped and left nearly paralysed.

A Kevin Muscat penalty in the 78th minute gave the Socceroos a slender advantage for the second leg in Montevideo five days later. A 3–0 defeat again extinguished the dream.

In November 2005, Australia and Uruguay were again pitched against each other in the South American-Oceania play-off for a place at Germany 2006.

The Socceroos, now coached by Dutchman Guus Hiddink, lost the first leg in Montevideo 1–0. Mark Bresciano scored in the 35th minute of the return leg four days later at Stadium Australia, built for the 2000 Olympic Games in Sydney, to send the match into a penalty shootout.

The previous year, shortly before Warren's death, Australian television personality John Safran had travelled to Mozambique and hired a new witch doctor to reverse the 'Socceroos' Curse'. According to Warren in *Sheilas, Wogs and Poofters*, this had been placed on the Australians after they failed to pay £50 to the witch doctor who had put a curse on the Rhodesian goalkeeper Robin Jordan during their campaign to qualify for the 1970 World Cup. It seemed ridiculous, but Warren believed in it, and so did many others.

In the same stadium where Australia had defeated Rhodesia in 1969, the new witch doctor channelled the spirit of his long-dead predecessor who had placed the original curse and performed a ritual to lift the hex, which included covering Safran in chicken's blood.

When Safran returned to Australia, he and Warren went to Stadium Australia and performed the second part of the ritual, which involved covering themselves in a special clay the witch doctor had provided. 'Johnny was really sincere about it,' Safran said. 'It really messed with his head a bit.'

Television personality John Safran returned to Mozambique in 2004 to try to get the Socceroos' 'curse' lifted

Whether it had any effect or not, who knows. It was left to John Aloisi to fulfil the role Mackay had in 1973 when he hit the decisive spot kick to give the Socceroos a 4-2 win over Uruguay on penalties.

Murray, commentating for SBS, struggled to hold his emotions. 'That was one of the most epic games I have witnessed, and I've seen a few,' Murray told viewers post-match. 'And one in which we were all emotionally involved, and

Australia qualified for the World Cup finals for the first time in 32 years at Germany 2006 when John Aloisi, left, scored the winning penalty in a shootout in the play-off against Uruguay

Johnny Warren told us so. I told you so. I told you so. And there it is: he has been proven right tonight.'

Then Murray looked up at the heavens. 'Johnny, we hear you,' he said.

For the draw for the qualifying rounds, held in Berlin in 2003, Warren's great friend Schaefer had been invited to return to Germany to represent Oceania. Schaefer had retired from international football after West Germany 1974, having played 49 times for the Socceroos. After quitting playing, he had enjoyed a successful coaching career. This included leading Sydney Olympic, the club founded as Pan-Hellenic by Greek immigrants, to twice finishing as runners-up in the National Soccer League in 1984 and 1986, respectively.

During his return to Germany, Schaefer got to spend time with old acquaintance Pele. The beginning of their friendship had started in unlikely circumstances, during the Socceroos' friendly with Santos in Sydney in 1972. During the game, Richards fouled Pele and Schaefer went over to help him up. The legendary Brazilian, recognising Schaefer, reportedly said, 'I know your name, you're Mr Bastard.'

Schaefer and Pele stayed connected down the years. 'When I ran into him again in West Germany during the 1974 World Cup, he greeted me with another "Mr Bastard",' Schaefer said. 'We had a cup of coffee and a chat. Later on in 2003, I even appeared with him on a television show for former World

Cup players. It was good, really nice. I see him as my best mate, believe it or not.'

Schaefer died in March 2023, at the age of 80. 'Der Milchmann', as he was still called in Germany, was remembered fondly for his kindness in retirement as well as his achievements on the field. 'My parents struggled financially and there were probably times the milk money wasn't there when Manfred delivered,' wrote Australian football journalist and Rasic's biographer Ray Gatt. 'But there were always two bottles at the front door, money or not.'

Tributes came flowing in from all over Australia, but it was probably the one from Rasic that would have meant

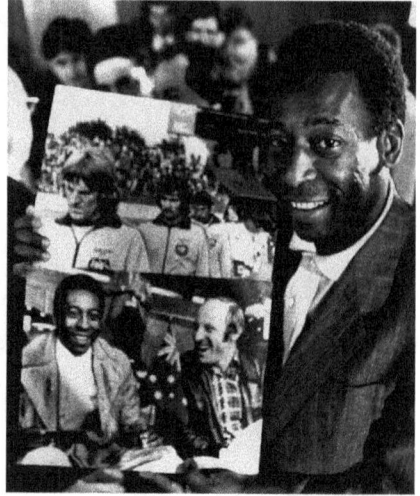

Pele and Socceroos defender Manfred Schaefer became close friends after first meeting during Santos's friendly in Sydney in 1972

the most. 'He was an extraordinary man, a wonderful footballer,' he said. 'He was tough on the outside, but kind and gentle on the inside.'

In July 2023, another member of the Socceroos' West Germany 1974 squad passed away when it was announced that Atti Abonyi had died at the age of 76. Abonyi, who, as Schaefer had done, first made his mark for Australia during the tour to South Vietnam in 1967, played his last match for the Socceroos in 1977. Like Alston, that also came in the 1978 World Cup qualifying match in Tehran, when Australia were beaten 1–0 by Iran.

Abonyi finished his career having appeared in 61 internationals and having scored 25 goals, a record until John Kosmina equalled it the following decade. In June 1975, Abonyi had made a guest appearance for the touring Manchester United side, coming on as a substitute for David McCreery against Queensland and scoring the third goal.

Abonyi spent seven years with St George Budapest after joining them from Melbourne Hungaria in 1969. He transferred to Sydney Croatia in 1977 and helped the club finish top of the New South Wales League for three consecutive seasons with 74 goals in 89 appearances. Abonyi spent the last two seasons, in 1978 and 1979, as player-coach. He also coached Melita Eagles to finish top of the New South Wales League 1980 and enjoyed stints at the helm of Canberra City and Sydney Croatia, again, in the National Soccer League.

Abonyi had been among the members of the 1974 squad who always cheered for the new Socceroos to join them in making the World Cup finals. Before the match against Uruguay in Sydney in 2005, he had said: 'I want nothing more than for Australia to qualify. If they don't qualify now, when will they qualify?'

The penalty spot at Stadium Australia, from which Aloisi had scored to send Australia to Germany 2006, was dug up after the match to be preserved and was later auctioned off with the proceeds donated to the Johnny Warren Football Foundation. Present at the grass-cutting ceremony were 1974 Socceroos Johnny Watkiss and Jim Fraser. Watkiss was given the honour of taking the last kick from the penalty spot before it was dug up.

Wilson, captain of the 1974 team, was a notable absentee from the celebrations of the Socceroos finally making it back to the World Cup finals. He continued playing in the green and gold, performing outstandingly as Australia failed to qualify for Argentina 1978. His last match was in 1979 in a friendly against New Zealand at Newmarket Park in Auckland. The Socceroos lost 1–0.

It was Wilson's 65th appearance for the Socceroos – and a record 61st as captain. Gutendorf tried, unsuccessfully, to get Wilson to come out of international retirement for the 1982 World Cup qualifying campaign.

After the World Cup in West Germany, Wilson travelled back to Australia, despite offers to return to Europe from both English Division One club Tottenham Hotspur and Hertha Berlin, who had wanted to sign him with Alston. Instead, Wilson joined Western Suburbs and remained when they were absorbed by APIA Leichhardt for the 1979 National Soccer League.

Wilson's performances at the World Cup did not insulate him from the realities of being a soccer player in Australia. He was fired from his job as a car salesman in Wollongong, a city south of Sydney along the Grand Pacific Drive, because his boss did not like him taking time off work to go training. In the end, he found employment as a miner in Wollongong's Nebo Colliery. When he was not captaining the Socceroos, Wilson was five miles underground cutting coal, working machinery and doing general labouring.

'If I'd been a cricketer or a rugby league player in a giant competition like the World Cup, I'd be rolling in money now,' Wilson said upon his return. 'We soccer players don't get the same press coverage they do, not that I really want the fame. I'm a pretty quiet sort of person. I like to keep myself to myself. I tend to shun parties and I haven't got much of a social life.'

Wilson's last season was as a player-coach with APIA Leichhardt in 1982, before walking away. Wilson still prefers a quiet existence living near Wollongong. His greatest joy is riding one of his Harley-Davidson motorbikes up into the mountains to spend the day there or visiting the local bowling club for a beer.

Wilson has resisted any invitations to get involved with reunions of the 1974 World Cup squad, including joining the lap of honour around the Melbourne

Cricket Ground before the fateful game against Iran in 1997. He told Rasic that he 'just wouldn't be able to handle all the fuss'.

The *Daily Telegraph* newspaper tracked Wilson down shortly before the 2006 World Cup. 'There's nothing I want to say,' he told them. 'I've got nothing to add.'

Andre Kruger, a German who fell in love with the Socceroos during the 1974 World Cup when he was a teenager and has been a lifelong fanatical supporter, has stayed connected with Wilson down the years. Kruger elaborated on the brief comments made by Wilson about not being involved in Socceroos reunions. 'I spoke with Peter, and he said that he hoped Australia would win the World Cup so that no one will talk about 1974 again,' he said.

Rasic claimed the *Daily Telegraph* journalist who tracked Wilson down 'should be embarrassed by what he did to Peter'.

In 2000, Sydney suburb Glenwood named a road after the Socceroos legend. But he did not attend the inauguration of 'Peter Wilson Street'.

Kruger, however, tries to make sure that memories of Wilson's performances at those 1974 World Cup finals are kept alive. On his website he sells tee-shirts with the legend 'Big Willie' emblazoned above a picture of Wilson's moustachioed image and the figure '3', his number at West Germany 1974. It is unlikely that Gerd Muller, the German striker who had claimed Wilson 'didn't care whether he kicked the ball, a leg or a head' after facing him in Hamburg, purchased one before his death in 2021.

One major difference between the World Cup held in West Germany in 1974 and the united Germany in 2006 was that the first one the Socceroos qualified for included only 16 countries. The second tournament, 32 years later, had double the amount of teams competing.

The Socceroos, by now all full-time professionals playing for some of Europe's leading clubs, were drawn in Group F alongside defending champions Brazil. In their opening match, against Japan at the Fritz-Walter-Stadion in Kaiserslautern, they were trailing to a 20th-minute goal until Tim Cahill equalised in the 84th minute with Australia's first goal in the World Cup finals. He scored a second five minutes later before Aloisi hit a third in injury time to give the Socceroos a historic 3–1 victory.

Australia reached the round of 16 and were only knocked out following a highly controversial penalty awarded to Italy in the fifth minute of injury time.

A road in a Sydney suburb was named after Socceroos 1974 World Cup captain Peter Wilson

The Socceroos have qualified for every World Cup finals since, at South Africa 2010, Brazil 2014, Russia 2018 and Qatar 2022. A large part of that is down to the fact that in 2006, the Asian Football Confederation finally voted to accept Australia as members, ending a 50-year plus campaign that had been started originally by *Soccer World*.

In Qatar, the Socceroos again reached the round of 16 and were unlucky to lose 2–1 to Argentina. The scorer of Argentina's first goal was Lionel Messi, who went on to inspire the South Americans to their third World Cup victory.

It had taken a goal from maybe the greatest footballer ever to beat the Socceroos. Australia had certainly come a long way since a German newspaper had asked nearly half a century earlier, 'Why have we got these kangaroos at the World Cup?'

There was no one prouder than Rasic. 'The green and gold power, our pride, our honour, is so great that when you put that jersey on, you are 60 percent a better player,' he said. 'Our country doesn't know what that magic means.'

Soccer is no longer on the periphery of Australian sport. Kids who have decided to kick a football around their streets and in the schoolyard are no longer told that they should be playing a proper sport, like Aussie rules, and not 'that wogball'. They no longer have to endure insults such as 'only poofters and wogs play soccer'. They can now play the sport they love without the fear of being ridiculed, mocked or beaten up.

It was Rasic's team of immigrants like Wilson, Schaefer, Mackay, Abonyi and Buljevic who came along and started the long process that made Australia realise that they were not the strange ones, but it was them failing to realise that football was the world's most popular game.

The Socceroos were a peek into Australia's multicultural future a long time before the rest of the country embraced it.

Farewell, Mr Wog

On 13th November 2023, a special reunion was held at Sydney Town Hall to celebrate the 50th anniversary of Australia qualifying for the 1974 World Cup finals, when Jimmy Mackay's 'goal in a million' had beaten South Korea in the play-off in Hong Kong.

Besides missing the late Mackay, Johnny Warren, Manfred Schaefer and Atti Abonyi, it was the first Socceroos reunion not to feature the mastermind of the famous victory. Rale Rasic had died on 8th June that year, at the age of 87. Tributes were led by Australia's prime minister, Anthony Albanese, who called Rasic a 'proud man who leaves a mighty legacy'.

The words 'trailblazer' and 'pioneer' were used in almost every obituary.

After leading the Socceroos to West Germany 1974, Rasic continued to be involved in the sport right until the end. He went on to coach a host of Australian clubs, including Pan-Hellenic, Marconi-Fairfield, Adelaide City, APIA Leichhardt and Canberra Cosmos. He was still acting as technical director for the Juventus Football Academy until a few weeks before he died.

In 1987, Rasic guided APIA Leichhardt to the National Soccer League title with the longest unbeaten streak in a national competition. But for all his success in domestic competition, Rasic was never given another opportunity to coach the Socceroos.

Rasic had fallen out too many times with Australian Soccer Federation president Sir Arthur George and the other blazers who ran the sport. Sir Arthur continued to serve as president of the Federation until 1988, when he was replaced by Ian Brusasco, the official that Rasic had thrown a pen at during a short ill-fated interview in 1977 when they were trying to find a replacement for convicted shoplifter Brian Green.

Rale Rasic died in June 2023 without getting another opportunity to coach his beloved Socceroos

Rasic once claimed he thought he was never given another chance because the Federation did not consider him a 'real Aussie'.

'They took from me something that I was doing better than anyone else,' he said. 'I was a true-blue Aussie, and nobody can deny that – I taught the players how to sing the national anthem.

'I made 16 million people very proud. I can now have a coffee and a sandwich anywhere in Australia free of charge. I'm the people's man.'

Before the 1974 World Cup, Rasic had taken time to look back on the impact that Australia's successful, record-breaking qualifying campaign had had on the sport back home, and how his group of mainly foreign-born players had come to identify themselves with the country they had made their homes.

'In four years of playing in Asia, we lost only one game and that was against Iran in Tehran before a highly-partisan crowd,' he said. 'But the biggest headache we had was playing in Australia. Being a multinational country, the Greeks would scream if there was no Greek in the team, the Italians if there was no Italian. The thing about the English is that they couldn't care less as long as they see good football. So, for four years, we never felt we were playing at home. The team never liked to play in Australia. Never.

'But in 1973, when we started in the World Cup tournament, Australia suddenly began to support the Australian team and there were capacity crowds at Sydney for the matches against Iran and Korea. Emotions went so far during the national anthem that some players had tears in their eyes. This meant it would affect their performances – something I hadn't thought of.'

The high profile that Rasic brought to soccer in his adopted country helped Sir Arthur become an influential figure in the sport internationally. He was the first Australian member of the FIFA Executive Committee under Joao Havelange, the Brazilian elected president of football's world governing body at West Germany 1974. FIFA later awarded Sir Arthur the Gold Order of Merit, the body's highest honour. Sir Arthur died in 2013, at the age of 98.

Rasic always partly blamed the influence of English football – the 'Pommie mafia', as he often called them – for his dismissal after West Germany 1974. 'We should have capitalised on the 1974 Socceroos and set the game up for 100 years, but Arthur George's mind had been poisoned,' he wrote in his autobiography.

'The English influence had reared its ugly head, and he was, in my opinion, a puppet for the likes of Englishman Eric Worthington. Worthington's view of the football world was totally one-eyed. It was everything English and nothing else mattered. He had no vision in regard to what the rest of the football world was doing.'

Mind you, Rasic did not have a higher opinion of Football Federation Australia, the newly reconstituted governing body, which in 2005 finally dropped the word 'soccer' from its title and adopted the one that the rest of the world used to describe the sport.

Rasic was furious in 2005 that for the match against Uruguay, the game where John Aloisi's famous penalty sent the Socceroos back to the World Cup finals for the first time in 32 years, the 1974 squad had been 'snubbed' by not being invited with their partners. Instead, he organised a reunion at a restaurant in Sydney for 'my boys'.

Rasic once claimed that it did not matter to him that he never got another chance to lead the Socceroos in a World Cup qualifying campaign because he had executed his four-year plan in making it to West Germany 1974. Few were convinced by this, however, and everyone knew he had wanted another crack, especially when he saw so many of his successors fail so abysmally.

Rasic's connection with the 1974 squad, who he called 'part of my family', remained strong for the rest of his life. He revealed that 'the secret to qualifying for the World Cup [was] the selection of the men. They must be prepared to give everything they can. According to Einstein, if you give 10 percent then we will have a better world. I asked for a bit more than 10 percent.'

In 2013, on the 40th anniversary of their play-off victory against South Korea, Rasic and 15 players headed back to Hong Kong for a series of celebrations. 'I had curly black hair in those days,' Rasic told guests at the Wombat Hole, the watering hole at the Australian High Commission. 'But when Jimmy scored in the 70th minute, that black hair became white.'

Rale Rasic and several members of the Socceroos World Cup team returned to Hong Kong in 2013 to celebrate the 40th anniversary of their play-off victory against South Korea

The following year, Rasic returned to Hamburg to relive the memories of the 1974 World Cup, where he met up with Andre Kruger, Germany's Socceroos super supporter, and Peter Bizer, the journalist with whom he had remained friends ever since he had travelled to Australia to make a film about the team qualifying for the finals.

'Rale wanted to see the 1974 locations again: the Olympic Stadium in Berlin, then Hamburg, the training camp and the Volksparkstadion, where his team lost 2–0 and 3–0 to the two German teams from East and West,' Bizer said. 'He also wanted to visit Frankfurt again to try the apple wine he had tasted in 1974. In the evening in Hamburg, we had a not very formal but delicious dinner with a full menu of questions, answers, discussions.'

Shortly after that meal, news came from Australia that Rasic's son, Simon, had died suddenly in Australia of a heart attack at the age of only 44 and he had to return home quickly. 'What a tragedy,' Bizer said. 'Many of his friends around the football world shared the pain with Rale when the sad news broke.'

Rasic's home housed the greatest collection of Socceroos 1974 memorabilia. The collection included an irreplaceable treasure trove of tracksuits and jerseys worn at the World Cup finals, as well as documents and souvenirs of Australian and world football. Among the framed jerseys was the one worn by Mackay in the play-off against South Korea in Hong Kong.

The 'Australian Football Museum', as Rasic called it, also contained a World Cup cashmere blanket and ball given to the coaches from the 16 competing countries, and even a bell from the Lord Mayor of Hamburg.

'It means the world,' Rasic said of his priceless collection. 'It's a memory that, as a human being, can never ever, ever, ever get taken away from me. I'm very proud of the country and to be the first team from the country to achieve World Cup qualification.

'In the line-up, you can see the picture of what it meant to be a Socceroo. Everybody is spotlessly dressed and is standing up and still. There were six different nationalities that I had in the team and they all proudly sang the national anthem.

'The Socceroos were the first professional unit in Australian sporting history, when pride and honour for the country and national flag meant "Amen". And they were taught by a wog. Mr Wog.'

Rasic had desperately wanted someone to make his vision of a proper football museum, that the public could visit, come true, but he claimed that Football Federation Australia were not interested. The hope is that others who shared Rasic's dream will keep it alive and, one day, it will come to fruition.

Rasic was inducted into the Sport Australia Hall of Fame in 1989 – the only soccer coach ever to be given the honour. He was chosen to carry the Olympic Torch before the 2000 Games in Sydney. In 2001, he was awarded the

Hopes that a museum could be established to help display Rale Rasic's collection of Socceroos memorabilia remained unfilled at the time of his death

Australian Sports Medal and the Centenary Medal for 'services to soccer'. He also received the Medal of the Order of Australia in the 2004 Australia Day Honours, for 'service to soccer as a player, coach and administrator'.

While he was in hospital, a few days before his death, Rasic asked a friend whether Mario Zagallo, the legendary Brazilian who was a member of his country's World Cup-winning teams at Sweden 1958 and Chile 1962, and their coach at West Germany 1974, was still alive.

Competitive until the end, Rasic wanted to be the last of the coaches from those World Cup finals alive. Zagallo, who had coached Brazil to its famous World Cup victory at Mexico 1970, died in January 2024.

Rasic may not have lifted the World Cup trophy, but the contribution he made to soccer in Australia was as great as that of Zagallo in Brazil. He may be gone, but Rale Rasic's legacy will live forever.

Acknowledgements

For a sport that for most of its existence has been on the periphery of Australian society, soccer has been remarkably well served by the small group of dedicated journalists and writers who have worked so valiantly down the years to ensure that it receives the coverage it deserves.

I have called heavily upon the archives of *Soccer World*, particularly the work of Andrew Dettre and Lou Gautier. This book would not have been anywhere near as comprehensive regarding the Socceroos' journey to the 1974 World Cup finals without their dedication, professionalism and insightfulness over many years when it must have felt like they were the only ones keeping the flame alive. Thanks to Andrew's son, Steve, for helping out with some photographs of his father.

The archive of Laurie Schwab, the former soccer writer for *The Age* newspaper in Melbourne, also provided valuable information.

Without the diligence of Roy Hay in documenting Australia's visits to Saigon during the Vietnam War, particularly in his booklet *Football and War: Australia and Vietnam 1967–1972*, an important part of the Socceroos story would have been lost.

This book would have been hard to write without some of the biographies written by people involved in the Socceroos 1974 World Cup adventure.

As you would expect, *Sheilas, Wogs and Poofters: An Incomplete Biography of Johnny Warren and Soccer in Australia* was the go-to source during my initial research and provided valuable historical insight.

The *Rale Rasic Story: The Socceroos' First World Cup Coach*: as Told to Ray Gatt was another major source of research, particularly about Rasic's early upbringing in Yugoslavia and, later, his relationship with Australian Soccer Federation president Sir Arthur George.

Noddy: the Untold Story of Adrian Alston by Philip Micallef provided a fabulous account of his journey from non-league footballer in England to one of the Socceroos' most important players. Adrian probably does not remember, but he arranged tickets for our family for Luton Town's match against Arsenal in Highbury in September 1974, where he scored in a 2–2 draw. I have attempted to repay him by trying to get him the credit he deserves for being the original inventor of the 'Cruyff turn', although I fear it is too late for it to be renamed the 'Alston turn'.

Philip Micallef's immensely entertaining series of interviews with members of the 1974 Socceroos squad for SBS's *The World Game* was also a rich source of information.

A unique perspective on a unique period of history in Australian soccer was provided by team doctor Brian Corrigan in his book *The Life of Brian*, particularly about the incident involving the witch doctor during the visit to Mozambique for the 1970 World Cup qualifying match against Rhodesia.

Thanks should also go to Jesse Fink for his book *15 Days in June*, the story of Australia's performance at the 2006 World Cup. It offered unprecedented background and information on Australia's first World Cup campaign and the ill-fated trip to Cambodia in 1965 to play North Korea over two legs.

On the same theme, *Sporting Memories of a Yorkshire Aussie* by Geoff Sleight, who participated in those matches, shone a light on how poorly prepared Australia were for that first bid. But without the lessons learnt then, it is unlikely that the planning would have been in place for 1974.

German journalist Peter Bizer was kind in sharing his memories of his visit to Australia in early 1974 to do a television programme on the Socceroos' preparations for the World Cup. It was the start of a lifelong friendship between him and Rale, and he has been generous in sharing those memories. Thanks to Helena Jasinski for putting us together.

John Maynard's *Socceroos – A World Cup Odyssey, 1965 to 2022* helped me check on match statistics involving Australia, as did ozfootball.net. Mark Boric's online historical library, Melbourne Soccer, was another valuable resource.

John Henderson at Airdrieonians helped greatly with providing statistics of Jimmy Mackay's brief spell with them before emigrating to Australia. Graeme McGinty also helped me track down matchday programmes of games involving my uncle in Scotland.

Also, thank you to everyone who follows the Australian Football History page on Facebook and who took the time to answer my questions.

Keir Radnedge, a former colleague at the *Guardian*, was also an invaluable help when answering questions about the 1970 and 1974 World Cups.

Of course, no book on the history of the 1974 Socceroos would have been possible without consulting Andre Kruger, whose unlikely love affair with Australian soccer has lasted more than half a century now. Thank you for answering my questions and providing the photographs from that historic night in Hong Kong when Jimmy scored the goal in the play-off against South Korea that earned the Socceroos their place at West Germany 1974.

Most importantly, thank you to my beautiful wife, Sarah, whose love and support allowed me the opportunity and time to fulfil the promise I had made to my father, David, nearly 30 years ago to write this book.

Finally, any mistakes are mine and mine alone.

Australia FIFA World Cup 1974 squad

Number	Position	Name	Born	Birthplace	Club
1	GK	Jack Reilly	27.08.45	Stonehaven, Scotland	Melbourne Hakoah
2	DF	Doug Utjesenovic	08.10.46	Belgrade, Yugoslavia	St George Budapest
3	DF	Peter Wilson	15.09.47	Felling, England	Safeway United
4	DF	Manfred Schaefer	12.02.43	Pillau, Germany	St George Budapest
5	DF	Colin Curran	21.08.47	Newcastle, Australia	Western Suburbs
6	MD	Ray Richards	18.05.46	Croydon, England	Marconi-Fairfield
7	MD	Jimmy Rooney	10.12.45	Dundee, Scotland	APIA Leichardt
8	MD	Jimmy Mackay	19.12.43	Edinburgh, Scotland	Sydney Hakoah
9	FW	Johnny Warren	17.05.43	Sydney, Australia	St George Budapest
10	FW	Garry Manuel	20.02.50	Sydney, Australia	Pan-Hellenic
11	FW	Attila Abonyi	16.08.46	Budapest, Hungary	St George Budapest
12	FW	Adrian Alston	06.02.49	Preston, England	Safeway United
13	FW	Peter Ollerton	20.05.51	Preston, England	APIA Leichardt
14	FW	Max Tolson	18.07.45	Wollongong, Australia	Safeway United
15	DF	Harry Williams	07.05.51	Sydney, Australia	St George Budapest
16	DF	Ivo Rudic	24.01.42	Split, Yugoslavia	Pan-Hellenic
17	MD	David Harding	14.08.46	Liverpool, England	Pan-Hellenic
18	DF	Johnny Watkiss	28.03.41	Willenhall, England	Sydney Hakoah
19	FW	Ernie Campbell	20.10.49	Sydney, Australia	Marconi-Fairfield
20	FW	Branko Buljevic	06.09.47	Split, Yugoslavia	Footscray JUST
21	GK	Jim Milisavljevic	15.04.51	Melbourne, Australia	Footscray JUST
22	GK	Allan Maher	21.07.50	Sydney, Australia	Sutherland Shire
	Coach	Rale Rasic	26.12.35	Mostar, Yugoslavia	
	Assistant	Les Scheinflug	01.10.38	Buckeburg, Germany	
	Manager	John Barclay	13.11.27	Rosyth, Scotland	
	Doctor	Brian Corrigan	06.05.41	Daylesford, Australia	
	Physio	Peter Van Ryn	18.05.17	The Hague, Netherlands	

Australia 1974 FIFA World Cup qualifying and finals results

Qualifying Asian and Oceanian zone

Zone B
Group B1

4th March 1973
Newmarket Ground, Auckland
New Zealand 1 (Turner 57)
Kevin Curtin, Maurice Tillotson, Colin Latimour, John Staines, Ron Armstrong, Brian Turner, Alan Vest, Dennis Tindall (Brian Armstrong 77), David Taylor, Alan Marley (Geoff Brand 85), Malcolm Bland
Australia 1 (Campbell 85)
Ron Corry, Doug Utjesenovic, Peter Wilson, Manfred Schaefer, Bobby Hogg, Ray Richards, Johnny Warren (Atti Abonyi 77), Ray Baartz, Adrian Alston, Max Tolson (Ernie Campbell 67), Branko Buljevic
Attendance: 12,000

11th March 1973
Sydney Sports Ground, Sydney
Australia 3 (Richards 49, Alston 80, 85)
Ron Corry, Doug Utjesenovic, Peter Wilson, Manfred Schaefer, Bobby Hogg, Ray Richards, Jimmy Mackay, Jimmy Rooney, Adrian Alston, Ray Baartz, Branko Buljevic (Ernie Campbell 23)
Iraq 1 (Nouri 89)
Jalal Abdul-Rahman, Mejbil Fartus, Abid Kadum, Douglas Aziz, Sahab Khazal, Shidrik Yousef, Riyadh Nouri, Ammo Yousef (Bashar Rasheed 78), Sabah Hatim (Abdul Razzaq Ahmed 67), Salah Obeid, Ali Adnan Kadim
Attendance: 28,514

13th March 1973
Sydney Sports Ground, Sydney
Australia 2 (Campbell 23, Alston 42)
Ron Corry, Doug Utjesenovic, Peter Wilson, Manfred Schaefer, Bobby Hogg, Ray Richards, Jimmy Mackay, Jimmy Rooney (Branko Buljevic 55), Adrian Alston, Ray Baartz, Ernie Campbell (Atti Abonyi 76)

Indonesia 1 (Iswadi Idris 36)
Ronny Pasla, Yuswardi, Sunarto, Anwar Udjang, Widodo H.S., Suaeb Rizal,
Ronny Pattinasarany, Sarman Panggabean (Waskito 80), Iswadi Idris (Asmara
79), Jacob Sihasale, Abdul Kadir
Attendance: 12,763

16th March 1973
Sydney Sports Ground, Sydney
Australia 3 (Utjesenovic 11, Baartz 19, Buljevic 26)
Ron Corry, Doug Utjesenovic, Peter Wilson, Manfred Schaefer, Bobby Hogg, Ray
Richards, Jimmy Mackay, Jimmy Rooney, Adrian Alston, Ray Baartz, Branko Buljevic
New Zealand 3 (Vest 10, Tindall 50, Hogg (own goal) 86)
Kevin Curtin, Maurice Tillotson, Colin Latimour, John Staines, Ron Armstrong,
Brian Turner, Tommy Randles, Dennis Tindall, Alan Vest, David Taylor (Max
Davies 75), Brian Hardman (Tony Sibley 46)
Attendance: 14,071

18th March 1973
Olympic Park, Melbourne
Australia 0
Jim Fraser, Doug Utjesenovic, Peter Wilson, Manfred Schaefer, Bobby Hogg,
Jimmy Mackay, Ray Baartz, Ray Richards, Adrian Alston, Max Tolson (Jimmy
Rooney 65), Branko Buljevic (Atti Abonyi 77)
Iraq 0
Sattar Khalef, Mejbil Fartous, Abid Kadim, Kuiser Abdul Hamid, Raheem Karim,
Douglas Aziz, Riyadh Nuri (Shedrak Yousif 87), Bashar Rasheed, Abdul Razzaq
Ahmed, Sabah Hatim (Ali Adnan Kadum 62), Salah Obied
Attendance: 10,684

24th March 1973
Sydney Sports Ground, Sydney
Australia 6 (Mackay 3, 40, Abonyi 23, 54, Richards 72, Baartz 78)
Jim Fraser, Doug Utjesenovic, Peter Wilson, Manfred Schaefer, Bobby Hogg,
Jimmy Mackay, Ray Baartz, Ray Richards, Atti Abonyi, Adrian Alston, Branko
Buljevic (Max Tolson 46)
Indonesia 0
Ronny Pasla (Yudo Hadianto 24), Sunarto, Anwar Udjang, Rachman Halim,
Widodo (Sutan Harhara 46), Anjas Asmara, Suaeb Rizal, Sarman Panggabean,
Waskito, Jacob Siharsale, Max Timisela
Attendance: 12,390

Group B1 final table

Pos	Team	Ply	W	D	L	GF	GA	Points
1	Australia	6	3	3	0	15	6	9
2	Iraq	6	3	2	1	11	6	8
3	Indonesia	6	1	2	3	6	13	4
4	New Zealand	6	0	3	3	5	12	3

Group B play-off

18th August 1973
Sydney Sports Ground, Sydney
Australia 3 (Alston 43, Abonyi 46, Wilson 85)
Jim Fraser, Doug Utjesenovic, Peter Wilson, Johnny Watkiss, Col Curran, Johnny Warren, Ray Richards, Jimmy Mackay, Atti Abonyi, Ray Baartz, Adrian Alston (Billy Vojtek 75)
Iran 0
Nasser Hejazi, Mehdi Monajati, Gholamhossein Mazloumi, Ebrahim Ashtiani, Jafar Kashani, Akbar Kargarjam, Reza Adelkhani, Javad Ghorab, Parviz Ghelichkhani, Esmail Haj Rahimipur (Safar Iranpak 23 (Mohammed Sadeghi 46)), Mehdi Lavasani
Attendance: 30,881

24th August 1973
Aryamehr Stadium, Tehran
Iran 2 (Ghelichkhani 14 pen, 31)
Mansour Rashidi, Ebrahim Ashtiani, Jafar Kashani, Akbar Kargarjam, Parviz Ghelichkhani, Ali Parvin, Karo Haghverdian (Javad Ghorab 76), Gholamhossein Mazloumi, Mohammad Sadeghi, Reza Adelkhani (Ashgar Sharafi 65)
Australia 0
Jim Fraser, Doug Utjesenovic, Peter Wilson, Johnny Watkiss, Col Curran, Ray Richards, Johnny Warren (Jimmy Rooney 71), Jimmy Mackay, Atti Abonyi, Ray Baartz, Adrian Alston (Max Tolson 46)
Attendance: 55,997

Australia won 3–2 on aggregate.

Final round

28th October 1973
Sydney Sports Ground, Sydney
Australia 0
Jim Fraser, Doug Utjesenevic, Peter Wilson, Johnny Watkiss, Col Curran, Ray Richards, Jimmy Mackay, Johnny Warren (Ernie Campbell 75), Ray Baartz, Atti Abonyi, Adrian Alston (Max Tolson 60)
South Korea 0
Byun Ho-Young, Kim Ho-Kon, Yoo Kee-Heung, Kang Kee-Wook, Park Yung-Tae, Cha Bum-Keun, Ko Jae-Wook, Park Byung-Chul, Park Ee-Chun (Kang Tae-Hyun 65), Kim Jae-Han, Chung Kyu-Goong
Attendance: 32,005

10th November 1973
Dongdaemun Stadium, Seoul
South Korea 2 (Kim Jae-Han 15, Ko Jae-Wook 30)
Byun Ho-Young, Kim Ho-Kon, Yoo Kee-Heung, Kang Kee-Wook, Park Yung-Tae, Cha Bum-Keun, Ko Jas-Wook, Park Byung-Chul, Park Ee-Chun, Kim Jae-Han, Chung Kyu-Poong
Australia 2 (Buljevic 31, Baartz 47)
Jim Fraser, Doug Utjesenovic, Peter Wilson, Manfred Schaefer, Col Curran, Ray Richards (Adrian Alston 76), Jimmy Mackay, Jimmy Rooney, Atti Abonyi, Ray Baartz, Branko Buljevic
Attendance: 32,000

Australia and South Korea tied 2-2 on aggregate; a final play-off was decided.

13th November 1973
Government Stadium, Hong Kong
Australia 1 (Mackay 70)
Jim Fraser, Doug Utjesenovic, Peter Wilson, Manfred Schaefer, Col Curran, Ray Richards, Jimmy Mackay, Jimmy Rooney, Atti Abonyi (Adrian Alston 56), Ray Baartz, Branko Buljevic
South Korea 0
Lee Sae-Yun, Kim Ho-Kon, Yoo Kae-Heung, Kang Kee-Wook (Park Ee-Chun 80), Park Yung-Tae, Cha Bum-Keun, Ko Jae-Wook, Park Byung-Chul, Kim Jin-Kook (Chung Kyu-Goong 59), Kim Jae-Han, Kang Tae-Hyun
Attendance: 27,284

Finals

Group 1

14th June 1974
Volksparkstadion, Hamburg
East Germany 2 (Curran (own goal) 58, Streich 72)
Jurgen Croy, Gerhard Kische, Bernd Bransch, Konrad Weise, Siegmar Waetzlich, Juergen Sparwasser, Harald Imscher, Jurgen Pommerenke, Wolfram Lowe (Martin Hoffmann 55), Joachim Streich, Eberhard Vogel
Australia 0
Jack Reilly, Doug Utjesenovic, Peter Wilson, Manfred Schaefer, Col Curran, Ray Richards, Jimmy Mackay, Jimmy Rooney, Johnny Warren, Adrian Alston, Branko Buljevic
Attendance: 17,000

18th June 1974
Volksparkstadion, Hamburg
West Germany 3 (Overath 13, Cullmann 34, Muller 53)
Sepp Maier, Berti Vogts, Hans-Georg Schwarzenbeck, Franz Beckenbauer, Paul Breitner, Uli Hoeness, Bernhard Cullmann (Herbert Wimmer 67), Wolfgang Overath, Jurgen Grabowski, Gerd Muller, Jupp Heynckes (Bernd Hoelzenbein 46)
Australia 0
Jack Reilly, Doug Utjesenovic, Peter Wilson, Manfred Schaefer, Col Curran, Ray Richards, Jimmy Rooney, Jimmy Mackay, Ernie Campbell (Atti Abonyi 46), Adrian Alston, Branko Buljevic (Peter Ollerton 61)
Attendance: 53,000

22nd June 1974
Olympic Stadium, West Berlin
Australia 0
Jack Reilly, Doug Utjesenovic, Peter Wilson, Manfred Schaefer, Col Curran (Harry Williams 83), Ray Richards, Jimmy Mackay, Jimmy Rooney, Atti Abonyi, Adrian Alston (Peter Ollerton 65), Branko Buljevic
Chile 0
Leopoldo Vallejos, Rolando Garcia, Alberto Quintano, Elias Figueroa, Antonio Arias, Guillermo Paez, Carlos Reinoso, Francisco Valdez (Rogello Farias 55), Carlos Caszely, Sergio Ahumada, Leonardo Veliz (Guillermo Yavar 72)
Attendance: 17,400

Group 1 final table

Pos	Team	Ply	W	D	L	GF	GA	Points
1	East Germany	3	2	1	0	4	1	5
2	West Germany	3	2	0	1	4	1	4
3	Chile	3	0	2	1	1	2	2
4	Australia	3	0	1	2	0	5	1

Bibliography

Alston, Adrian with Philip Micallef, *Noddy: The Untold Story of Adrian Alston* (Fair Play Publishing, 2023)

Andrews, Neil, Zaire '74: *The Rise and Fall of Mobutu's Leopards* (Empire Publications, 2022)

Corrigan, Brian, *The Life of Brian: Confessions of an Olympic Doctor* (ABC Books, 2004)

Cruyff, Johan, *My Turn: The Autobiography* (Macmillan, 2017)

Didulica, John, *Football Belongs: Eight Matches That Explain Australia* (John Didulica, 2021)

Ferguson, Sir Alex, *Alex Ferguson: My Autobiography* (Hodder & Stoughton, 2013)

Fink, Jesse, *15 Days in June* (Hardie Grant Books, 2017)

Gorman, Joe, *The Death and Life of Australian Soccer* (University of Queensland Press, 2017)

Hallinan, Christopher and Hughson, John, *The Containment of Soccer in Australia: Fencing Off the World Game (Sport in the Global Society – Contemporary Perspectives)* (Routledge, 2013)

Hay, Roy, *Football and War: Australia and Vietnam 1967–1972* (Sports & Editorial Services Australia, 2016)

Hay, Roy and Murray, Bill, *History of Football in Australia, A Game of Two Halves* (Hardie Grant Books, 2016)

Hesse, Uli, *The Three Lives of the Kaiser: A Biography of Franz Beckenbauer* (Simon & Schuster, 2024)

Kunz, Peter, *Chronicles of Australian Soccer: The Foundation Years – 1859 to 1949* (Fair Play Publishing, 2019)

Maynard, John, *Socceroos – A World Cup Odyssey, Volume 1, 1965–2002* (Fair Play Publishing, 2023)

McDevitt, Ronnie, *Scotland in the Sixties: The Definitive Account of the Scotland Football Team 1960–69* (Pitch Publishing, 2019)

O'Halloran, Brendan Francis, *Soccer in Australia: An analytical view* (CreateSpace Independent Publishing Platform, 2016)

Peacock, Adam, *That Night: A Decade On, The Story Of Australian Football's Greatest Night* (Random House Australia, 2015)

Rasic, Rale with Roy Gatt, *The Rale Rasic Story. The Socceroos' First World Cup Coach* (New Holland Publishers, 2006)

Rous, Sir Stanley, *Football Worlds: A Lifetime in Sport* (Faber & Faber, 1978)

Sleight, Geoff, *Sporting Memories of a Yorkshire Aussie* (Geoff Sleight, 2023)

Stephen, Craig, *Boots and Bombs: How New Zealand football grew up in the 1960s and 70s* (Craig Stephen, 2023)

Tomlinson, Alan, *Sir Stanley Rous and the Growth of World Football: An Englishman Abroad* (Cambridge Scholars Publishing, 2020)

Warren, Johnny with Andrew Dettre, *Soccer in Australia* (Paul Hamlyn, 1974)

Warren, Johnny with Andy Harper and Josh Whittington, *Sheilas, Wogs and Poofters: An Incomplete Biography of Johnny Warren and Soccer in Australia* (Random House Australia, 2002)

www.ingramcontent.com/pod-product-compliance
Lightning Source LLC
Chambersburg PA
CBHW060420100426
42812CB00030B/3251/J